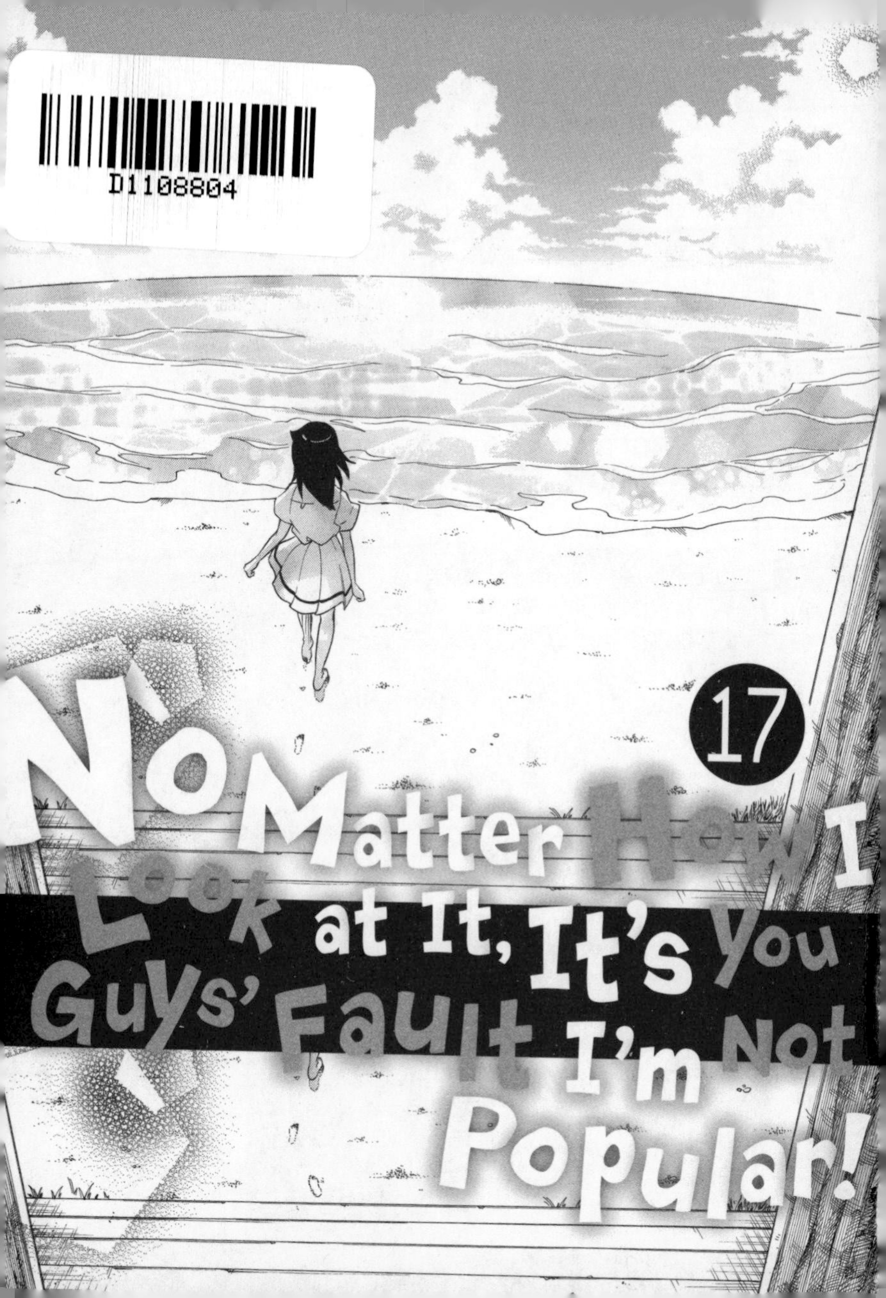
17
No Matter How I Look at It, It's You Guys' Fault I'm Not Popular!

...AWW, IF I'D BEEN A WORM, I WOULD'VE HAD A MAN FROM THE GET-GO AND DEFINITELY HAVE HAD S●X, NOT TO MENTION KIDS...

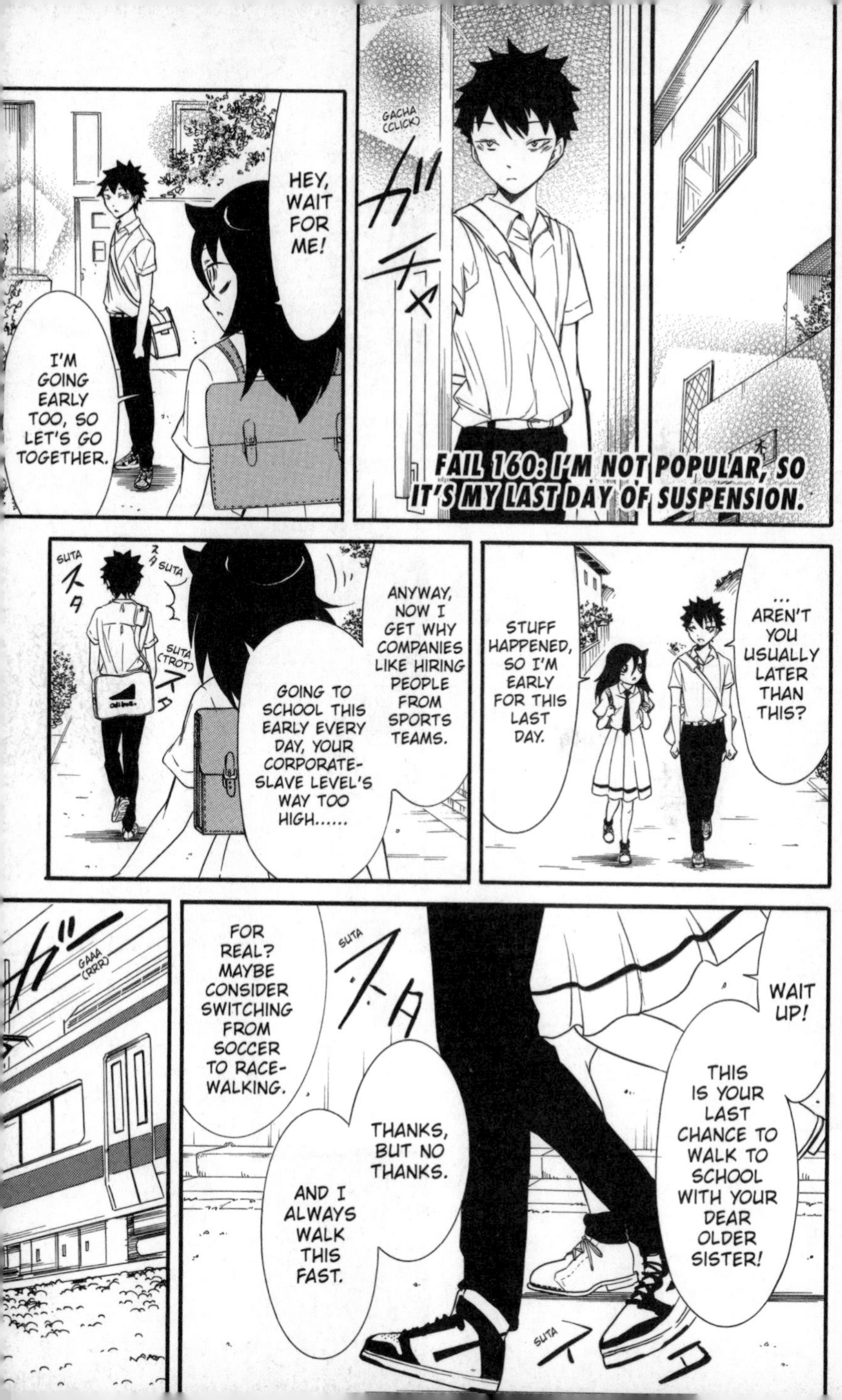
GACHA (CLICK)
FAIL 160: I'M NOT POPULAR, SO IT'S MY LAST DAY OF SUSPENSION.
HEY, WAIT FOR ME!
I'M GOING EARLY TOO, SO LET'S GO TOGETHER.
... AREN'T YOU USUALLY LATER THAN THIS?
STUFF HAPPENED, SO I'M EARLY FOR THIS LAST DAY.
SUTA
SUTA
ANYWAY, NOW I GET WHY COMPANIES LIKE HIRING PEOPLE FROM SPORTS TEAMS.
SUTA (TROT)
GOING TO SCHOOL THIS EARLY EVERY DAY, YOUR CORPORATE-SLAVE LEVEL'S WAY TOO HIGH......
WAIT UP!
THIS IS YOUR LAST CHANCE TO WALK TO SCHOOL WITH YOUR DEAR OLDER SISTER!
SUTA
FOR REAL? MAYBE CONSIDER SWITCHING FROM SOCCER TO RACE-WALKING.
THANKS, BUT NO THANKS.
AND I ALWAYS WALK THIS FAST.
SUTA
GAAA (RRR)

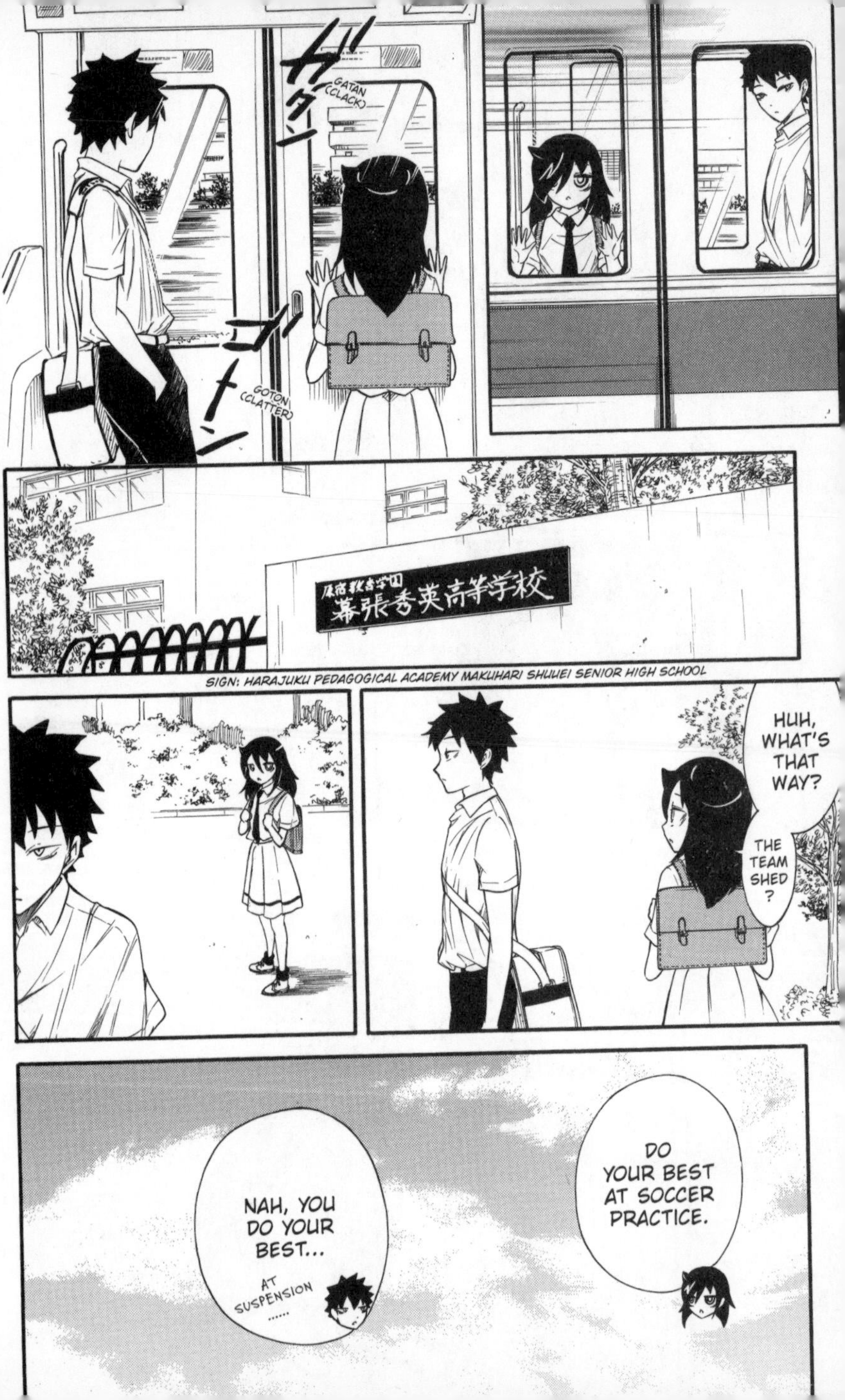
ガタン
GATAN (CLACK)
ゴトン
GOTON (CLATTER)
原宿教育学園
幕張秀英高等学校
SIGN: HARAJUKU PEDAGOGICAL ACADEMY MAKUHARI SHUUEI SENIOR HIGH SCHOOL
HUH, WHAT'S THAT WAY?
THE TEAM SHED?
DO YOUR BEST AT SOCCER PRACTICE.
NAH, YOU DO YOUR BEST...
AT SUSPENSION ......

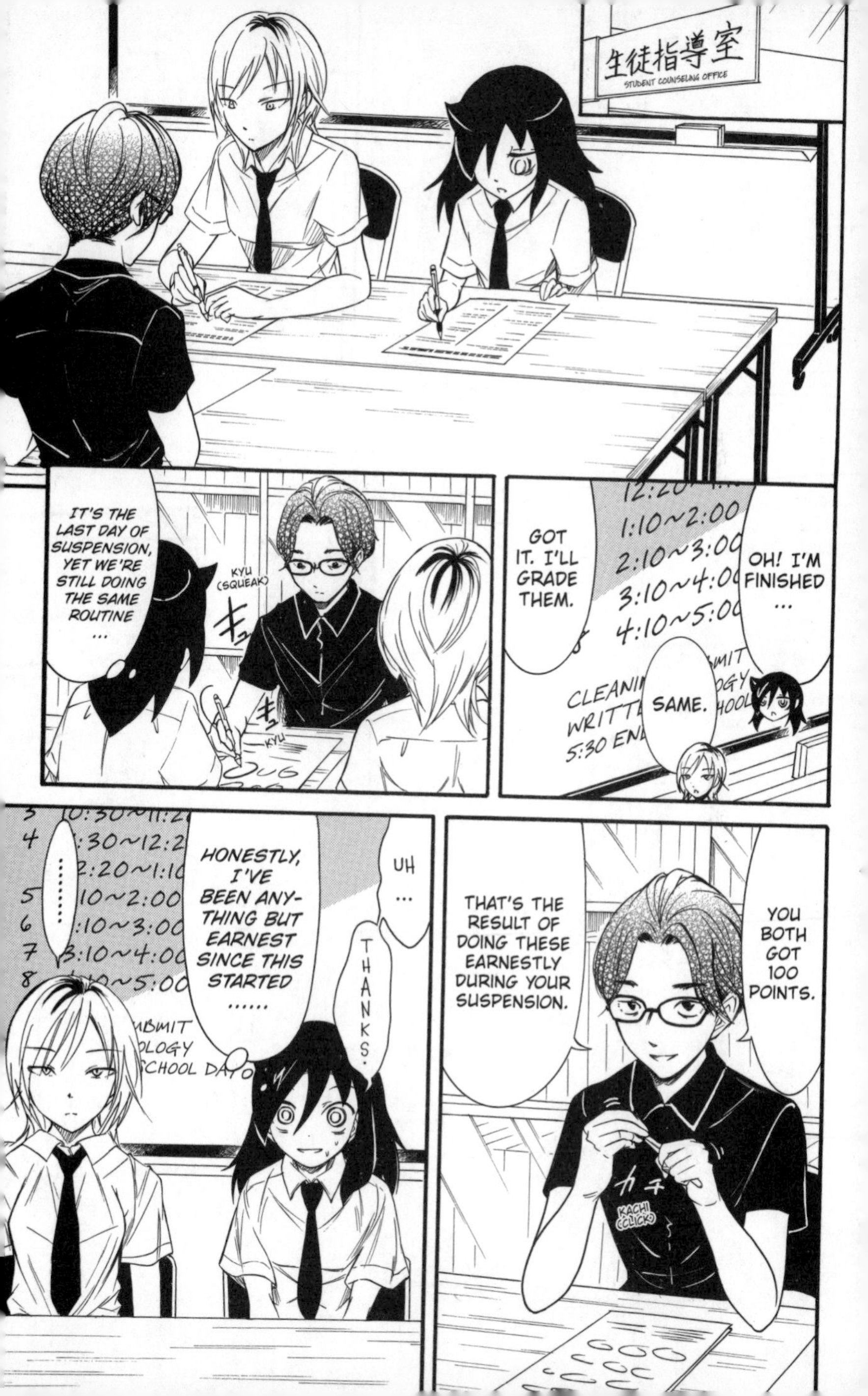
生徒指導室
STUDENT COUNSELING OFFICE
OH! I'M FINISHED ...
SAME.
GOT IT. I'LL GRADE THEM.
IT'S THE LAST DAY OF SUSPENSION, YET WE'RE STILL DOING THE SAME ROUTINE ...
KYU (SQUEAK)
YOU BOTH GOT 100 POINTS.
THAT'S THE RESULT OF DOING THESE EARNESTLY DURING YOUR SUSPENSION.
KACHI (CLICK)
UH ...
THANKS.
HONESTLY, I'VE BEEN ANYTHING BUT EARNEST SINCE THIS STARTED ......
......

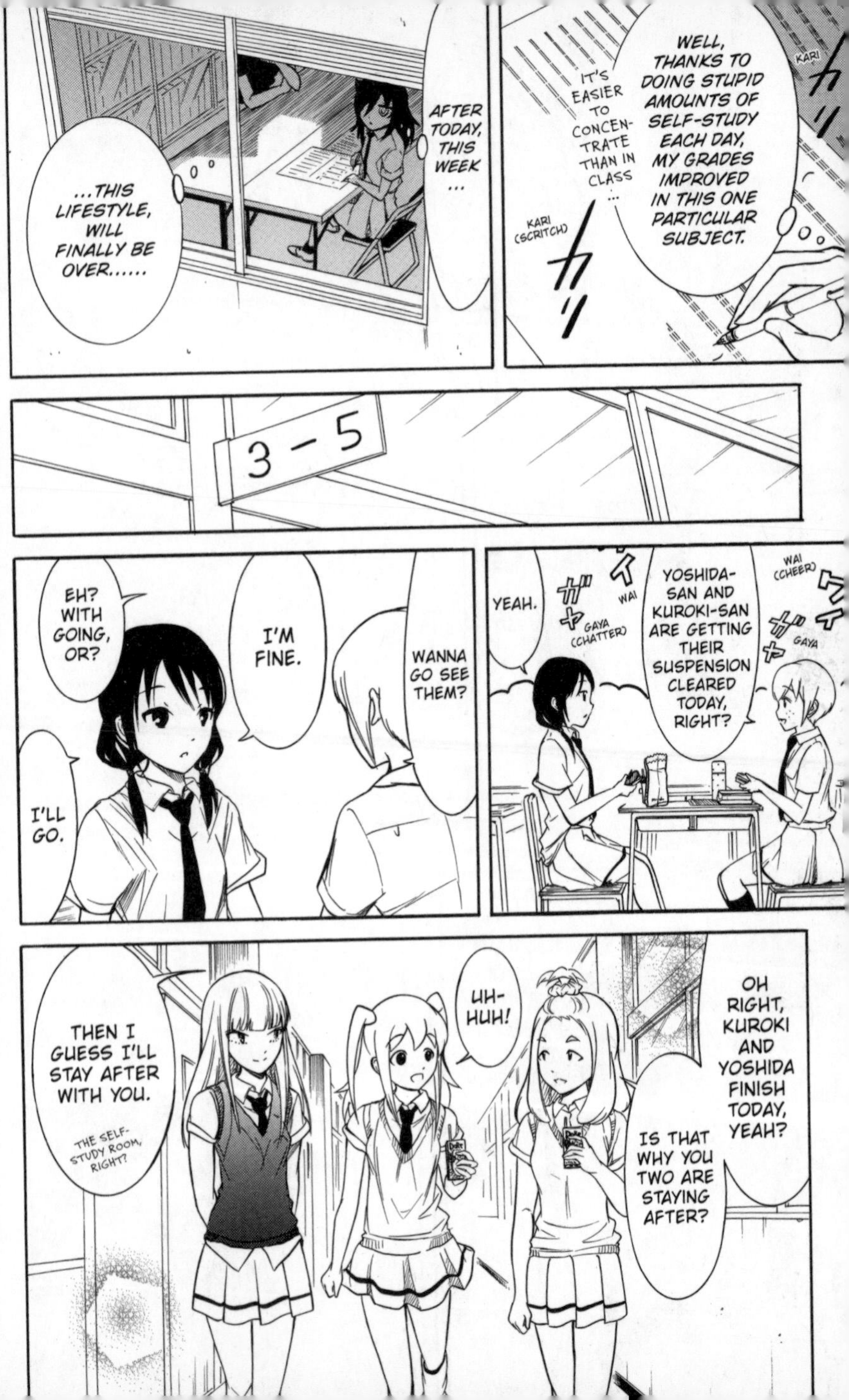
KARI
WELL, THANKS TO DOING STUPID AMOUNTS OF SELF-STUDY EACH DAY, MY GRADES IMPROVED IN THIS ONE PARTICULAR SUBJECT.
IT'S EASIER TO CONCEN-TRATE THAN IN CLASS...
KARI (SCRITCH)
AFTER TODAY, THIS WEEK...
...THIS LIFESTYLE, WILL FINALLY BE OVER......
3 - 5
WAI (CHEER)
GAYA
YOSHIDA-SAN AND KUROKI-SAN ARE GETTING THEIR SUSPENSION CLEARED TODAY, RIGHT?
WAI
GAYA (CHATTER)
YEAH.
WANNA GO SEE THEM?
I'M FINE.
EH? WITH GOING, OR?
I'LL GO.
OH RIGHT, KUROKI AND YOSHIDA FINISH TODAY, YEAH?
IS THAT WHY YOU TWO ARE STAYING AFTER?
UH-HUH!
THEN I GUESS I'LL STAY AFTER WITH YOU.
THE SELF-STUDY ROOM, RIGHT?

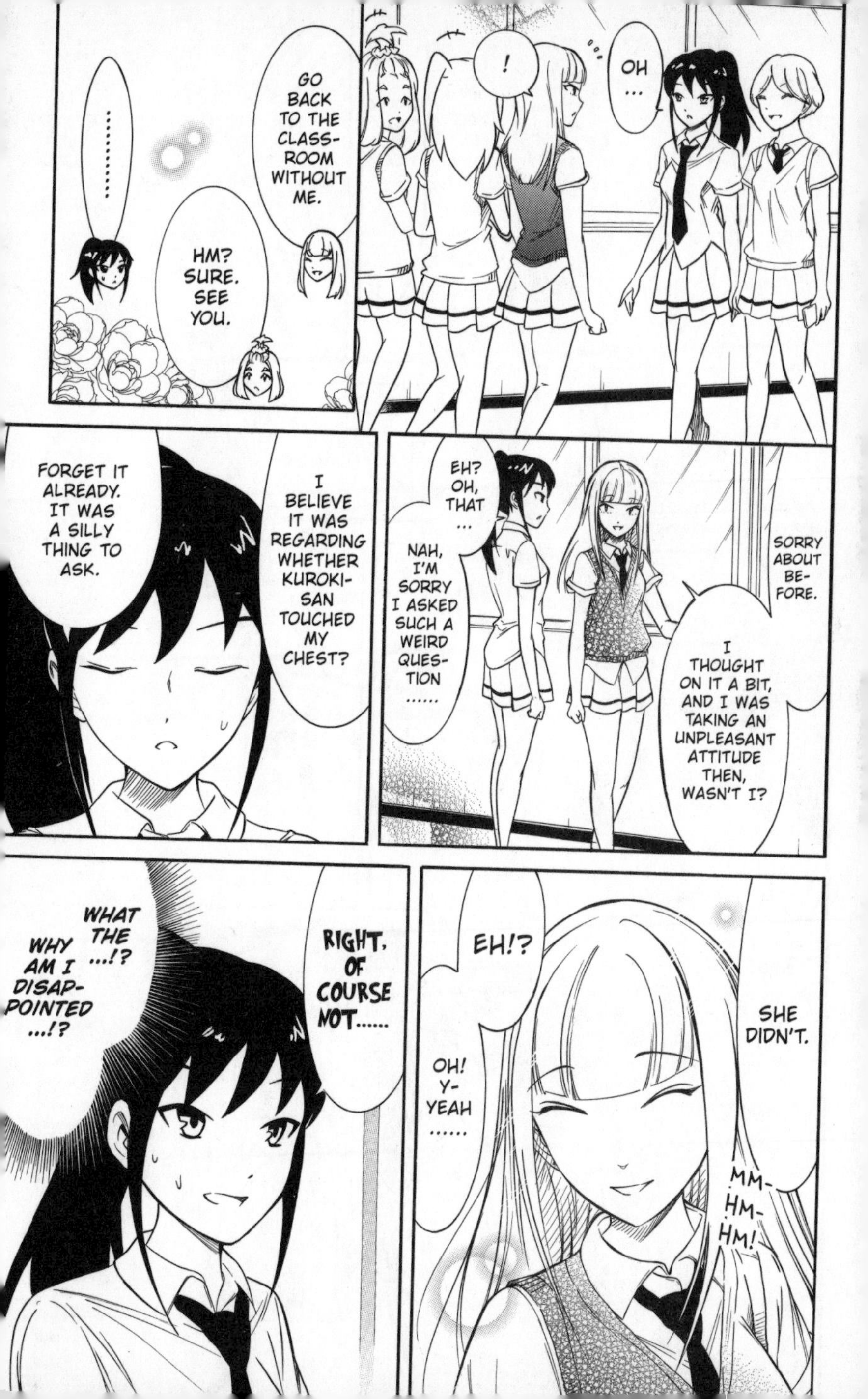
OH ...
!
GO BACK TO THE CLASS-ROOM WITHOUT ME.
HM? SURE. SEE YOU.
......
SORRY ABOUT BE-FORE.
I THOUGHT ON IT A BIT, AND I WAS TAKING AN UNPLEASANT ATTITUDE THEN, WASN'T I?
EH? OH, THAT ...
NAH, I'M SORRY I ASKED SUCH A WEIRD QUES-TION ......
I BELIEVE IT WAS REGARDING WHETHER KUROKI-SAN TOUCHED MY CHEST?
FORGET IT ALREADY. IT WAS A SILLY THING TO ASK.
SHE DIDN'T.
MM-HM-HM!
EH!?
OH! Y-YEAH ......
RIGHT, OF COURSE NOT......
WHAT THE ...!?
WHY AM I DISAP-POINTED ...!?

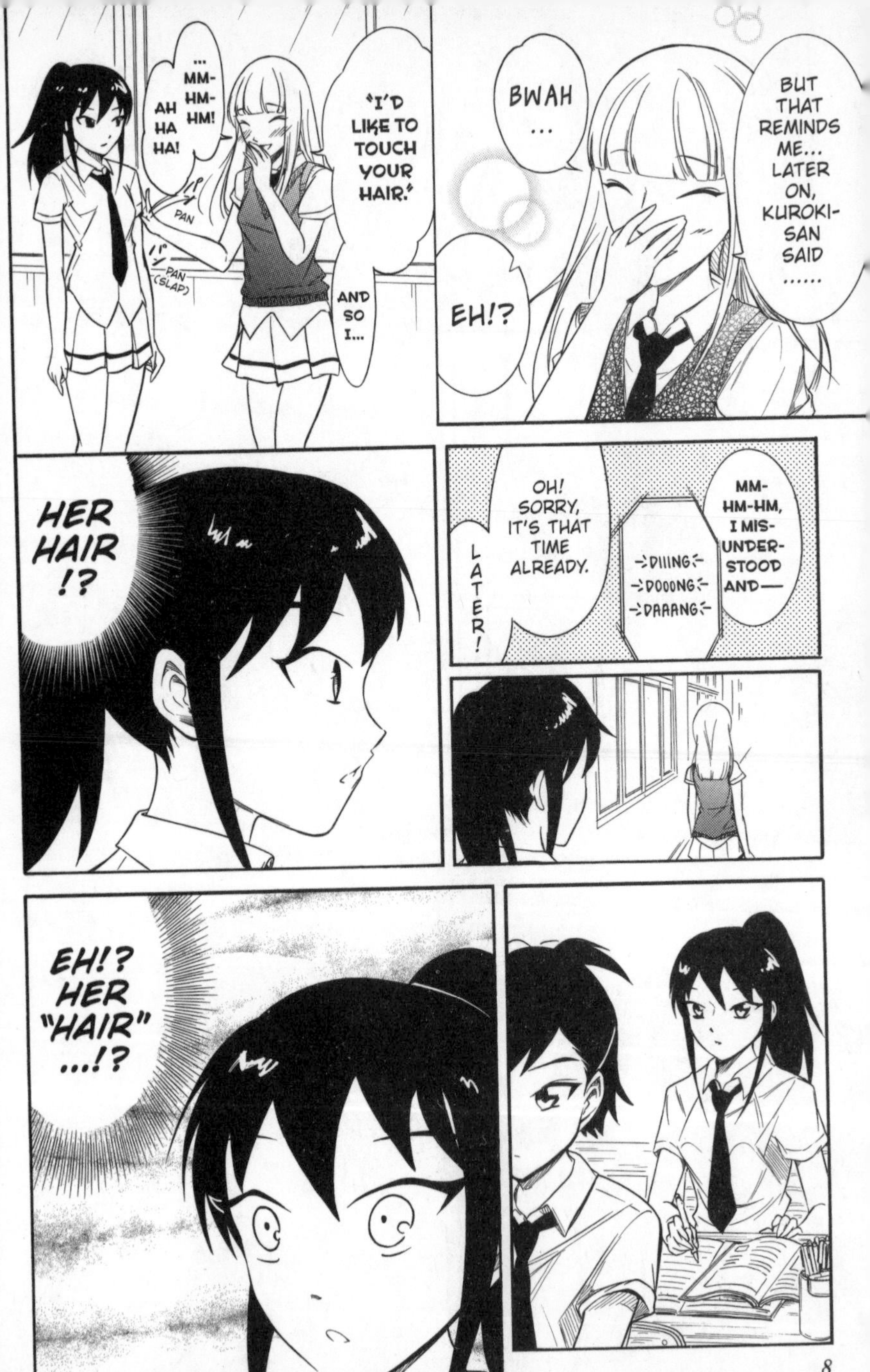
BUT THAT REMINDS ME... LATER ON, KUROKI-SAN SAID ......
BWAH ...
EH!?
"I'D LIKE TO TOUCH YOUR HAIR."
AND SO I...
... MM-HM-HM!
AH HA HA!
PAN
PAN (SLAP)
MM-HM-HM, I MISUNDERSTOOD AND—
DIIING
DOOONG
DAAANG
OH! SORRY, IT'S THAT TIME ALREADY.
LATER!
HER HAIR!?
EH!? HER "HAIR" ...!?

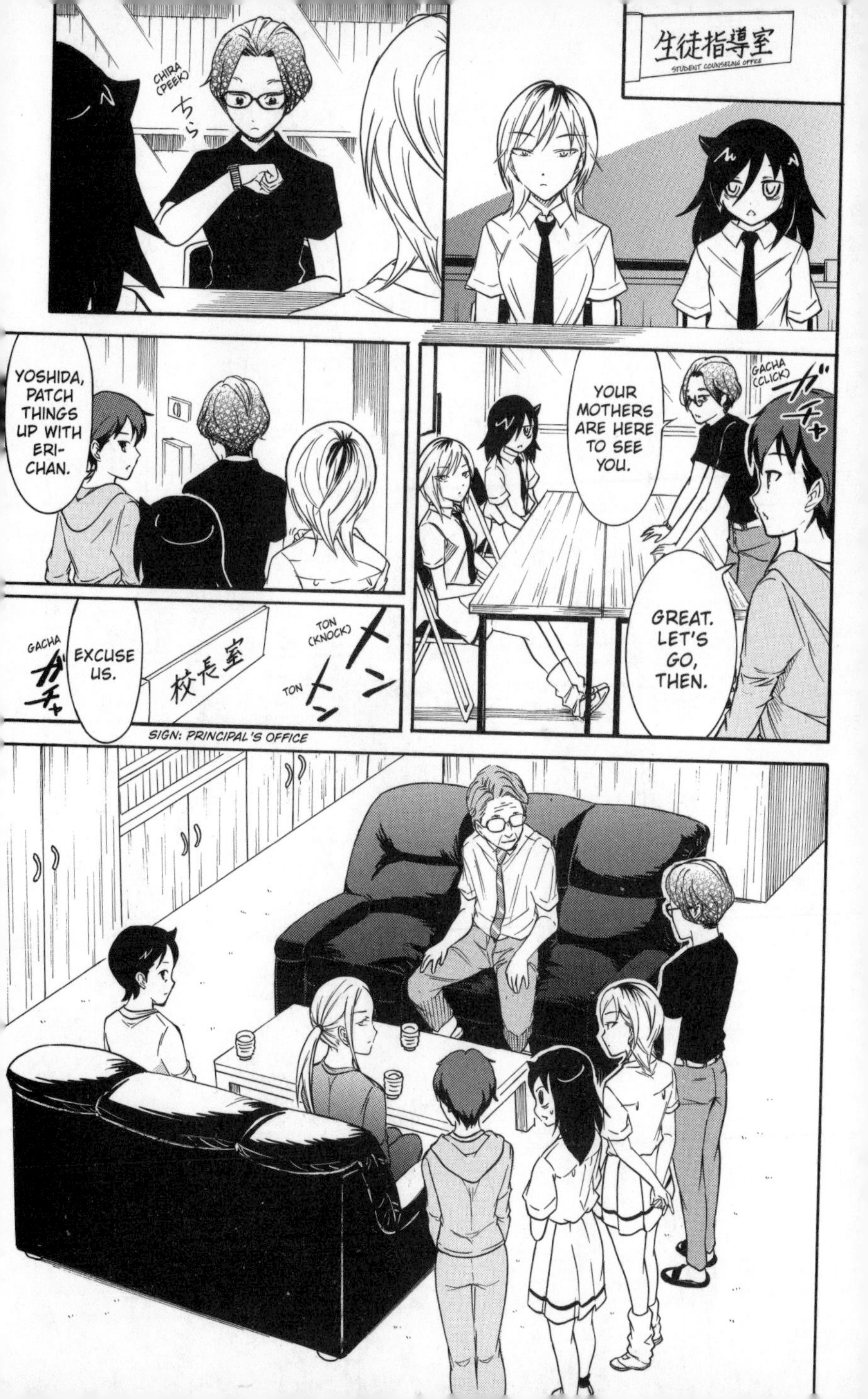
生徒指導室
STUDENT COUNSELING OFFICE
CHIRA (PEEK)
ちら
GACHA (CLICK)
ガチャ
YOUR MOTHERS ARE HERE TO SEE YOU.
GREAT. LET'S GO, THEN.
YOSHIDA, PATCH THINGS UP WITH ERI-CHAN.
TON (KNOCK)
トン
TON
トン
校長室
EXCUSE US.
GACHA
ガチャ
SIGN: PRINCIPAL'S OFFICE

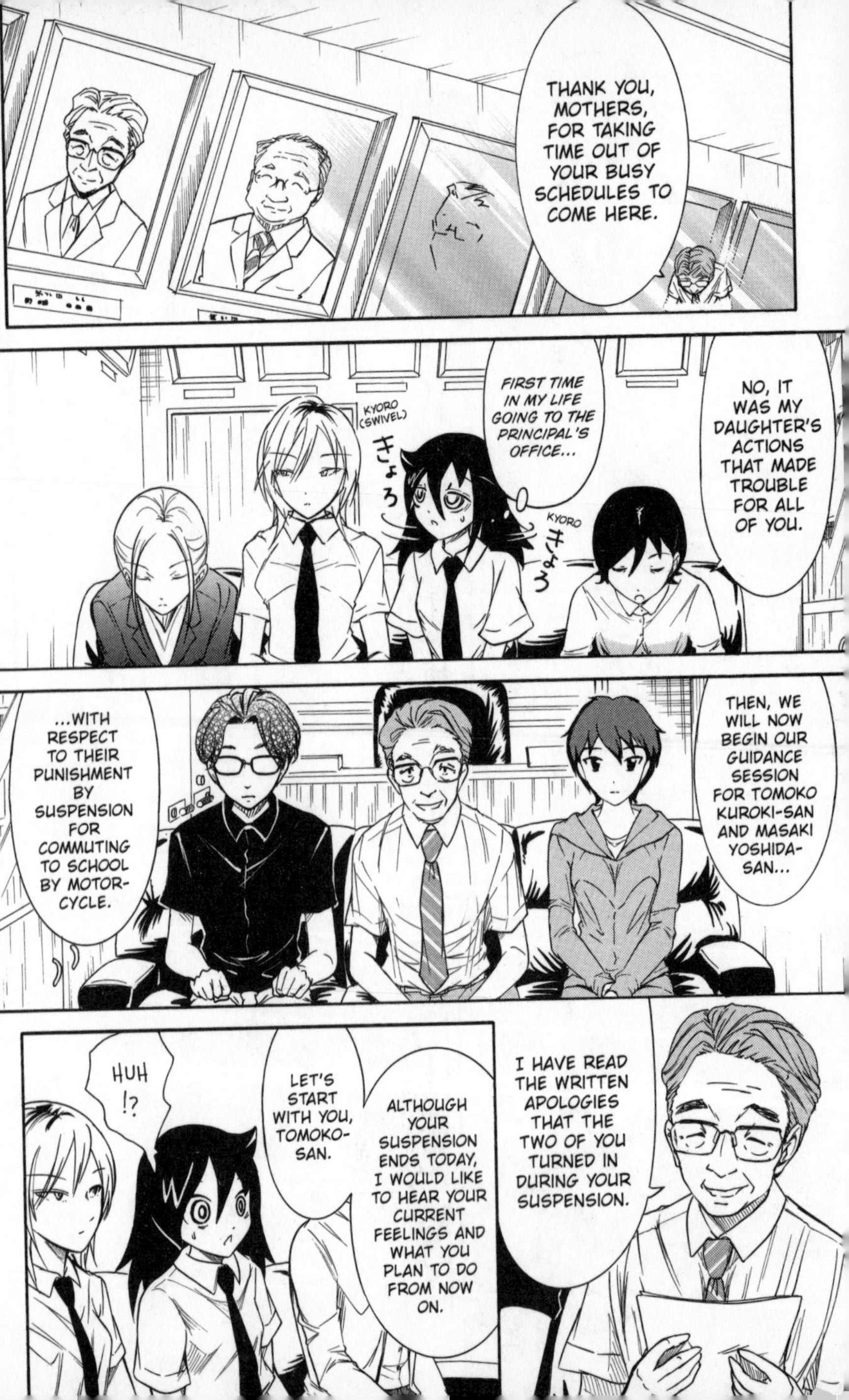
THANK YOU, MOTHERS, FOR TAKING TIME OUT OF YOUR BUSY SCHEDULES TO COME HERE.
NO, IT WAS MY DAUGHTER'S ACTIONS THAT MADE TROUBLE FOR ALL OF YOU.
FIRST TIME IN MY LIFE GOING TO THE PRINCIPAL'S OFFICE...
KYORO きょろ
KYORO (SWIVEL) きょろ
THEN, WE WILL NOW BEGIN OUR GUIDANCE SESSION FOR TOMOKO KUROKI-SAN AND MASAKI YOSHIDA-SAN...
...WITH RESPECT TO THEIR PUNISHMENT BY SUSPENSION FOR COMMUTING TO SCHOOL BY MOTOR-CYCLE.
I HAVE READ THE WRITTEN APOLOGIES THAT THE TWO OF YOU TURNED IN DURING YOUR SUSPENSION.
ALTHOUGH YOUR SUSPENSION ENDS TODAY, I WOULD LIKE TO HEAR YOUR CURRENT FEELINGS AND WHAT YOU PLAN TO DO FROM NOW ON.
LET'S START WITH YOU, TOMOKO-SAN.
HUH !?

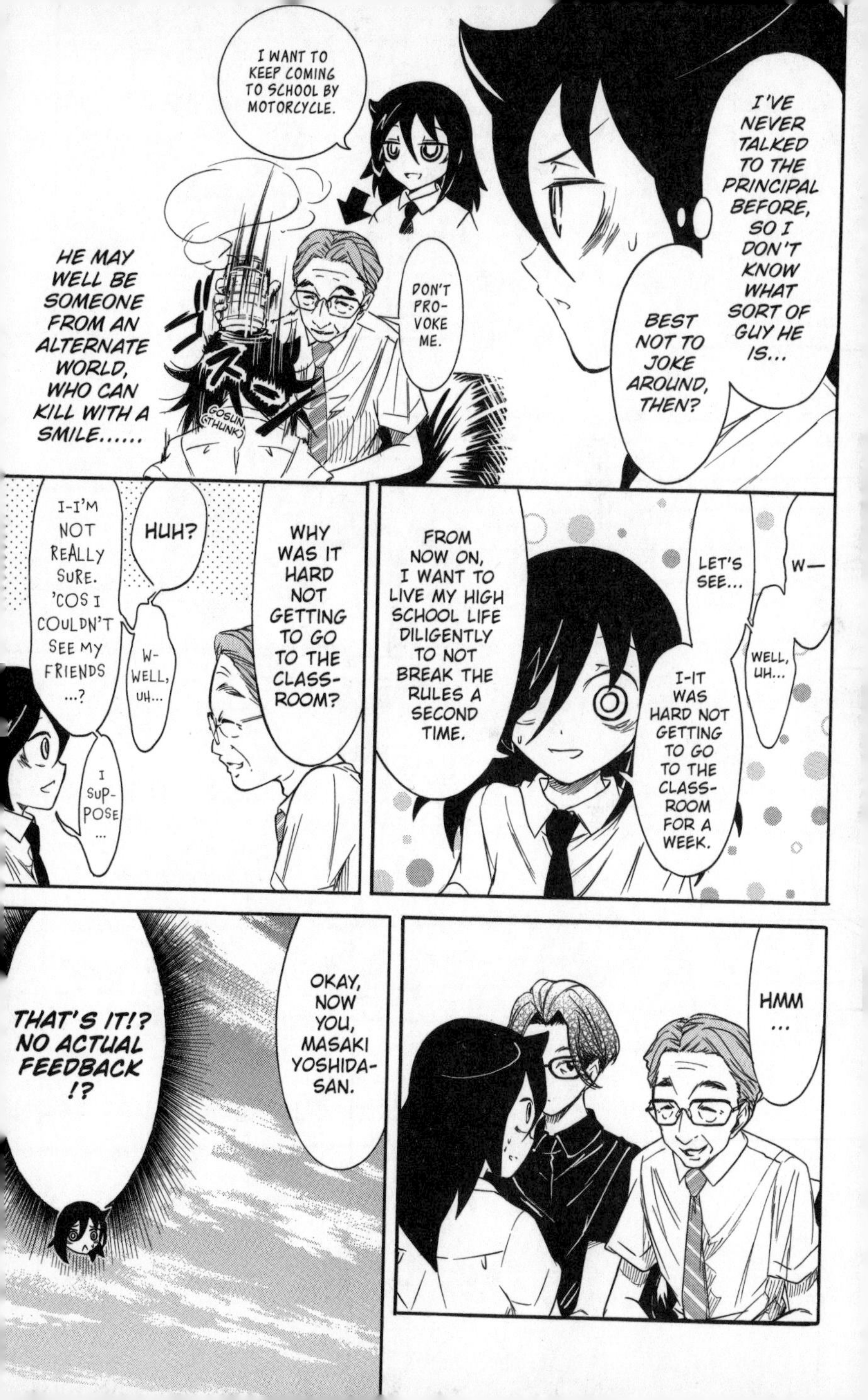
I'VE NEVER TALKED TO THE PRINCIPAL BEFORE, SO I DON'T KNOW WHAT SORT OF GUY HE IS...
BEST NOT TO JOKE AROUND, THEN?
I WANT TO KEEP COMING TO SCHOOL BY MOTORCYCLE.
DON'T PROVOKE ME.
GOSUN (THUNK)
HE MAY WELL BE SOMEONE FROM AN ALTERNATE WORLD, WHO CAN KILL WITH A SMILE......
W—
WELL, UH...
LET'S SEE...
I-IT WAS HARD NOT GETTING TO GO TO THE CLASSROOM FOR A WEEK.
FROM NOW ON, I WANT TO LIVE MY HIGH SCHOOL LIFE DILIGENTLY TO NOT BREAK THE RULES A SECOND TIME.
WHY WAS IT HARD NOT GETTING TO GO TO THE CLASSROOM?
HUH?
W-WELL, UH...
I-I'M NOT REALLY SURE. 'COS I COULDN'T SEE MY FRIENDS...?
I SUPPOSE...
HMM...
OKAY, NOW YOU, MASAKI YOSHIDA-SAN.
THAT'S IT!? NO ACTUAL FEEDBACK!?

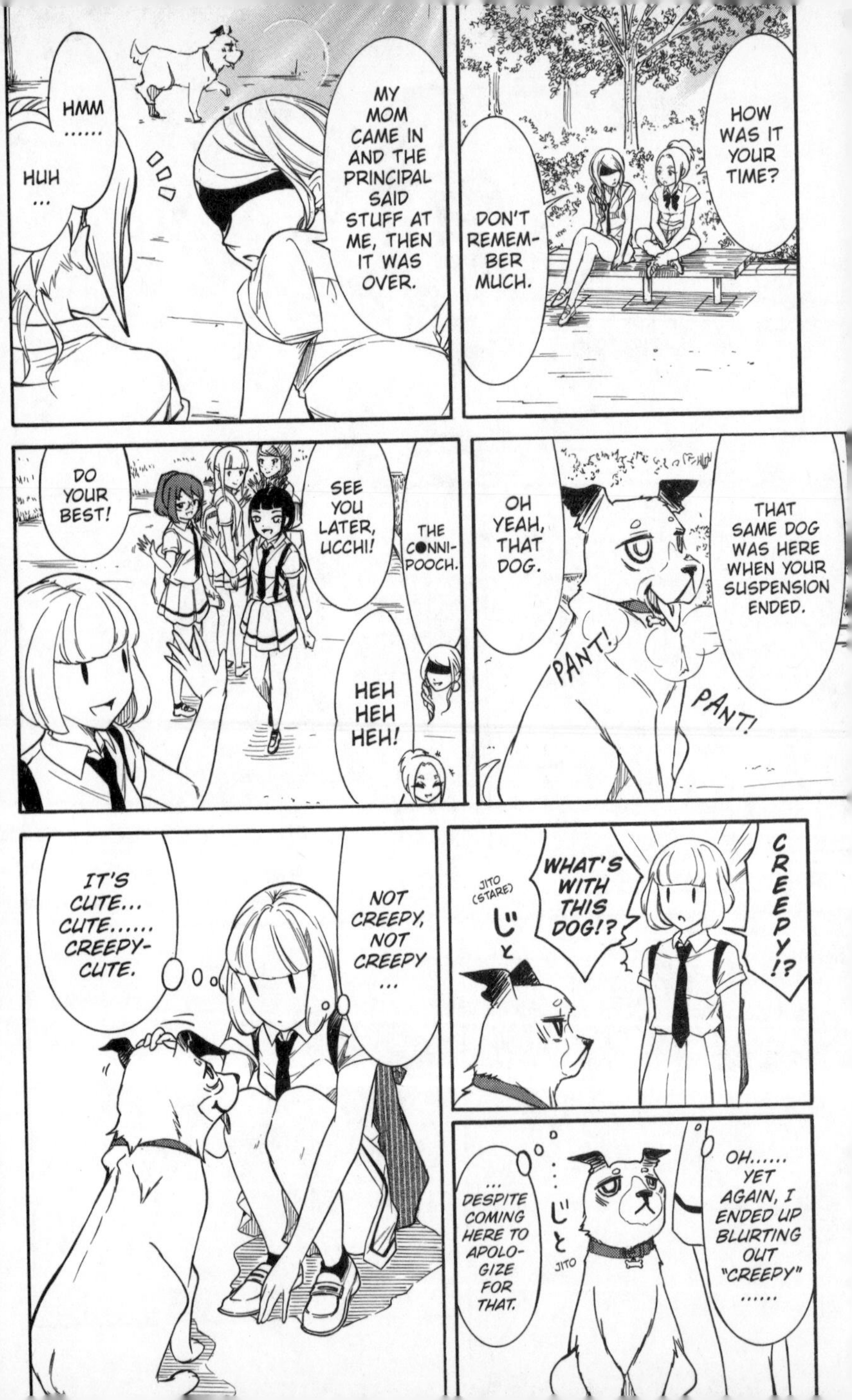
HOW WAS IT YOUR TIME?
DON'T REMEMBER MUCH.
MY MOM CAME IN AND THE PRINCIPAL SAID STUFF AT ME, THEN IT WAS OVER.
HMM......
HUH...
THAT SAME DOG WAS HERE WHEN YOUR SUSPENSION ENDED.
OH YEAH, THAT DOG.
PANT!
PANT!
THE CONNI-POOCH.
SEE YOU LATER, UCCHI!
HEH HEH HEH!
DO YOUR BEST!
CREEPY!?
WHAT'S WITH THIS DOG!?
JITO (STARE) じと
OH...... YET AGAIN, I ENDED UP BLURTING OUT "CREEPY"......
...じと JITO
...DESPITE COMING HERE TO APOLOGIZE FOR THAT.
NOT CREEPY, NOT CREEPY...
IT'S CUTE... CUTE...... CREEPY-CUTE.

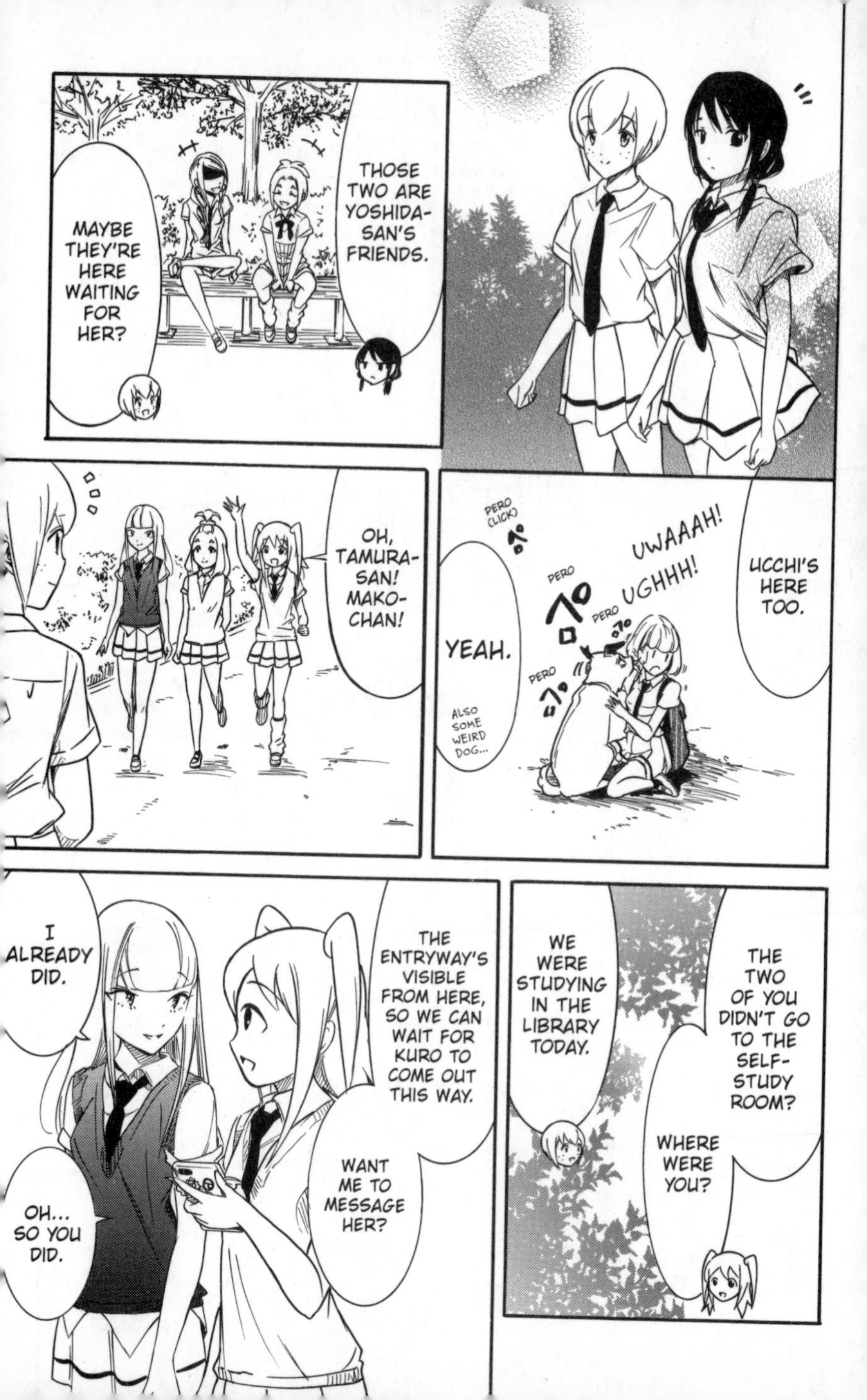
THOSE TWO ARE YOSHIDA-SAN'S FRIENDS.
MAYBE THEY'RE HERE WAITING FOR HER?
UCCHI'S HERE TOO.
UWAAAH! UGHHH!
PERO (CLICK)
PERO
PERO
PERO
YEAH.
ALSO SOME WEIRD DOG...
OH, TAMURA-SAN! MAKO-CHAN!
THE TWO OF YOU DIDN'T GO TO THE SELF-STUDY ROOM?
WHERE WERE YOU?
WE WERE STUDYING IN THE LIBRARY TODAY.
THE ENTRYWAY'S VISIBLE FROM HERE, SO WE CAN WAIT FOR KURO TO COME OUT THIS WAY.
WANT ME TO MESSAGE HER?
I ALREADY DID.
OH... SO YOU DID.

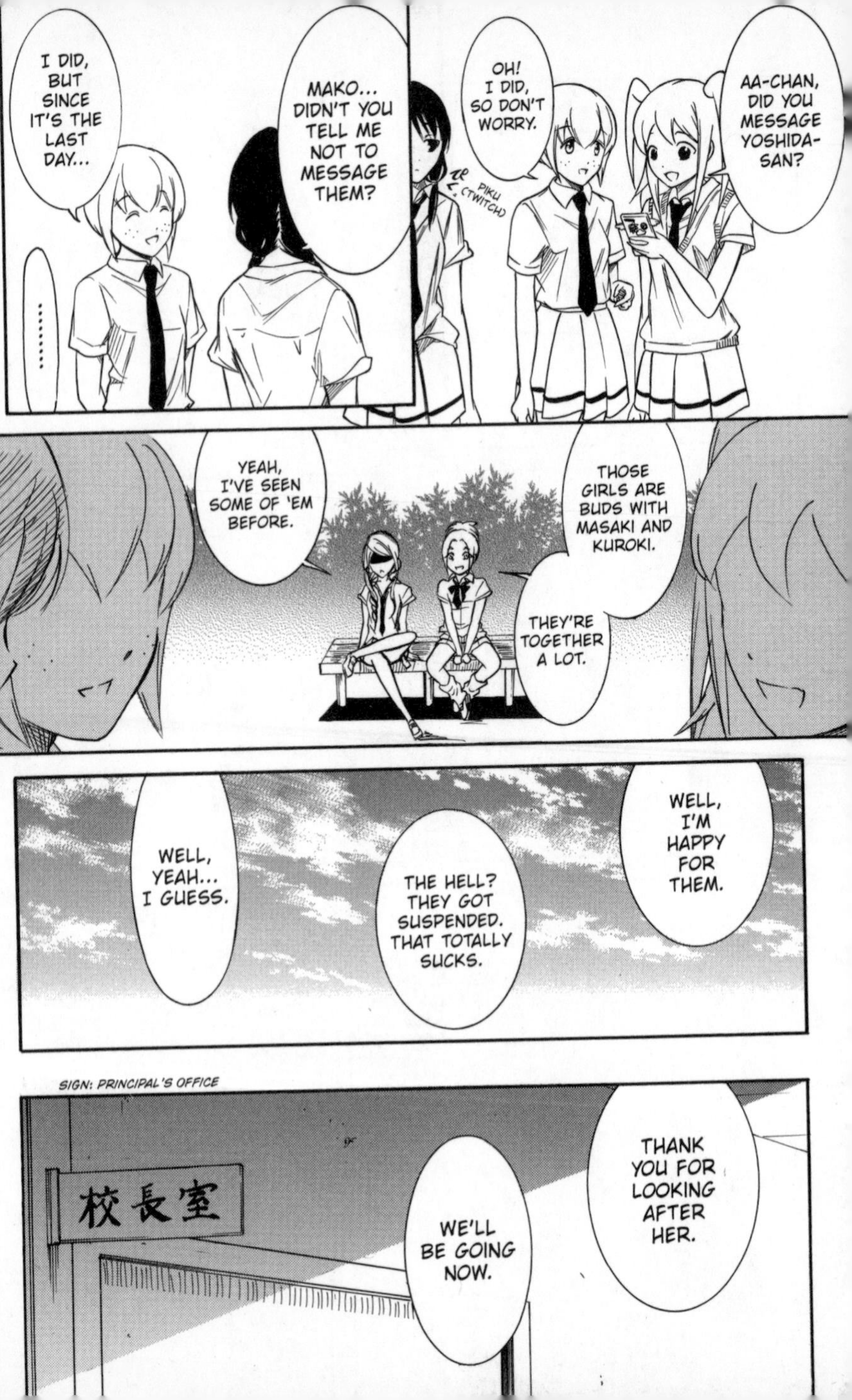
AA-CHAN, DID YOU MESSAGE YOSHIDA-SAN?
OH! I DID, SO DON'T WORRY.
PIKU (TWITCH)
MAKO... DIDN'T YOU TELL ME NOT TO MESSAGE THEM?
I DID, BUT SINCE IT'S THE LAST DAY...
......
THOSE GIRLS ARE BUDS WITH MASAKI AND KUROKI.
THEY'RE TOGETHER A LOT.
YEAH, I'VE SEEN SOME OF 'EM BEFORE.
WELL, I'M HAPPY FOR THEM.
THE HELL? THEY GOT SUSPENDED. THAT TOTALLY SUCKS.
WELL, YEAH... I GUESS.
SIGN: PRINCIPAL'S OFFICE
校長室
THANK YOU FOR LOOKING AFTER HER.
WE'LL BE GOING NOW.

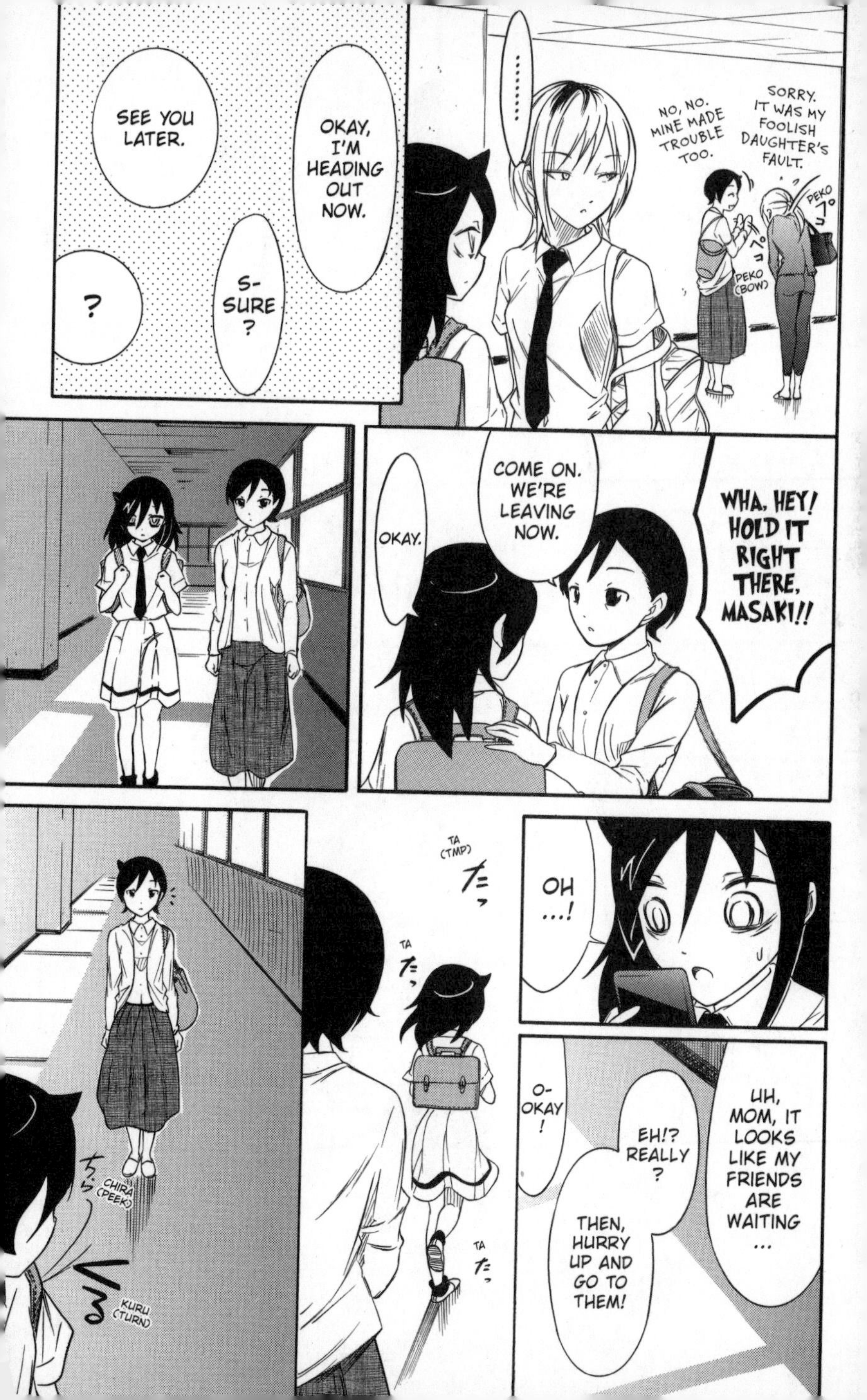
SORRY. IT WAS MY FOOLISH DAUGHTER'S FAULT.
PEKO
PEKO (BOW)
NO, NO. MINE MADE TROUBLE TOO.
......
OKAY, I'M HEADING OUT NOW.
SEE YOU LATER.
S-SURE?
?
WHA, HEY! HOLD IT RIGHT THERE, MASAKI!!
COME ON. WE'RE LEAVING NOW.
OKAY.
OH...!
UH, MOM, IT LOOKS LIKE MY FRIENDS ARE WAITING...
EH!? REALLY?
THEN, HURRY UP AND GO TO THEM!
O-OKAY!
TA (TMP)
TA
TA
CHIRA (PEEK)
KURU (TURN)

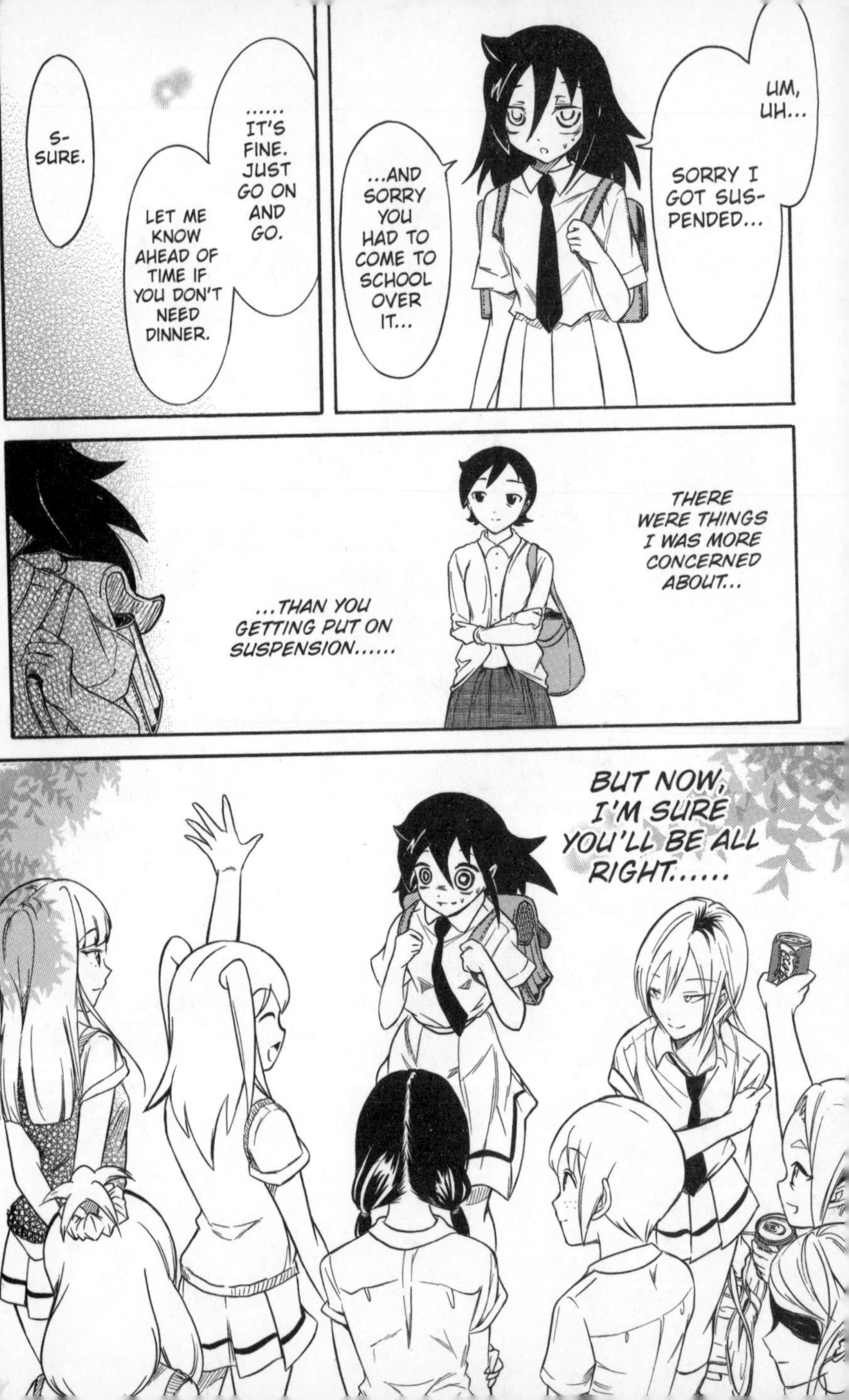
UM, UH...
SORRY I GOT SUS-PENDED...
...AND SORRY YOU HAD TO COME TO SCHOOL OVER IT...
......IT'S FINE. JUST GO ON AND GO.
LET ME KNOW AHEAD OF TIME IF YOU DON'T NEED DINNER.
S-SURE.
THERE WERE THINGS I WAS MORE CONCERNED ABOUT...
...THAN YOU GETTING PUT ON SUSPENSION......
BUT NOW, I'M SURE YOU'LL BE ALL RIGHT......

No Matter How I Look at It, It's You Guys' Fault I'm Not Popular!

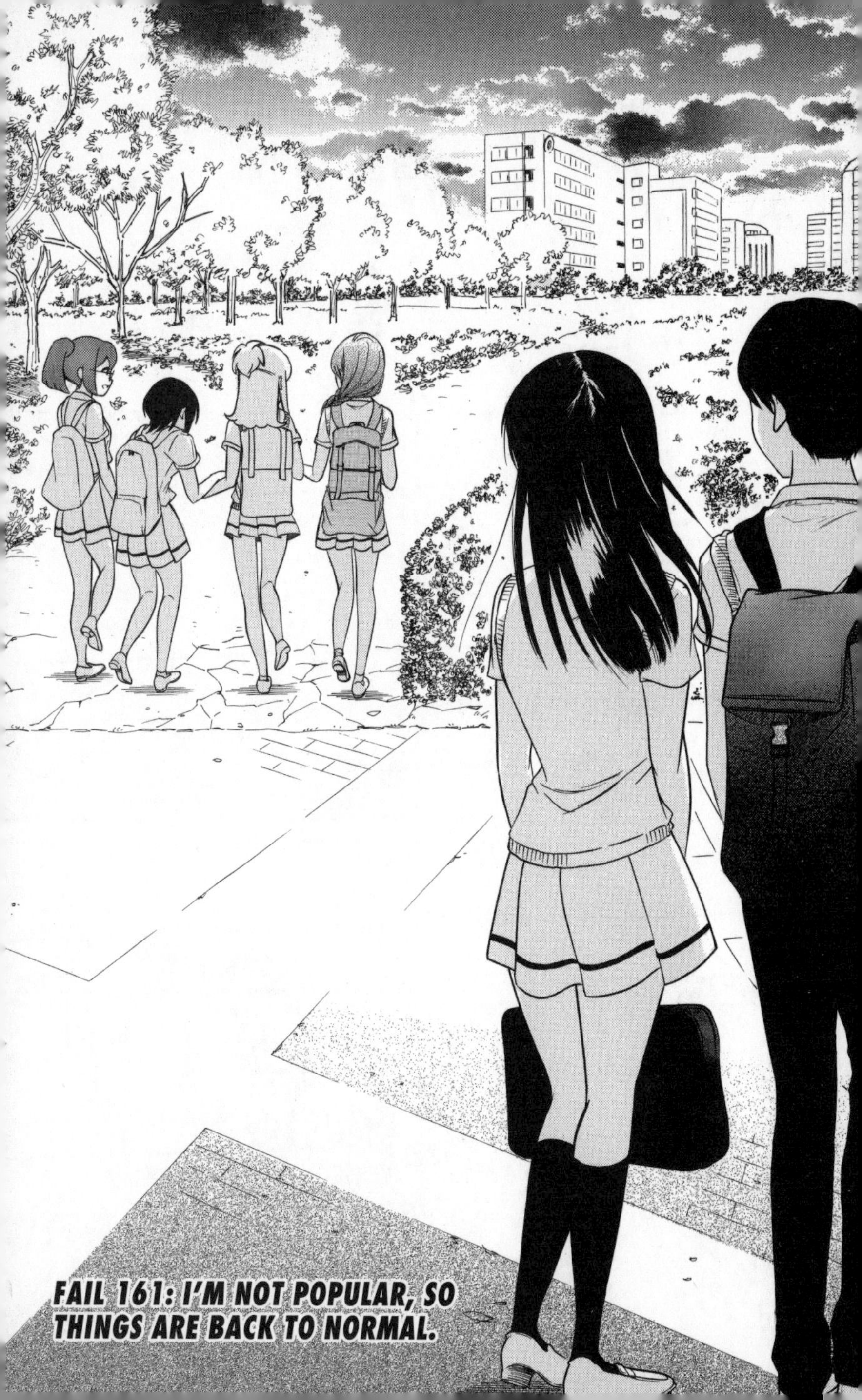
FAIL 161: I'M NOT POPULAR, SO THINGS ARE BACK TO NORMAL.

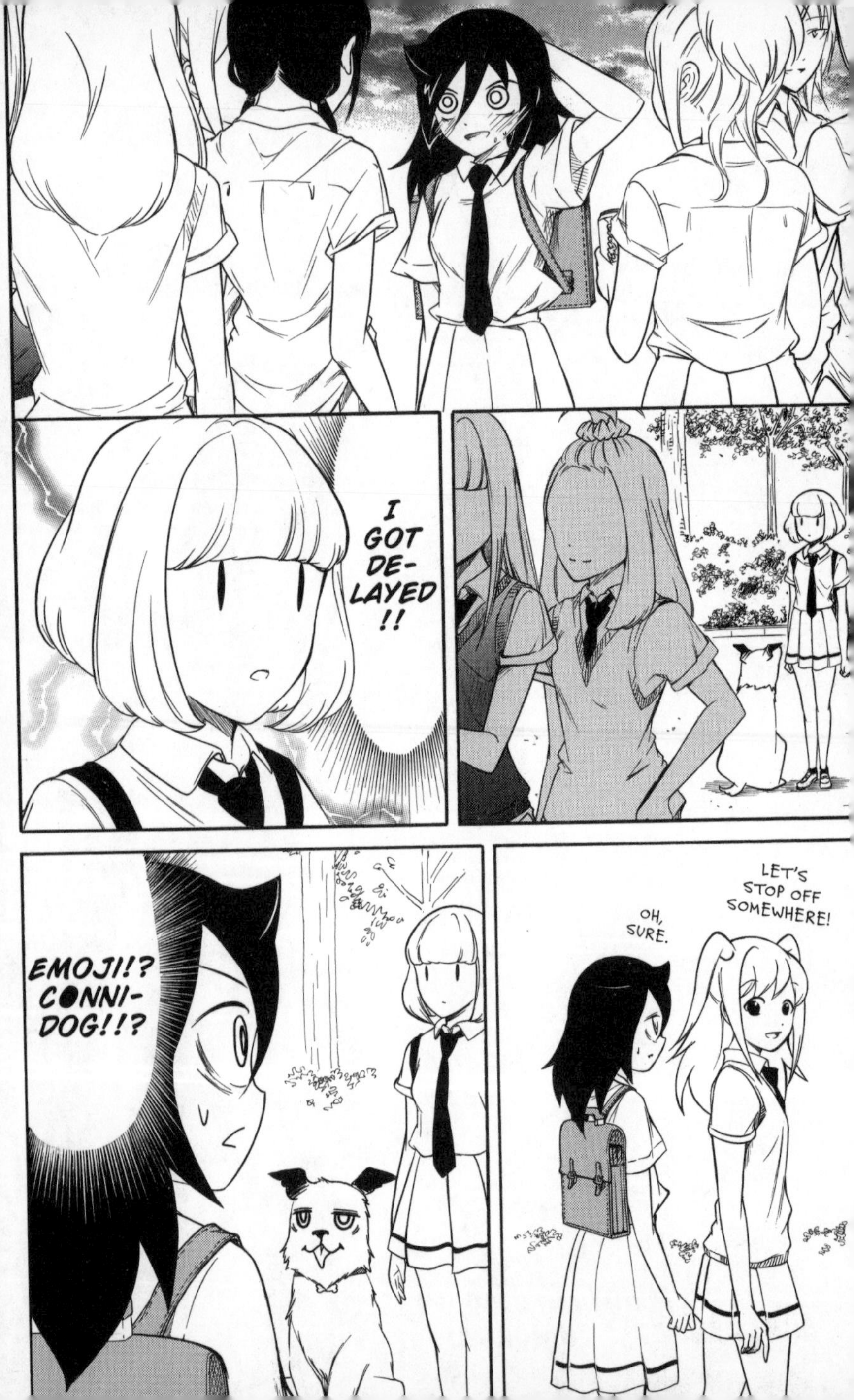
I GOT DE-LAYED!!
LET'S STOP OFF SOMEWHERE!
OH, SURE.
EMOJI!? CONNI-DOG!!?

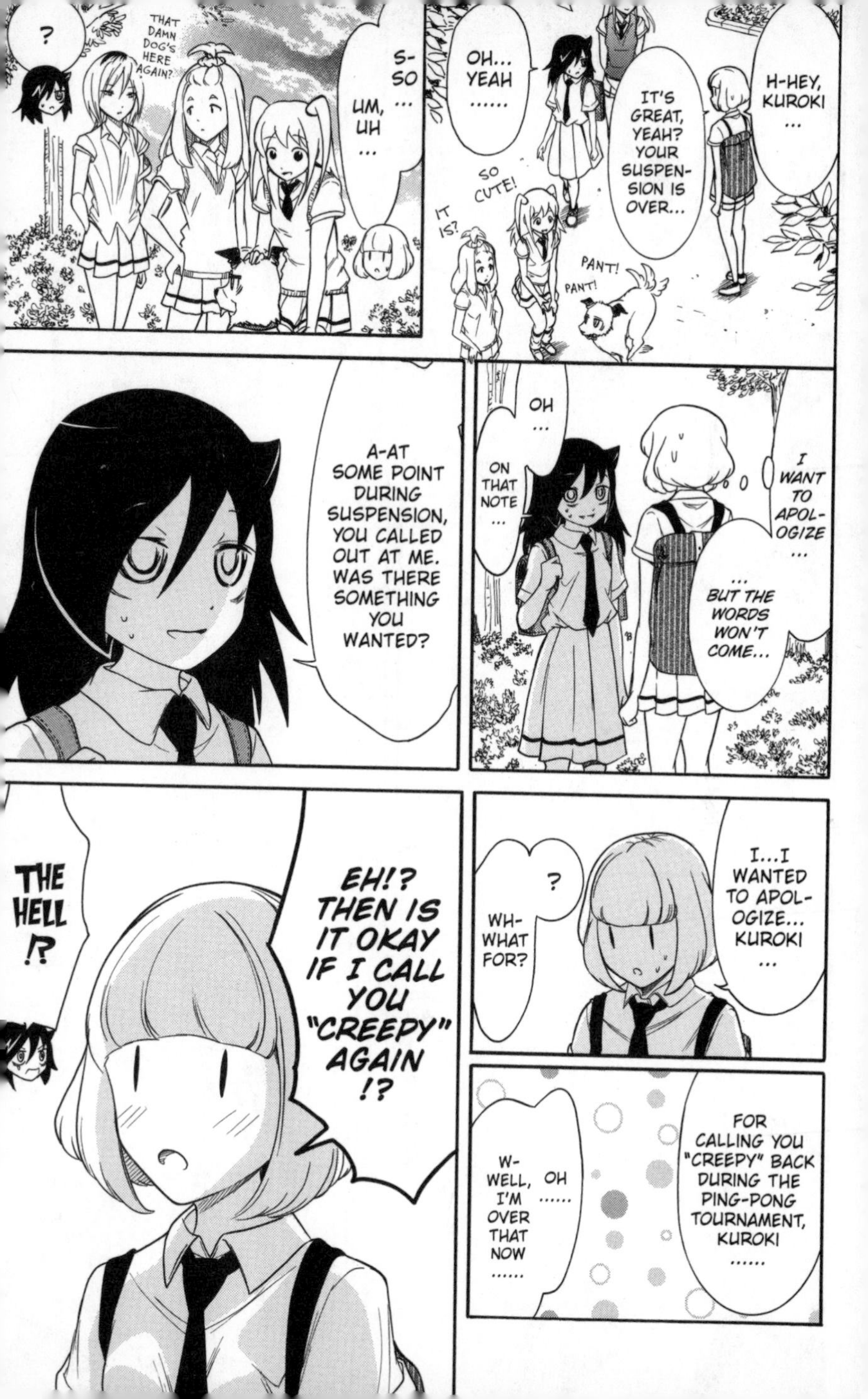
H-HEY, KUROKI ...
IT'S GREAT, YEAH? YOUR SUSPENSION IS OVER...
OH... YEAH ......
SO CUTE!
IT IS?
PANT! PANT!
S-SO ... UM, UH ...
THAT DAMN DOG'S HERE AGAIN?
?
I WANT TO APOLOGIZE ...
... BUT THE WORDS WON'T COME...
OH ... ON THAT NOTE ...
A-AT SOME POINT DURING SUSPENSION, YOU CALLED OUT AT ME. WAS THERE SOMETHING YOU WANTED?
I...I WANTED TO APOLOGIZE... KUROKI ...
? WH-WHAT FOR?
FOR CALLING YOU "CREEPY" BACK DURING THE PING-PONG TOURNAMENT, KUROKI ......
OH ......
W-WELL, I'M OVER THAT NOW ......
EH!? THEN IS IT OKAY IF I CALL YOU "CREEPY" AGAIN !?
THE HELL !?

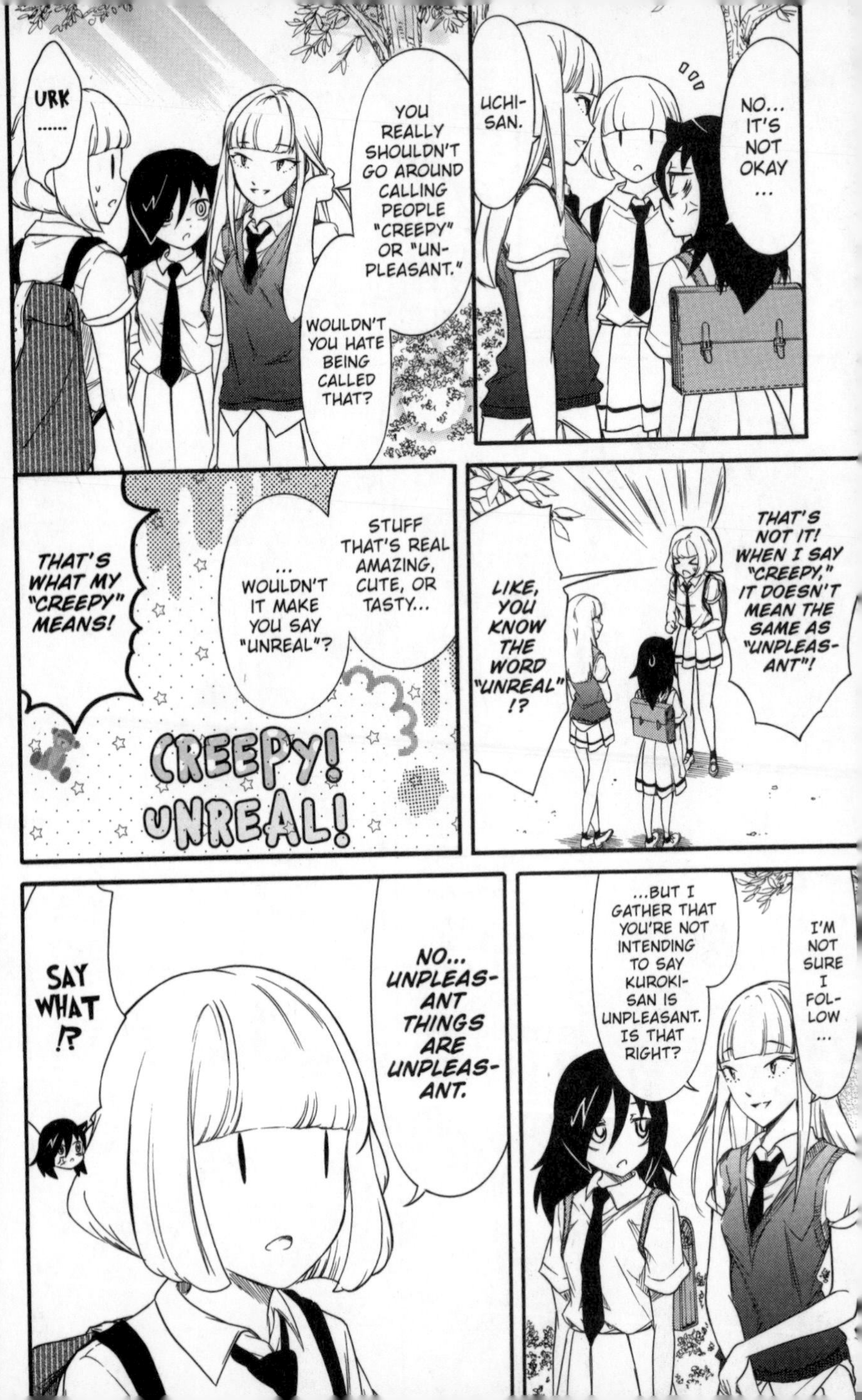
NO... IT'S NOT OKAY ...
UCHI-SAN.
YOU REALLY SHOULDN'T GO AROUND CALLING PEOPLE "CREEPY" OR "UN-PLEASANT."
WOULDN'T YOU HATE BEING CALLED THAT?
URK ......
THAT'S NOT IT! WHEN I SAY "CREEPY," IT DOESN'T MEAN THE SAME AS "UNPLEAS-ANT"!
LIKE, YOU KNOW THE WORD "UNREAL" !?
STUFF THAT'S REAL AMAZING, CUTE, OR TASTY...
... WOULDN'T IT MAKE YOU SAY "UNREAL"?
THAT'S WHAT MY "CREEPY" MEANS!
CREEPY! UNREAL!
I'M NOT SURE I FOL-LOW ...
...BUT I GATHER THAT YOU'RE NOT INTENDING TO SAY KUROKI-SAN IS UNPLEASANT. IS THAT RIGHT?
NO... UNPLEAS-ANT THINGS ARE UNPLEAS-ANT.
SAY WHAT !?

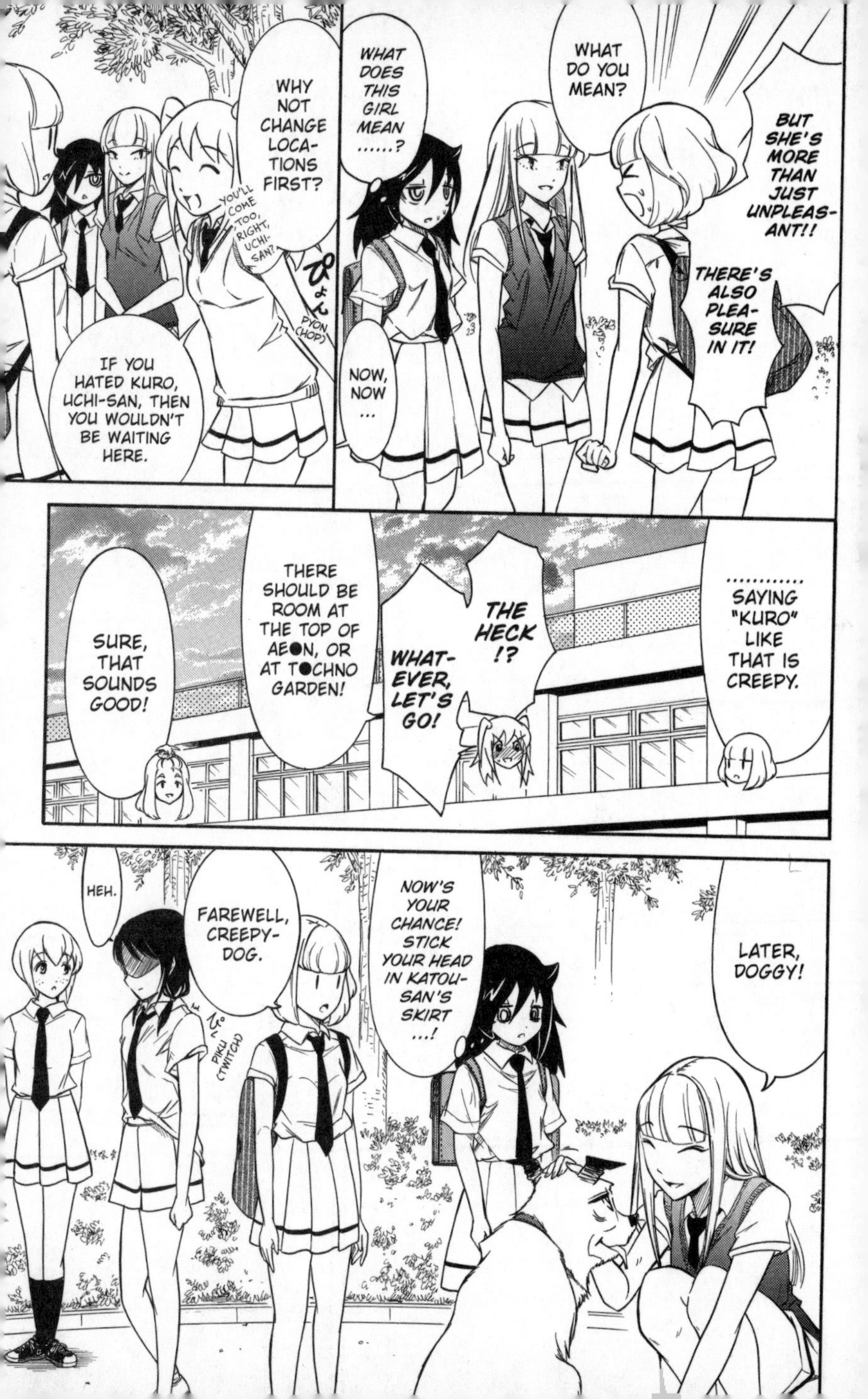
WHAT DO YOU MEAN?
BUT SHE'S MORE THAN JUST UNPLEASANT!!
THERE'S ALSO PLEASURE IN IT!
WHAT DOES THIS GIRL MEAN ......?
NOW, NOW ...
WHY NOT CHANGE LOCATIONS FIRST?
YOU'LL COME TOO, RIGHT, UCHI-SAN?
ぴょん
PYON (HOP)
IF YOU HATED KURO, UCHI-SAN, THEN YOU WOULDN'T BE WAITING HERE.
.... SAYING "KURO" LIKE THAT IS CREEPY.
THE HECK!?
WHATEVER, LET'S GO!
THERE SHOULD BE ROOM AT THE TOP OF AE●N, OR AT T●CHNO GARDEN!
SURE, THAT SOUNDS GOOD!
LATER, DOGGY!
NOW'S YOUR CHANCE! STICK YOUR HEAD IN KATOU-SAN'S SKIRT ...!
FAREWELL, CREEPY-DOG.
ぴく
PIKU (TWITCH)
HEH.

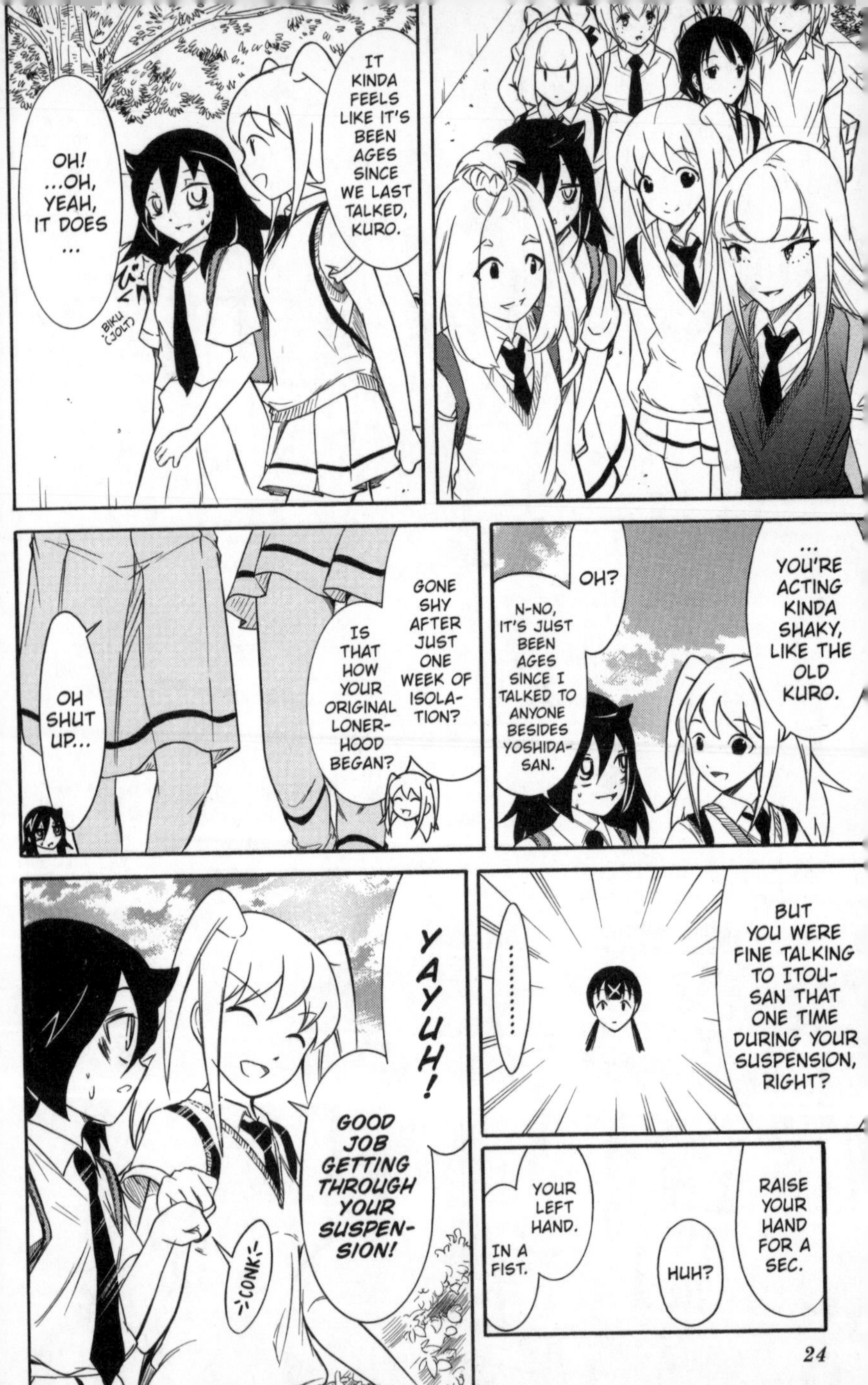
IT KINDA FEELS LIKE IT'S BEEN AGES SINCE WE LAST TALKED, KURO.
OH! ...OH, YEAH, IT DOES ...
BIKU (JOLT)
... YOU'RE ACTING KINDA SHAKY, LIKE THE OLD KURO.
OH?
N-NO, IT'S JUST BEEN AGES SINCE I TALKED TO ANYONE BESIDES YOSHIDA-SAN.
GONE SHY AFTER JUST ONE WEEK OF ISOLATION?
IS THAT HOW YOUR ORIGINAL LONER-HOOD BEGAN?
OH SHUT UP...
BUT YOU WERE FINE TALKING TO ITOU-SAN THAT ONE TIME DURING YOUR SUSPENSION, RIGHT?
....
RAISE YOUR HAND FOR A SEC.
HUH?
YOUR LEFT HAND.
IN A FIST.
YAYUH!
GOOD JOB GETTING THROUGH YOUR SUSPEN-SION!
CONK

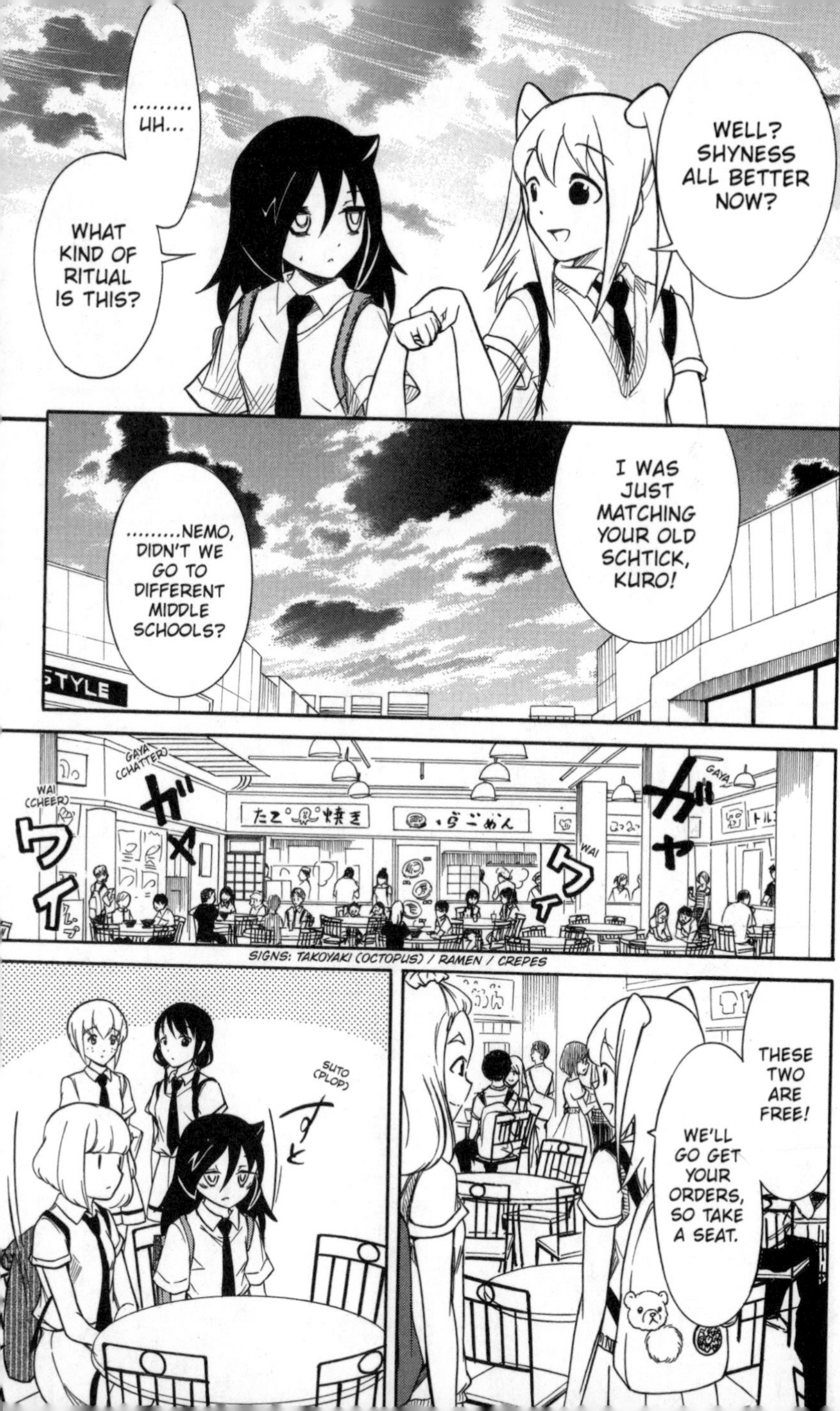
WELL? SHYNESS ALL BETTER NOW?
....
UH...
WHAT KIND OF RITUAL IS THIS?
I WAS JUST MATCHING YOUR OLD SCHTICK, KURO!
.........NEMO, DIDN'T WE GO TO DIFFERENT MIDDLE SCHOOLS?
STYLE
GAYA
WAI
GAYA (CHATTER)
WAI (CHEER)
SIGNS: TAKOYAKI (OCTOPUS) / RAMEN / CREPES
THESE TWO ARE FREE!
WE'LL GO GET YOUR ORDERS, SO TAKE A SEAT.
SUTO (PLOP)

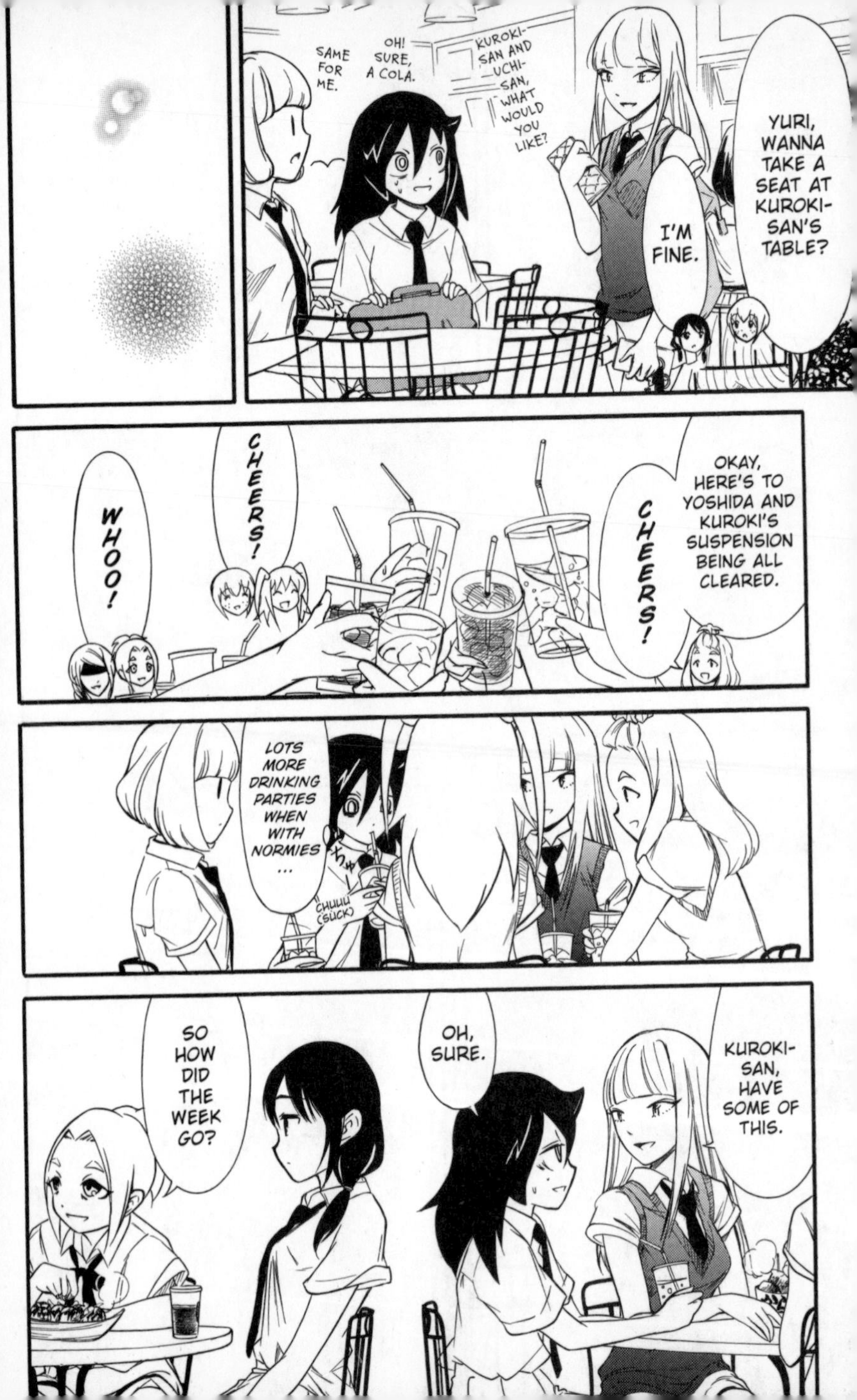
YURI, WANNA TAKE A SEAT AT KUROKI-SAN'S TABLE?
I'M FINE.
KUROKI-SAN AND UCHI-SAN, WHAT WOULD YOU LIKE?
OH! SURE, A COLA.
SAME FOR ME.
OKAY, HERE'S TO YOSHIDA AND KUROKI'S SUSPENSION BEING ALL CLEARED.
CHEERS!
CHEERS!
WHOO!
LOTS MORE DRINKING PARTIES WHEN WITH NORMIES ...
CHUUU (SUCK)
KUROKI-SAN, HAVE SOME OF THIS.
OH, SURE.
SO HOW DID THE WEEK GO?

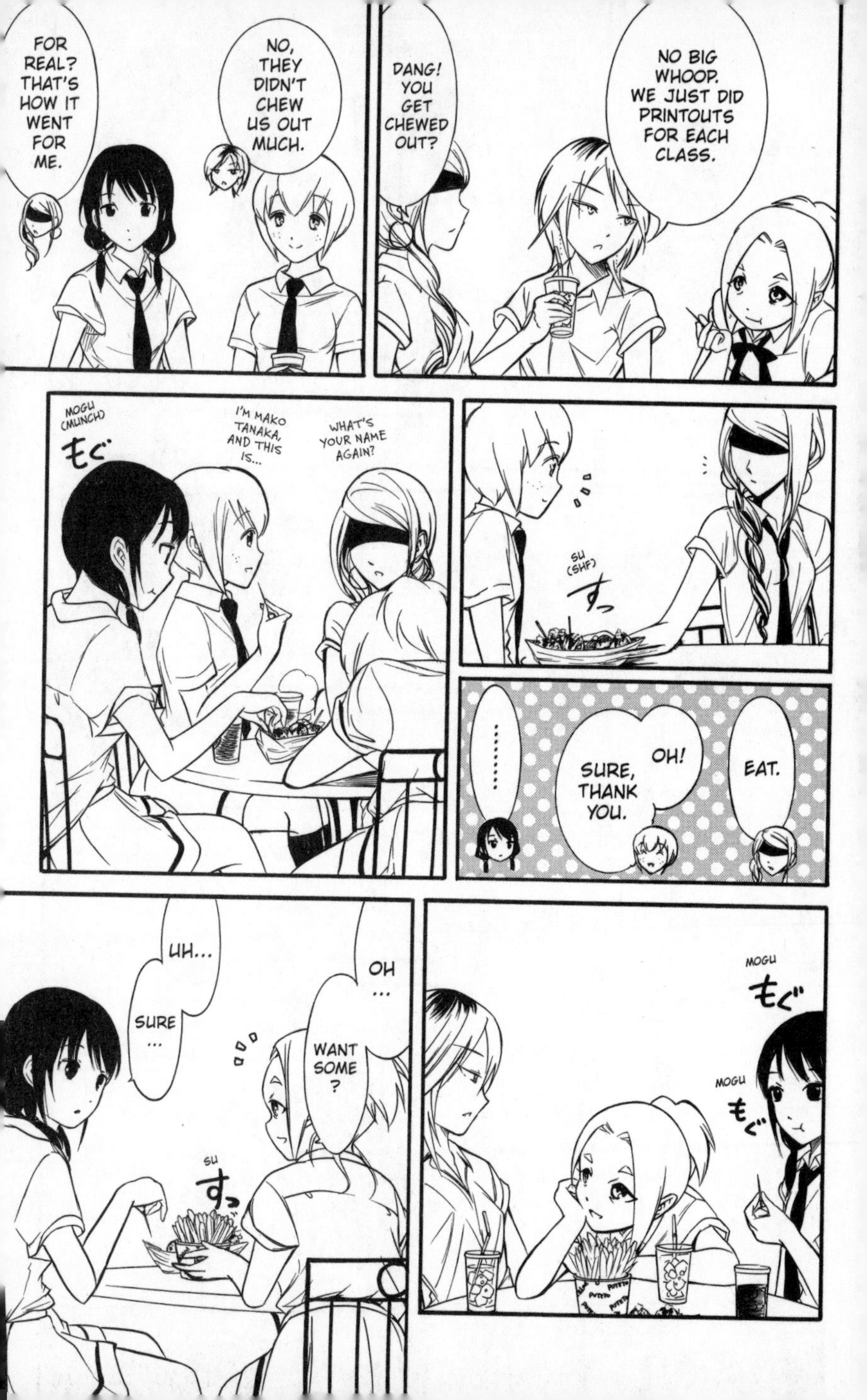
NO BIG WHOOP. WE JUST DID PRINTOUTS FOR EACH CLASS.
DANG! YOU GET CHEWED OUT?
NO, THEY DIDN'T CHEW US OUT MUCH.
FOR REAL? THAT'S HOW IT WENT FOR ME.
SU (SHF)
すっ
EAT.
OH!
SURE, THANK YOU.
......
WHAT'S YOUR NAME AGAIN?
I'M MAKO TANAKA, AND THIS IS...
MOGU (MUNCH)
もぐ
MOGU
もぐ
MOGU
もぐ
OH...
WANT SOME?
SU
すっ
UH...
SURE...

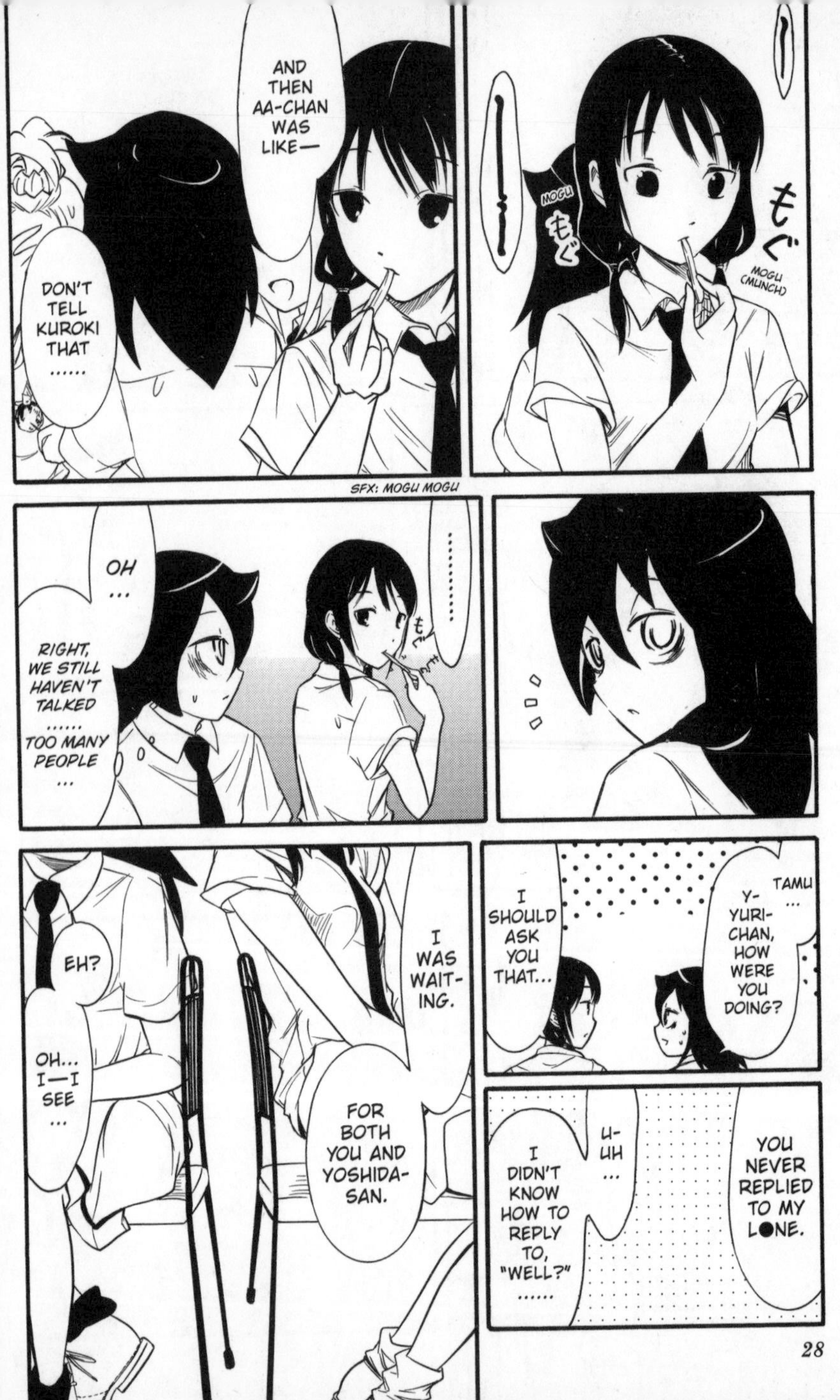
!
—
MOGU
もぐ
もぐ
MOGU (MUNCH)
AND THEN AA-CHAN WAS LIKE—
DON'T TELL KUROKI THAT ......
SFX: MOGU MOGU
......
OH ...
RIGHT, WE STILL HAVEN'T TALKED ...... TOO MANY PEOPLE ...
TAMU ...
Y-YURI-CHAN, HOW WERE YOU DOING?
I SHOULD ASK YOU THAT...
YOU NEVER REPLIED TO MY LONE.
U-UH ...
I DIDN'T KNOW HOW TO REPLY TO, "WELL?" ......
I WAS WAIT-ING.
FOR BOTH YOU AND YOSHIDA-SAN.
EH?
OH... I—I SEE ...

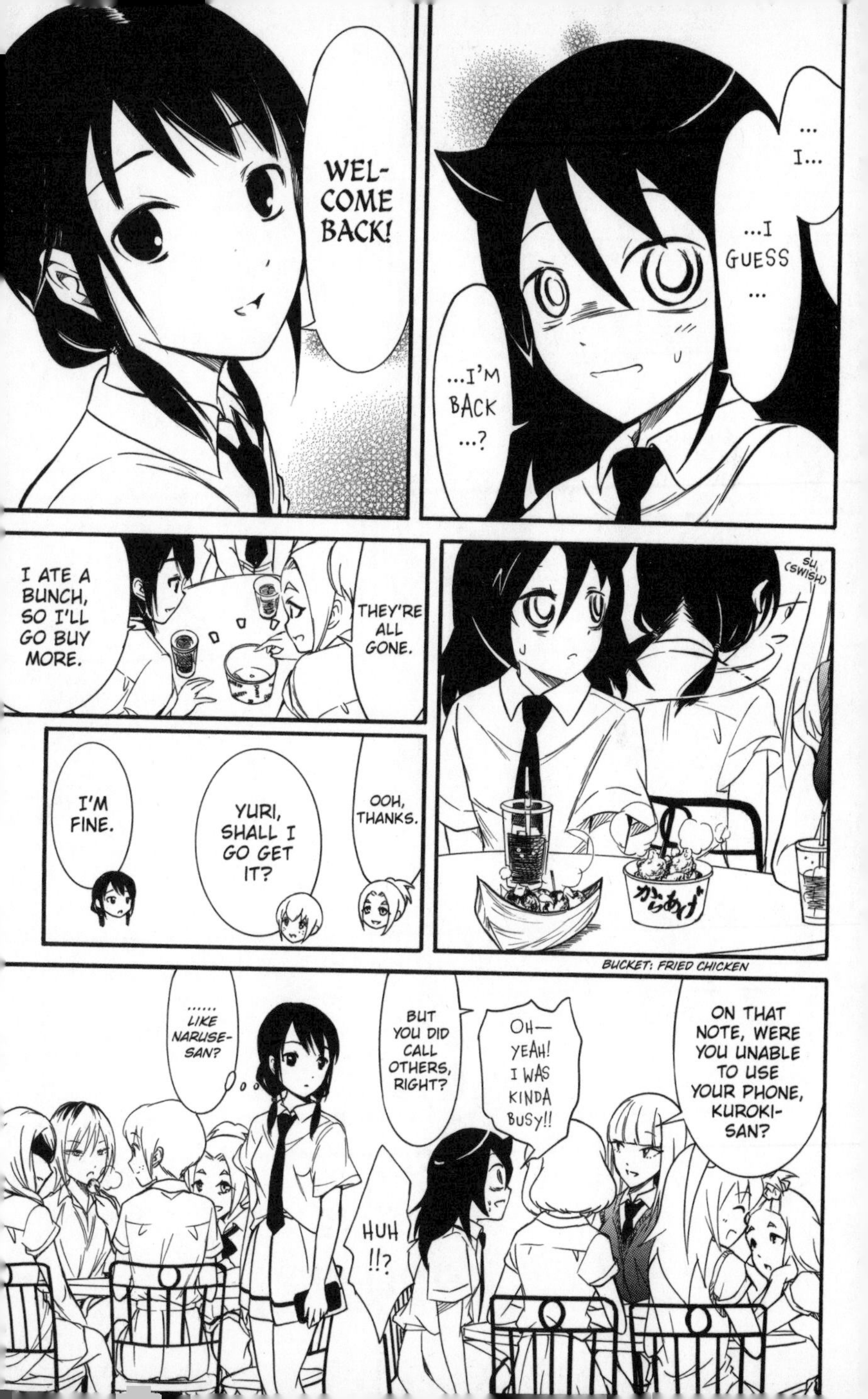
... I...
...I GUESS ...
...I'M BACK ...?
WEL-COME BACK!
SU (SWISH)
BUCKET: FRIED CHICKEN
THEY'RE ALL GONE.
I ATE A BUNCH, SO I'LL GO BUY MORE.
OOH, THANKS.
YURI, SHALL I GO GET IT?
I'M FINE.
ON THAT NOTE, WERE YOU UNABLE TO USE YOUR PHONE, KUROKI-SAN?
OH— YEAH! I WAS KINDA BUSY!!
BUT YOU DID CALL OTHERS, RIGHT?
...... LIKE NARUSE-SAN?
HUH !!?

NO Matter HOW I Look at It, It's You Guys' Fault I'm Not Popular!

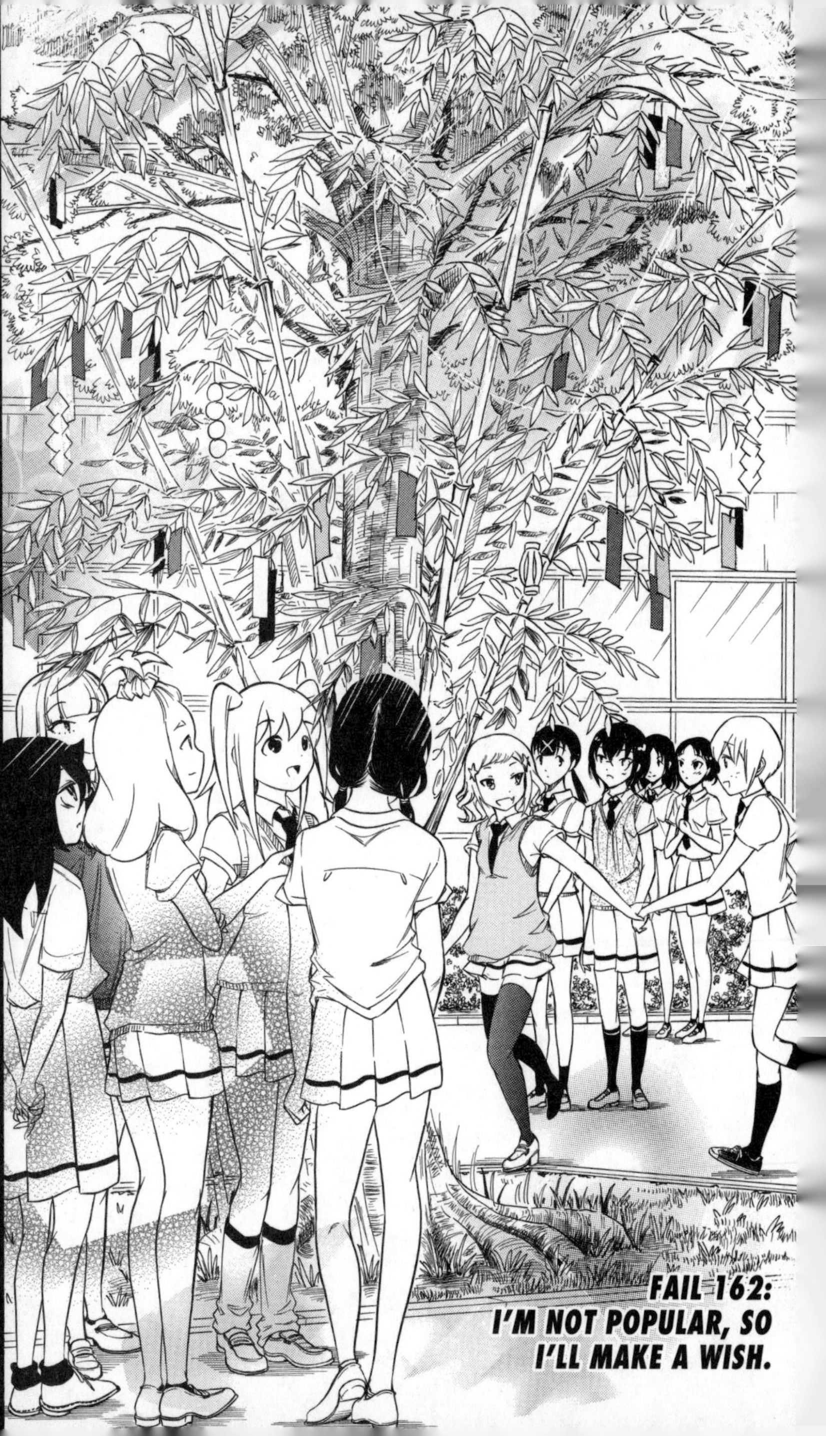
FAIL 162:
I'M NOT POPULAR, SO
I'LL MAKE A WISH.

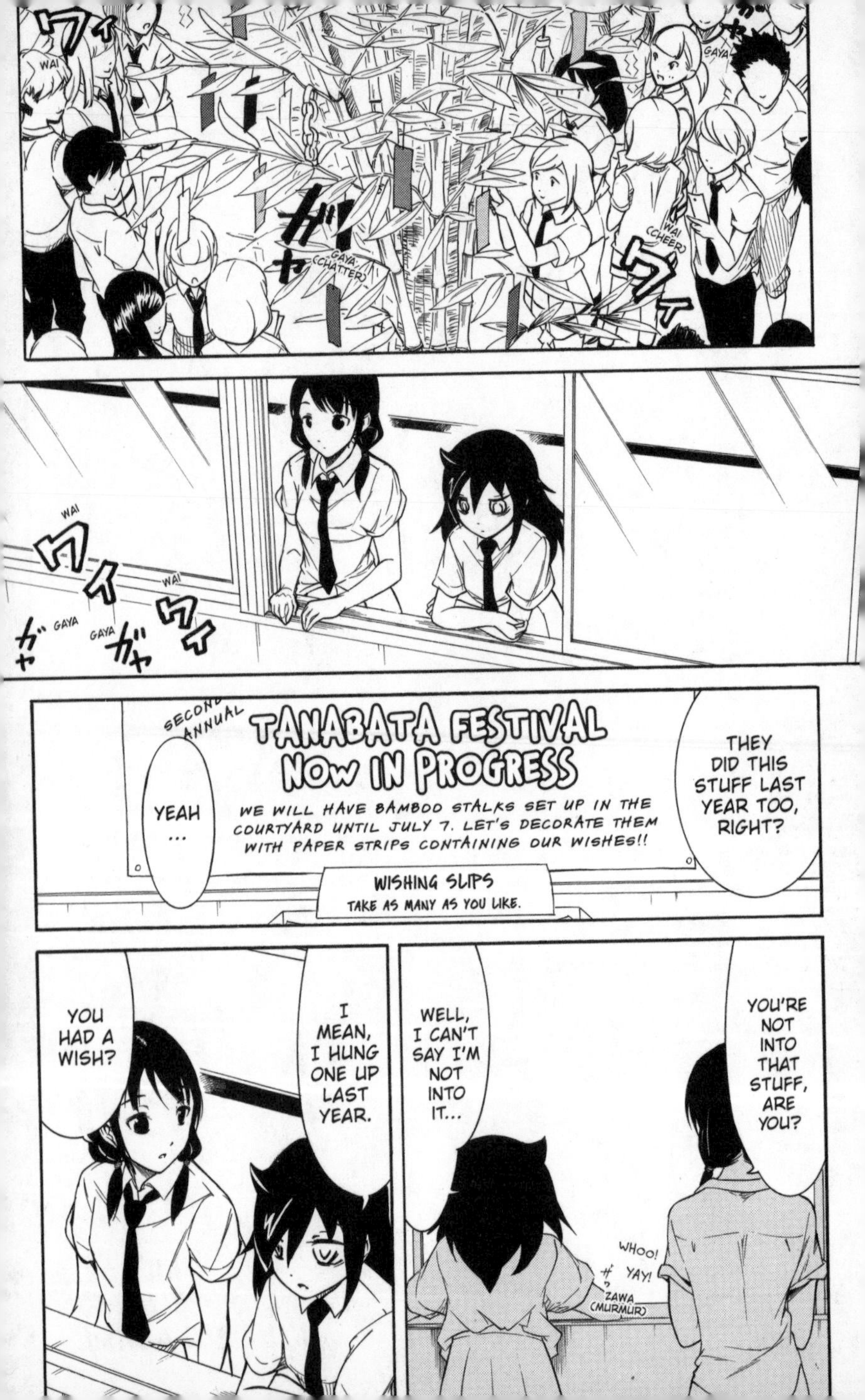
ガヤ GAYA
ワィ WAI (CHEER)
ガヤ GAYA (CHATTER)
ワィ WAI
ワィ WAI
ワィ WAI
ガヤ GAYA
ガヤ GAYA
THEY DID THIS STUFF LAST YEAR TOO, RIGHT?
SECOND ANNUAL
TANABATA FESTIVAL NOW IN PROGRESS
WE WILL HAVE BAMBOO STALKS SET UP IN THE COURTYARD UNTIL JULY 7. LET'S DECORATE THEM WITH PAPER STRIPS CONTAINING OUR WISHES!!
WISHING SLIPS
TAKE AS MANY AS YOU LIKE.
YEAH ...
YOU'RE NOT INTO THAT STUFF, ARE YOU?
WELL, I CAN'T SAY I'M NOT INTO IT...
WHOO!
YAY!
ZAWA (MURMUR)
I MEAN, I HUNG ONE UP LAST YEAR.
YOU HAD A WISH?

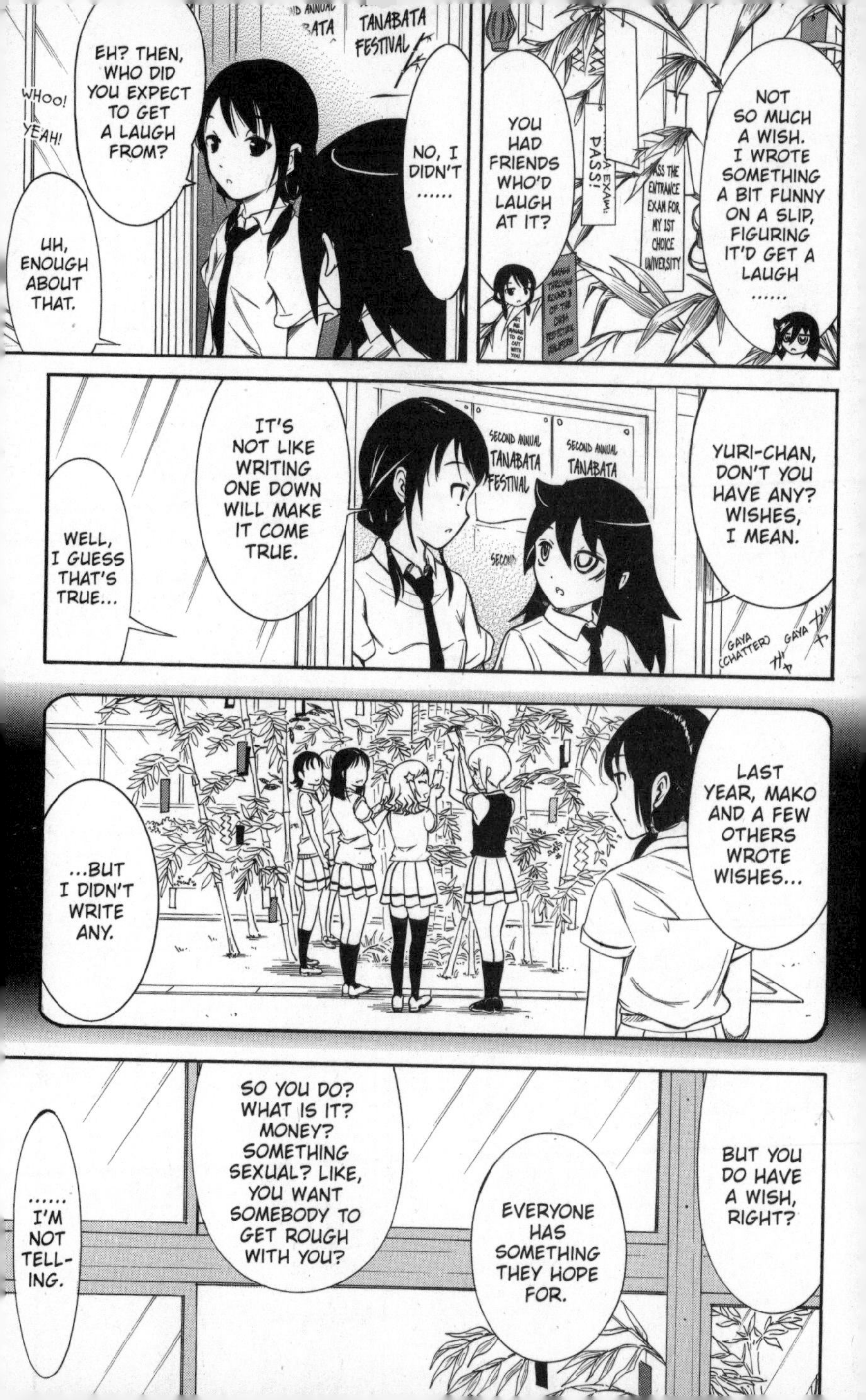
NOT SO MUCH A WISH. I WROTE SOMETHING A BIT FUNNY ON A SLIP, FIGURING IT'D GET A LAUGH ......
PASS THE ENTRANCE EXAM FOR MY 1ST CHOICE UNIVERSITY
PASS!
YOU HAD FRIENDS WHO'D LAUGH AT IT?
TANABATA FESTIVAL
NO, I DIDN'T ......
EH? THEN, WHO DID YOU EXPECT TO GET A LAUGH FROM?
WHOO!
YEAH!
UH, ENOUGH ABOUT THAT.
YURI-CHAN, DON'T YOU HAVE ANY? WISHES, I MEAN.
GAYA (CHATTER) GAYA
SECOND ANNUAL TANABATA
SECOND ANNUAL TANABATA FESTIVAL
IT'S NOT LIKE WRITING ONE DOWN WILL MAKE IT COME TRUE.
WELL, I GUESS THAT'S TRUE...
LAST YEAR, MAKO AND A FEW OTHERS WROTE WISHES...
...BUT I DIDN'T WRITE ANY.
BUT YOU DO HAVE A WISH, RIGHT?
EVERYONE HAS SOMETHING THEY HOPE FOR.
SO YOU DO? WHAT IS IT? MONEY? SOMETHING SEXUAL? LIKE, YOU WANT SOMEBODY TO GET ROUGH WITH YOU?
...... I'M NOT TELL-ING.

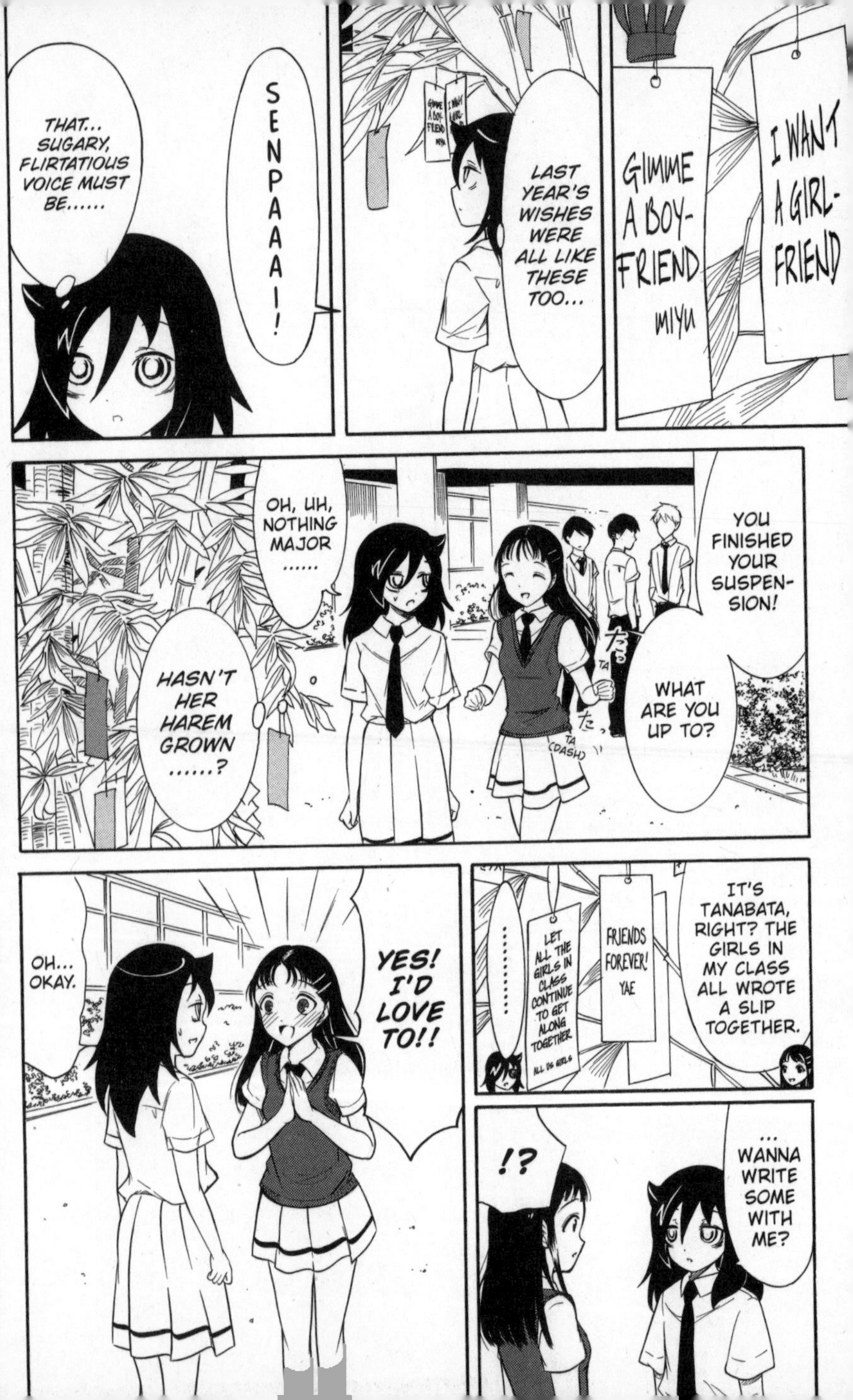
I WANT A GIRL-FRIEND
GIMME A BOY-FRIEND MIYU
LAST YEAR'S WISHES WERE ALL LIKE THESE TOO...
SENPAAAAI!
THAT... SUGARY, FLIRTATIOUS VOICE MUST BE......
YOU FINISHED YOUR SUSPENSION!
WHAT ARE YOU UP TO?
TA TA (DASH)
OH, UH, NOTHING MAJOR ......
HASN'T HER HAREM GROWN ......?
IT'S TANABATA, RIGHT? THE GIRLS IN MY CLASS ALL WROTE A SLIP TOGETHER.
FRIENDS FOREVER! YAE
LET ALL THE GIRLS IN CLASS CONTINUE TO GET ALONG TOGETHER
ALL US GIRLS
......
... WANNA WRITE SOME WITH ME?
!?
YES! I'D LOVE TO!!
OH... OKAY.

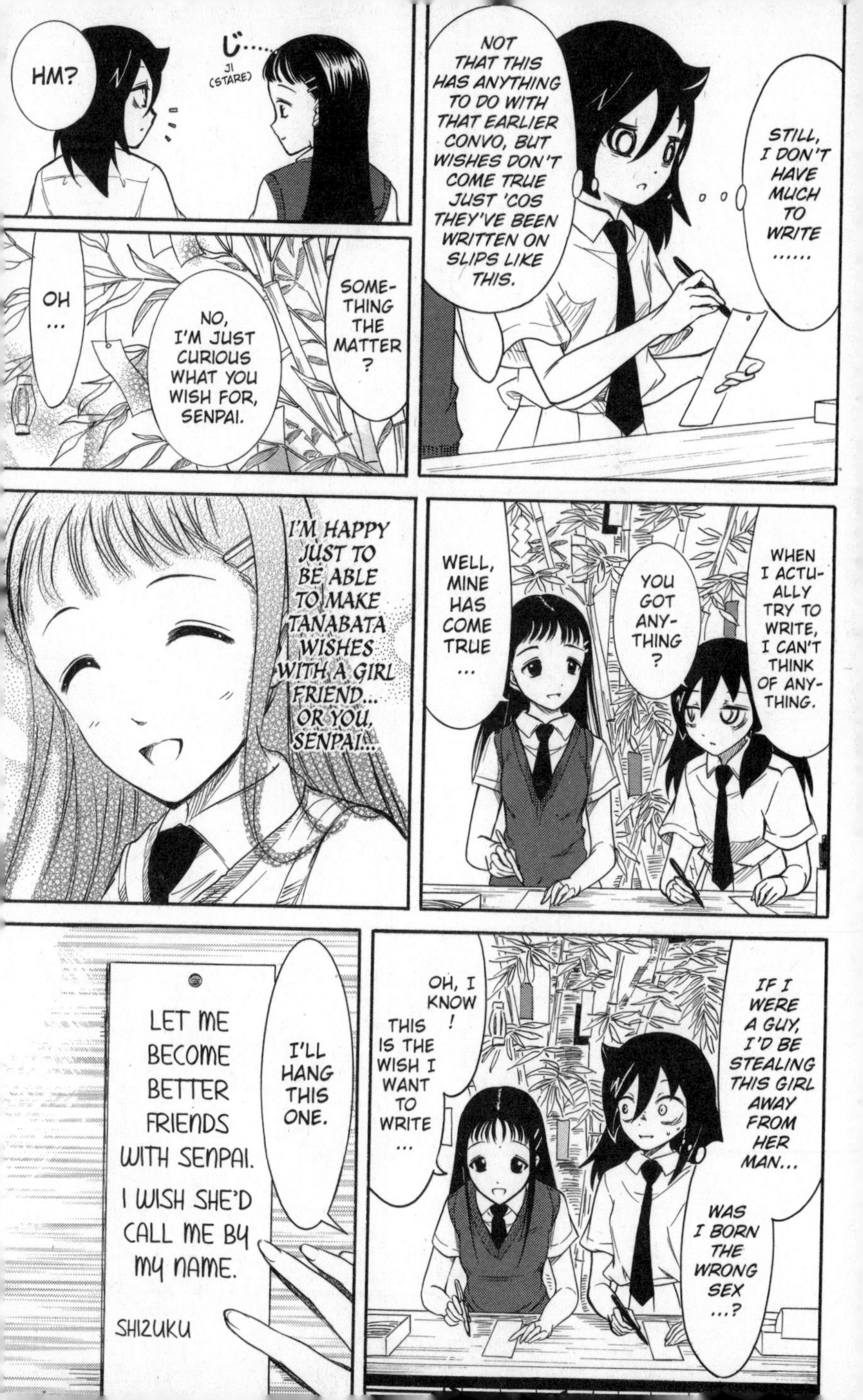
STILL, I DON'T HAVE MUCH TO WRITE......
NOT THAT THIS HAS ANYTHING TO DO WITH THAT EARLIER CONVO, BUT WISHES DON'T COME TRUE JUST 'COS THEY'VE BEEN WRITTEN ON SLIPS LIKE THIS.
じ……
JI (STARE)
HM?
SOME-THING THE MATTER?
NO, I'M JUST CURIOUS WHAT YOU WISH FOR, SENPAI.
OH ...
WHEN I ACTU-ALLY TRY TO WRITE, I CAN'T THINK OF ANY-THING.
YOU GOT ANY-THING?
WELL, MINE HAS COME TRUE ...
I'M HAPPY JUST TO BE ABLE TO MAKE TANABATA WISHES WITH A GIRL FRIEND... OR YOU, SENPAI...
IF I WERE A GUY, I'D BE STEALING THIS GIRL AWAY FROM HER MAN...
WAS I BORN THE WRONG SEX ...?
OH, I KNOW!
THIS IS THE WISH I WANT TO WRITE ...
I'LL HANG THIS ONE.
LET ME BECOME BETTER FRIENDS WITH SENPAI.
I WISH SHE'D CALL ME BY MY NAME.
SHIZUKU

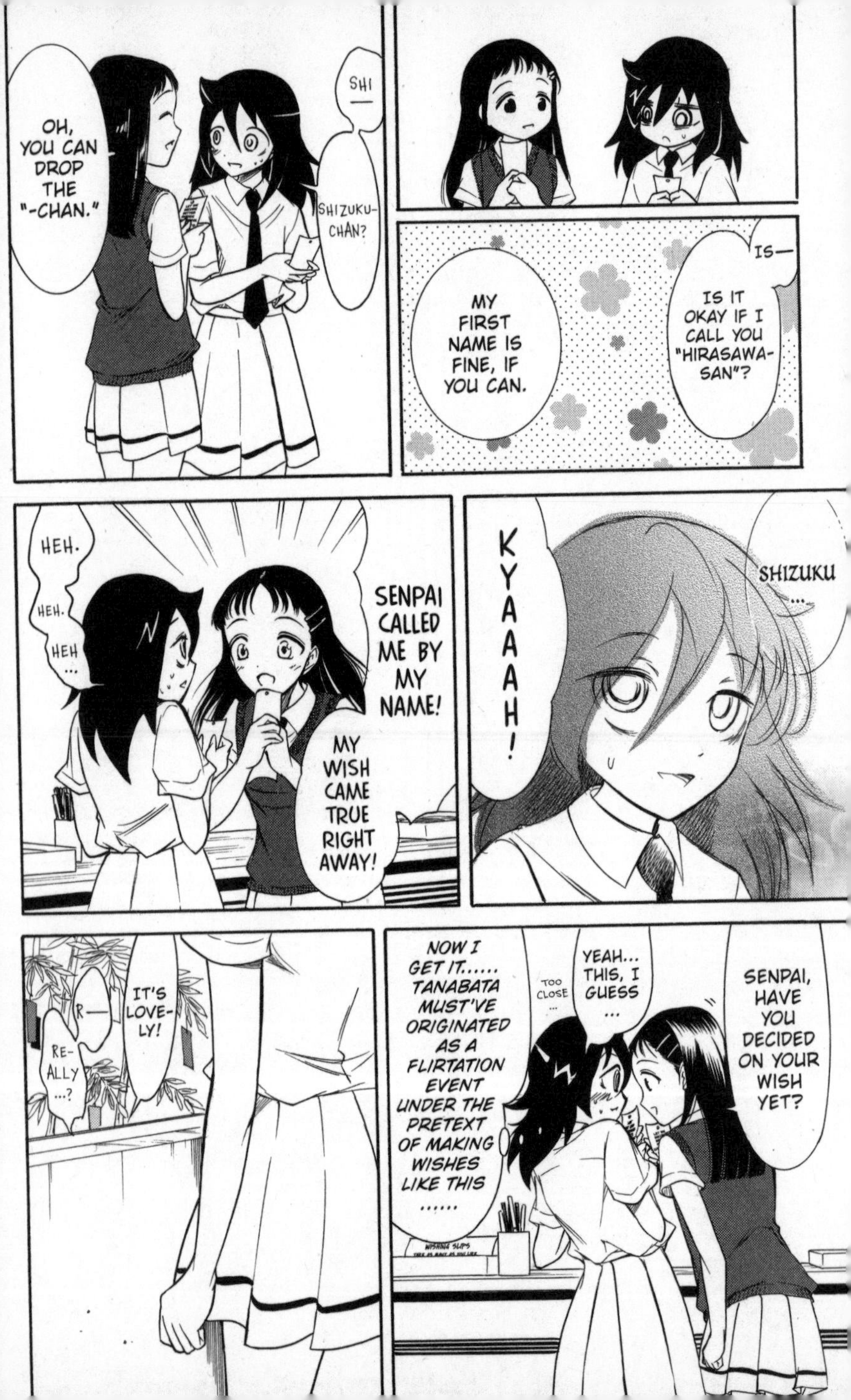
IS— IS IT OKAY IF I CALL YOU "HIRASAWA-SAN"?
MY FIRST NAME IS FINE, IF YOU CAN.
SHI— SHIZUKU-CHAN?
OH, YOU CAN DROP THE "-CHAN."
SHIZUKU...
KYAAAAH!
SENPAI CALLED ME BY MY NAME!
MY WISH CAME TRUE RIGHT AWAY!
HEH. HEH. HEH...
SENPAI, HAVE YOU DECIDED ON YOUR WISH YET?
YEAH... THIS, I GUESS...
TOO CLOSE...
NOW I GET IT...... TANABATA MUST'VE ORIGINATED AS A FLIRTATION EVENT UNDER THE PRETEXT OF MAKING WISHES LIKE THIS ......
WISHING SLIPS
IT'S LOVE-LY!
R— RE-ALLY...?

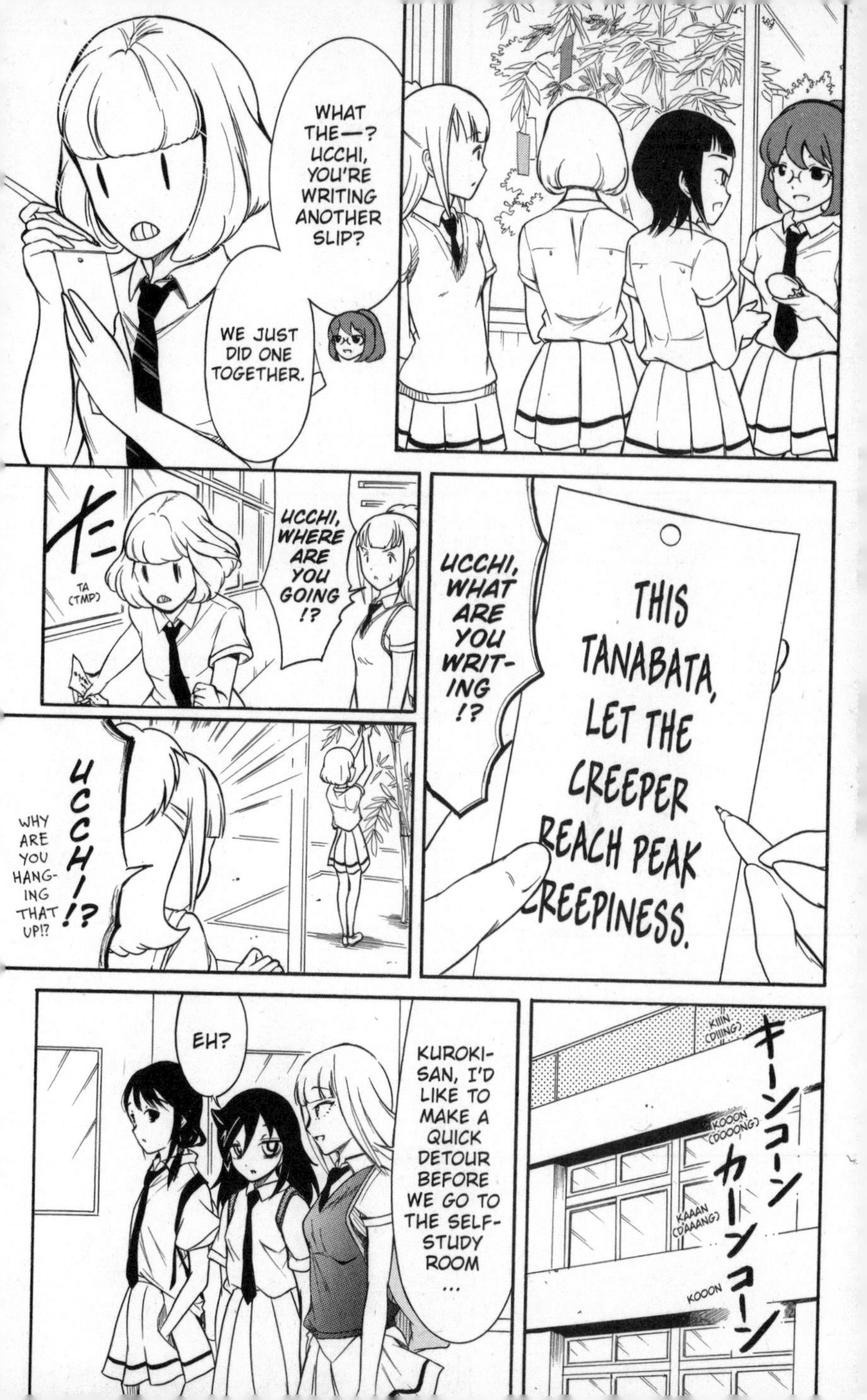
WHAT THE—? UCCHI, YOU'RE WRITING ANOTHER SLIP?
WE JUST DID ONE TOGETHER.
UCCHI, WHAT ARE YOU WRITING!?
THIS TANABATA, LET THE CREEPER REACH PEAK CREEPINESS.
TA (TMP)
UCCHI, WHERE ARE YOU GOING!?
UCCHI!?
WHY ARE YOU HANGING THAT UP!?
KIIN (DIIING)
KOOON (DOOONG)
KAAAN (DAAANG)
KOOON
KUROKI-SAN, I'D LIKE TO MAKE A QUICK DETOUR BEFORE WE GO TO THE SELF-STUDY ROOM...
EH?

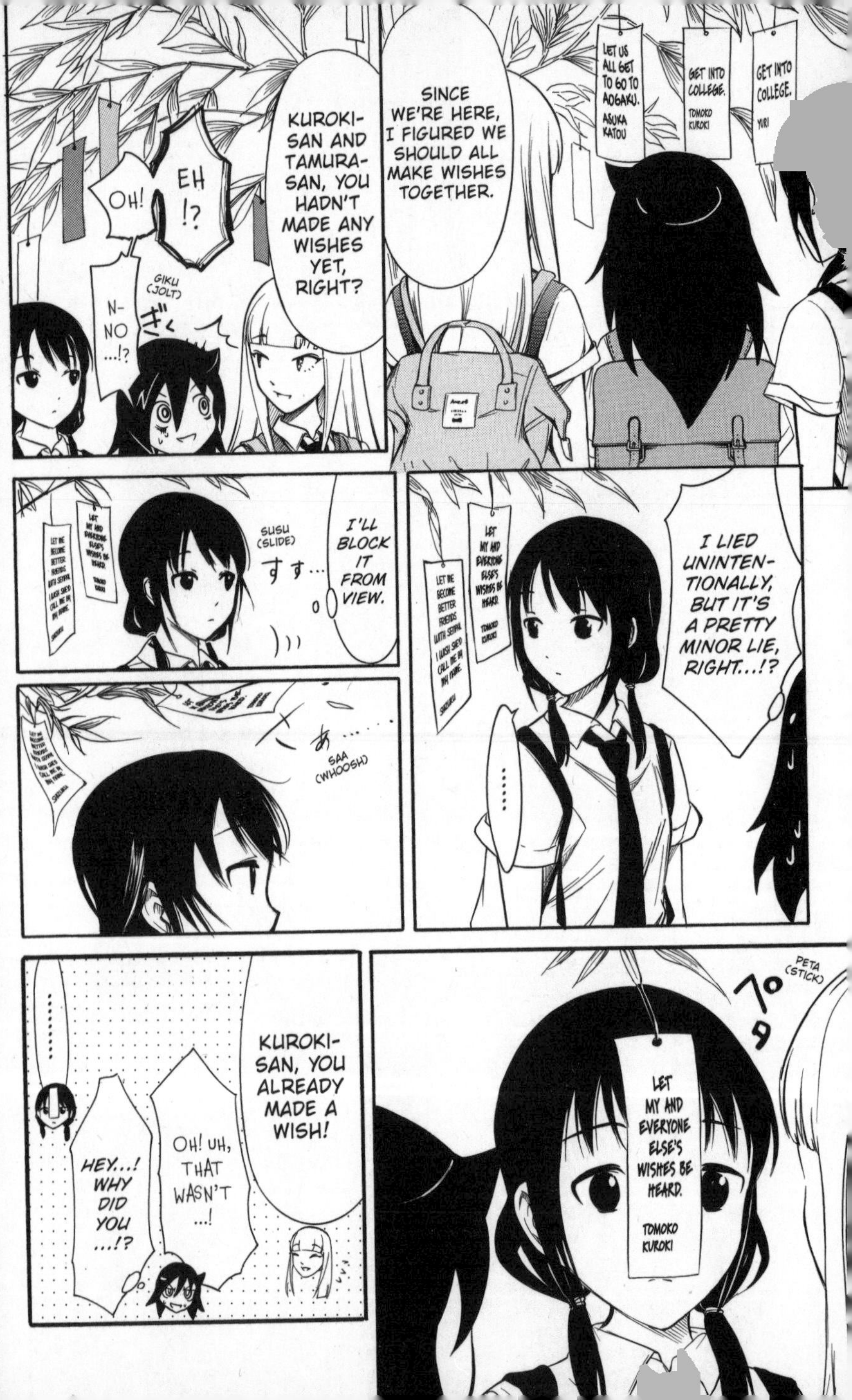
LET US ALL GET TO GO TO AOGAKU. ASUKA KATOU
GET INTO COLLEGE. TOMOKO KUROKI
GET INTO COLLEGE. YURI
SINCE WE'RE HERE, I FIGURED WE SHOULD ALL MAKE WISHES TOGETHER.
KUROKI-SAN AND TAMURA-SAN, YOU HADN'T MADE ANY WISHES YET, RIGHT?
EH !?
OH!
GIKU (JOLT)
ぎく
N-NO ...!?
I LIED UNINTENTIONALLY, BUT IT'S A PRETTY MINOR LIE, RIGHT...!?
LET MY AND EVERYONE ELSE'S WISHES BE HEARD. TOMOKO KUROKI
LET ME BECOME BETTER FRIENDS WITH SENPAI. I WISH SHE'D CALL ME BY MY NAME. SHIZUKU
......
I'LL BLOCK IT FROM VIEW.
SUSU (SLIDE)
すす...
SAA (WHOOSH)
さあ......
PETA (STICK)
ぺタ
LET MY AND EVERYONE ELSE'S WISHES BE HEARD. TOMOKO KUROKI
KUROKI-SAN, YOU ALREADY MADE A WISH!
OH! UH, THAT WASN'T ...!
HEY...! WHY DID YOU ...!?
......

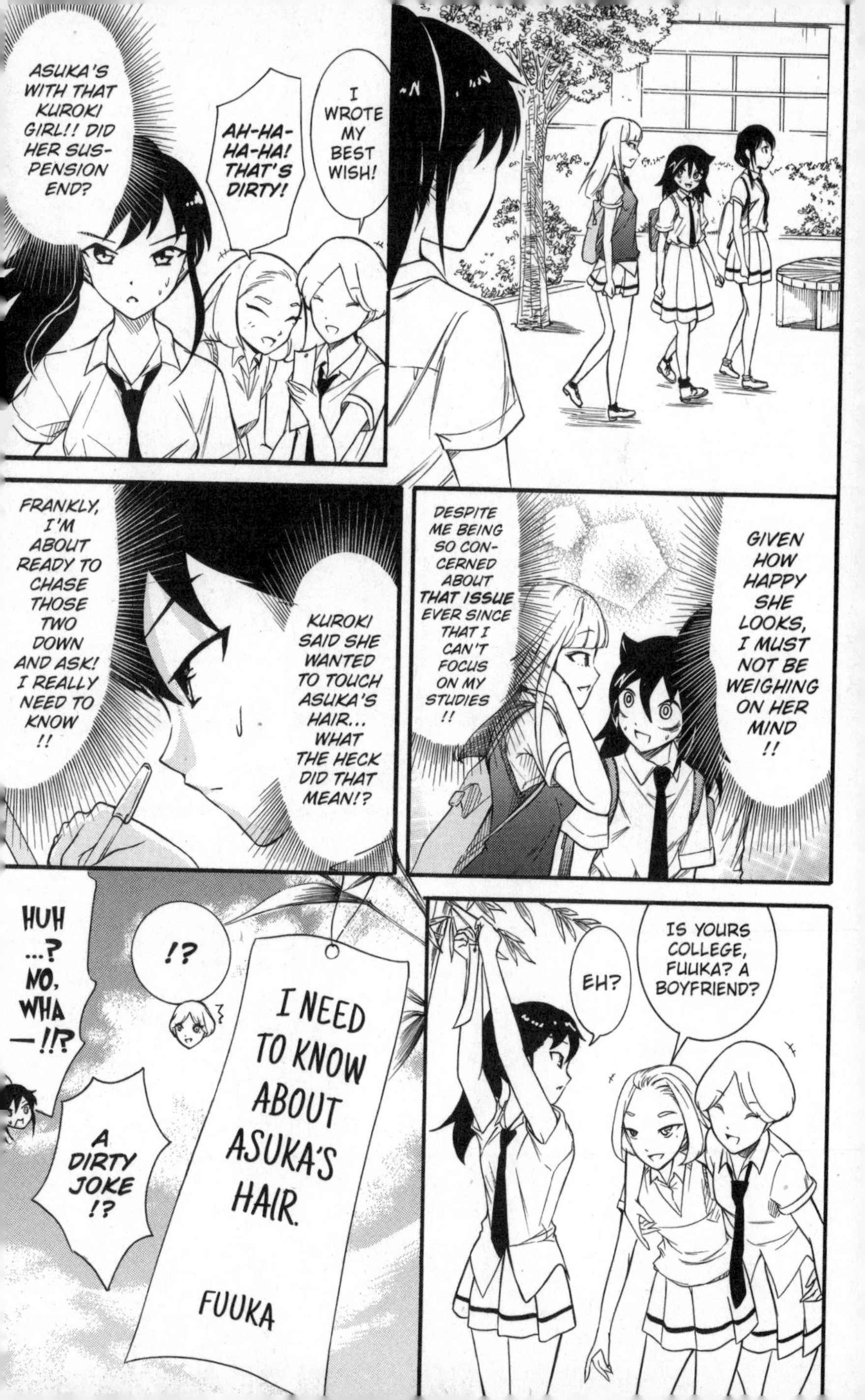
I WROTE MY BEST WISH!
AH-HA-HA-HA! THAT'S DIRTY!
ASUKA'S WITH THAT KUROKI GIRL!! DID HER SUSPENSION END?
GIVEN HOW HAPPY SHE LOOKS, I MUST NOT BE WEIGHING ON HER MIND!!
DESPITE ME BEING SO CONCERNED ABOUT THAT ISSUE EVER SINCE THAT I CAN'T FOCUS ON MY STUDIES!!
KUROKI SAID SHE WANTED TO TOUCH ASUKA'S HAIR... WHAT THE HECK DID THAT MEAN!?
FRANKLY, I'M ABOUT READY TO CHASE THOSE TWO DOWN AND ASK! I REALLY NEED TO KNOW!!
IS YOURS COLLEGE, FUUKA? A BOYFRIEND?
EH?
!?
I NEED TO KNOW ABOUT ASUKA'S HAIR.
FUUKA
HUH...? NO. WHA—!!?
A DIRTY JOKE!?

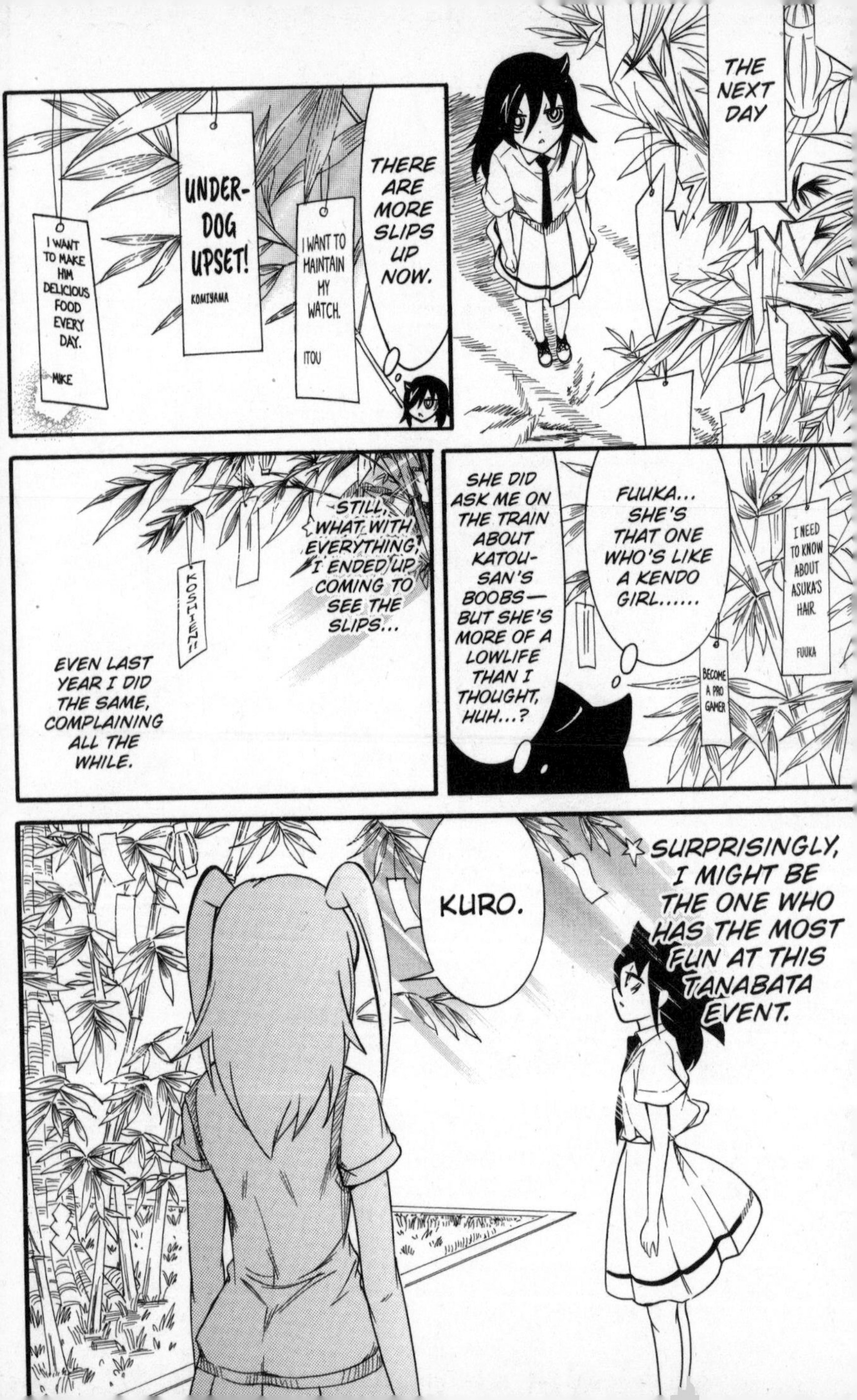
THE NEXT DAY
THERE ARE MORE SLIPS UP NOW.
I WANT TO MAINTAIN MY WATCH. ITOU
UNDER-DOG UPSET! KOMIYAMA
I WANT TO MAKE HIM DELICIOUS FOOD EVERY DAY. MIKE
I NEED TO KNOW ABOUT ASUKA'S HAIR FUUKA
FUUKA... SHE'S THAT ONE WHO'S LIKE A KENDO GIRL......
SHE DID ASK ME ON THE TRAIN ABOUT KATOU-SAN'S BOOBS—BUT SHE'S MORE OF A LOWLIFE THAN I THOUGHT, HUH...?
BECOME A PRO GAMER
STILL, WHAT WITH EVERYTHING, I ENDED UP COMING TO SEE THE SLIPS...
KOSHIEN!!
EVEN LAST YEAR I DID THE SAME, COMPLAINING ALL THE WHILE.
SURPRISINGLY, I MIGHT BE THE ONE WHO HAS THE MOST FUN AT THIS TANABATA EVENT.
KURO.

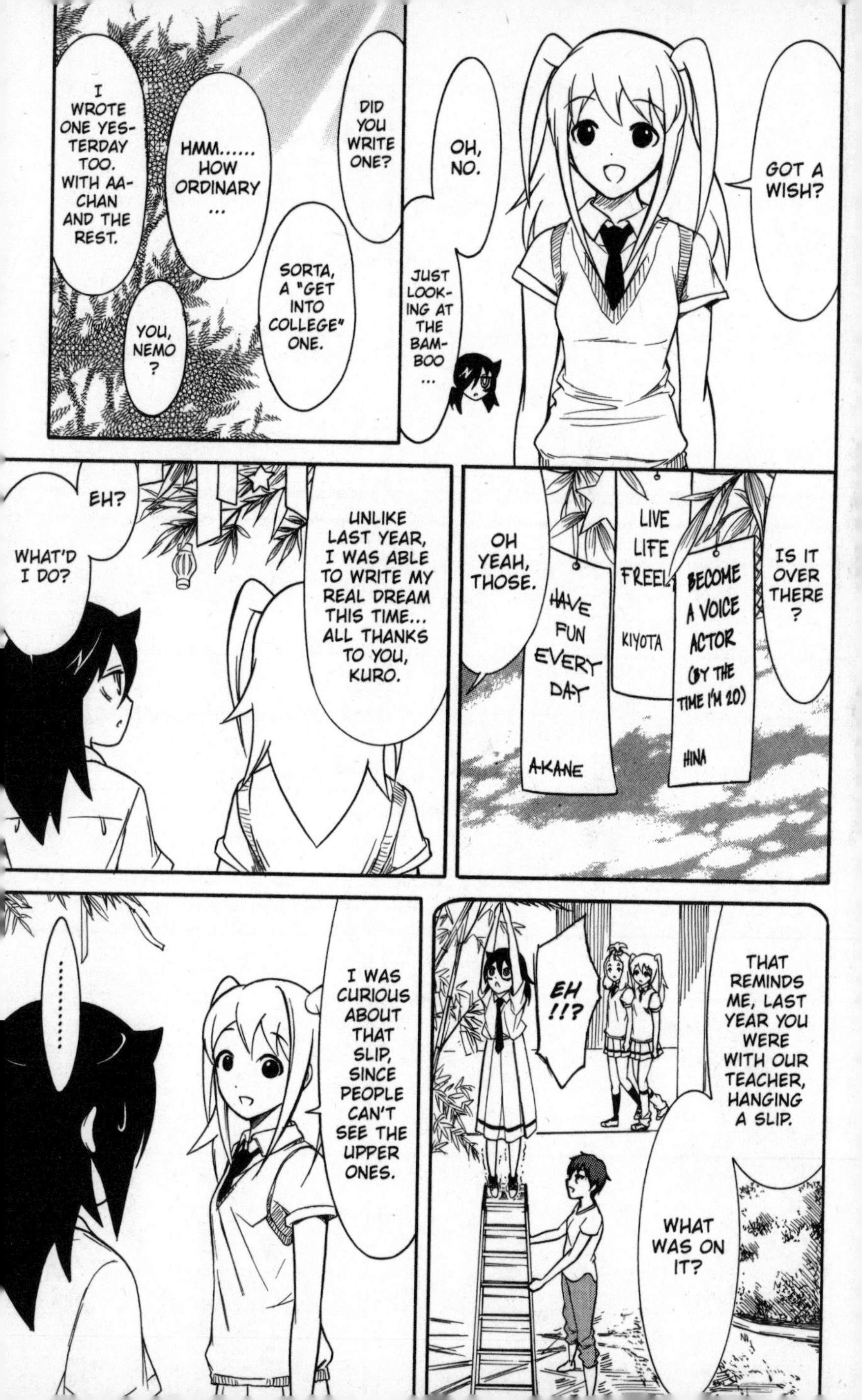
GOT A WISH?
OH, NO.
JUST LOOKING AT THE BAMBOO...
DID YOU WRITE ONE?
SORTA, A "GET INTO COLLEGE" ONE.
HMM...... HOW ORDINARY...
I WROTE ONE YESTERDAY TOO. WITH AA-CHAN AND THE REST.
YOU, NEMO?
IS IT OVER THERE?
OH YEAH, THOSE.
BECOME A VOICE ACTOR (BY THE TIME I'M 20)
HINA
LIVE LIFE FREELY
KIYOTA
HAVE FUN EVERY DAY
AKANE
UNLIKE LAST YEAR, I WAS ABLE TO WRITE MY REAL DREAM THIS TIME... ALL THANKS TO YOU, KURO.
EH?
WHAT'D I DO?
THAT REMINDS ME, LAST YEAR YOU WERE WITH OUR TEACHER, HANGING A SLIP.
WHAT WAS ON IT?
EH!!?
I WAS CURIOUS ABOUT THAT SLIP, SINCE PEOPLE CAN'T SEE THE UPPER ONES.
......

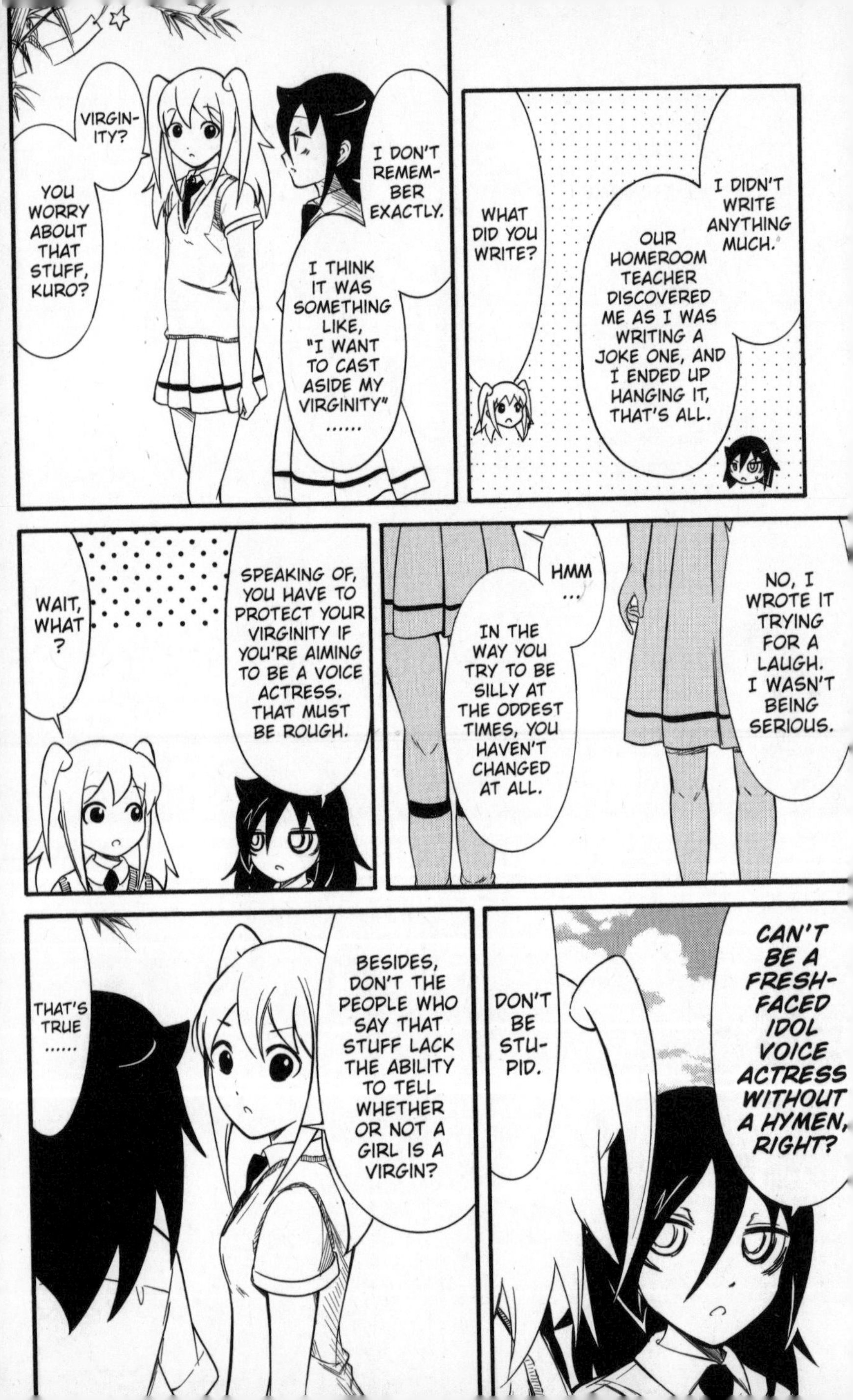
I DIDN'T WRITE ANYTHING MUCH.
OUR HOMEROOM TEACHER DISCOVERED ME AS I WAS WRITING A JOKE ONE, AND I ENDED UP HANGING IT, THAT'S ALL.
WHAT DID YOU WRITE?
I DON'T REMEMBER EXACTLY.
I THINK IT WAS SOMETHING LIKE, "I WANT TO CAST ASIDE MY VIRGINITY" ......
VIRGINITY?
YOU WORRY ABOUT THAT STUFF, KURO?
NO, I WROTE IT TRYING FOR A LAUGH. I WASN'T BEING SERIOUS.
HMM ...
IN THE WAY YOU TRY TO BE SILLY AT THE ODDEST TIMES, YOU HAVEN'T CHANGED AT ALL.
SPEAKING OF, YOU HAVE TO PROTECT YOUR VIRGINITY IF YOU'RE AIMING TO BE A VOICE ACTRESS. THAT MUST BE ROUGH.
WAIT, WHAT?
CAN'T BE A FRESH-FACED IDOL VOICE ACTRESS WITHOUT A HYMEN, RIGHT?
DON'T BE STUPID.
BESIDES, DON'T THE PEOPLE WHO SAY THAT STUFF LACK THE ABILITY TO TELL WHETHER OR NOT A GIRL IS A VIRGIN?
THAT'S TRUE ......

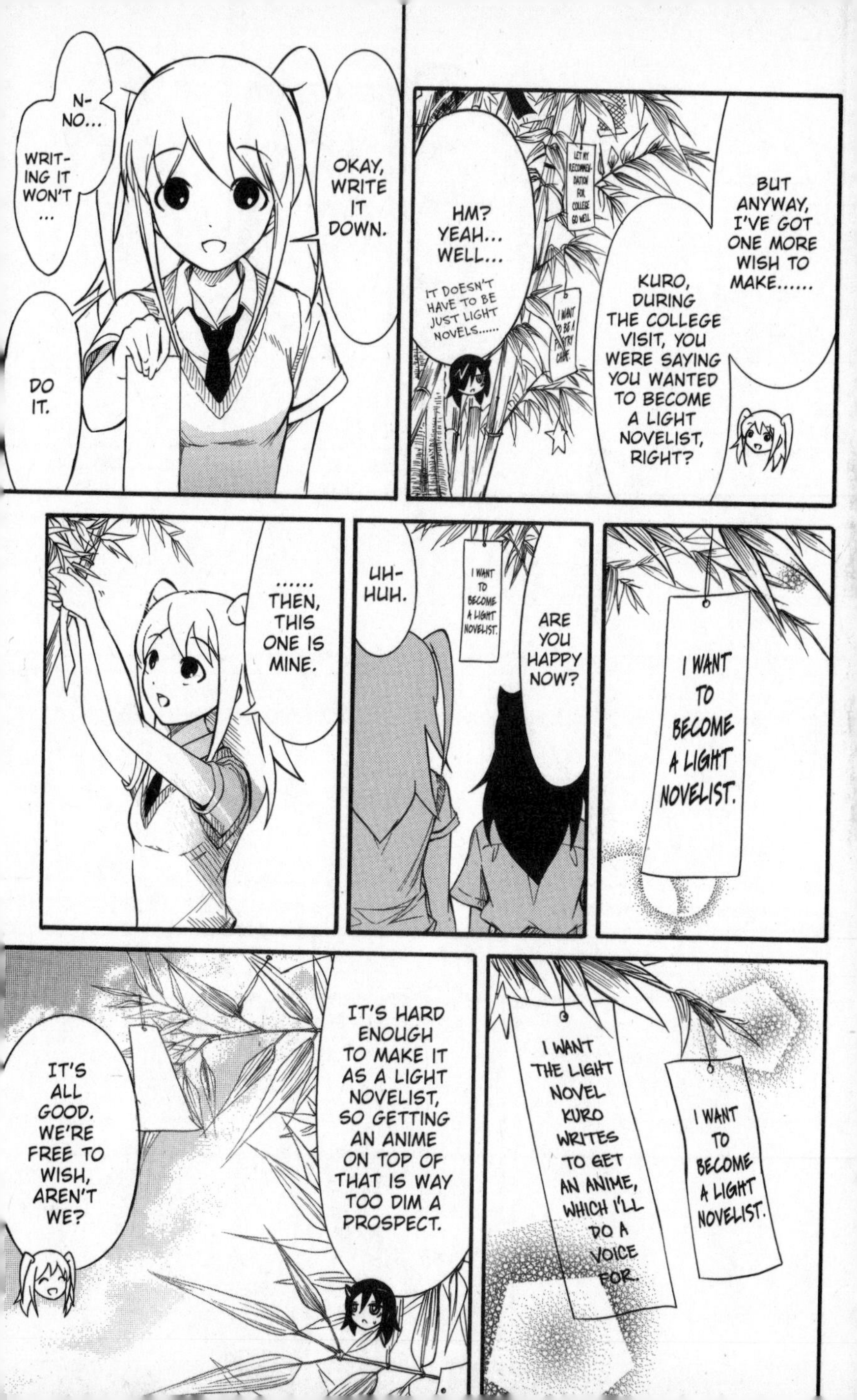
BUT ANYWAY, I'VE GOT ONE MORE WISH TO MAKE......
KURO, DURING THE COLLEGE VISIT, YOU WERE SAYING YOU WANTED TO BECOME A LIGHT NOVELIST, RIGHT?
LET MY RECOMMENDATION FOR COLLEGE GO WELL
HM? YEAH... WELL...
IT DOESN'T HAVE TO BE JUST LIGHT NOVELS......
OKAY, WRITE IT DOWN.
N-NO... WRITING IT WON'T ...
DO IT.
I WANT TO BECOME A LIGHT NOVELIST.
I WANT TO BECOME A LIGHT NOVELIST.
ARE YOU HAPPY NOW?
UH-HUH.
......THEN, THIS ONE IS MINE.
I WANT TO BECOME A LIGHT NOVELIST.
I WANT THE LIGHT NOVEL KURO WRITES TO GET AN ANIME, WHICH I'LL DO A VOICE FOR.
IT'S HARD ENOUGH TO MAKE IT AS A LIGHT NOVELIST, SO GETTING AN ANIME ON TOP OF THAT IS WAY TOO DIM A PROSPECT.
IT'S ALL GOOD. WE'RE FREE TO WISH, AREN'T WE?

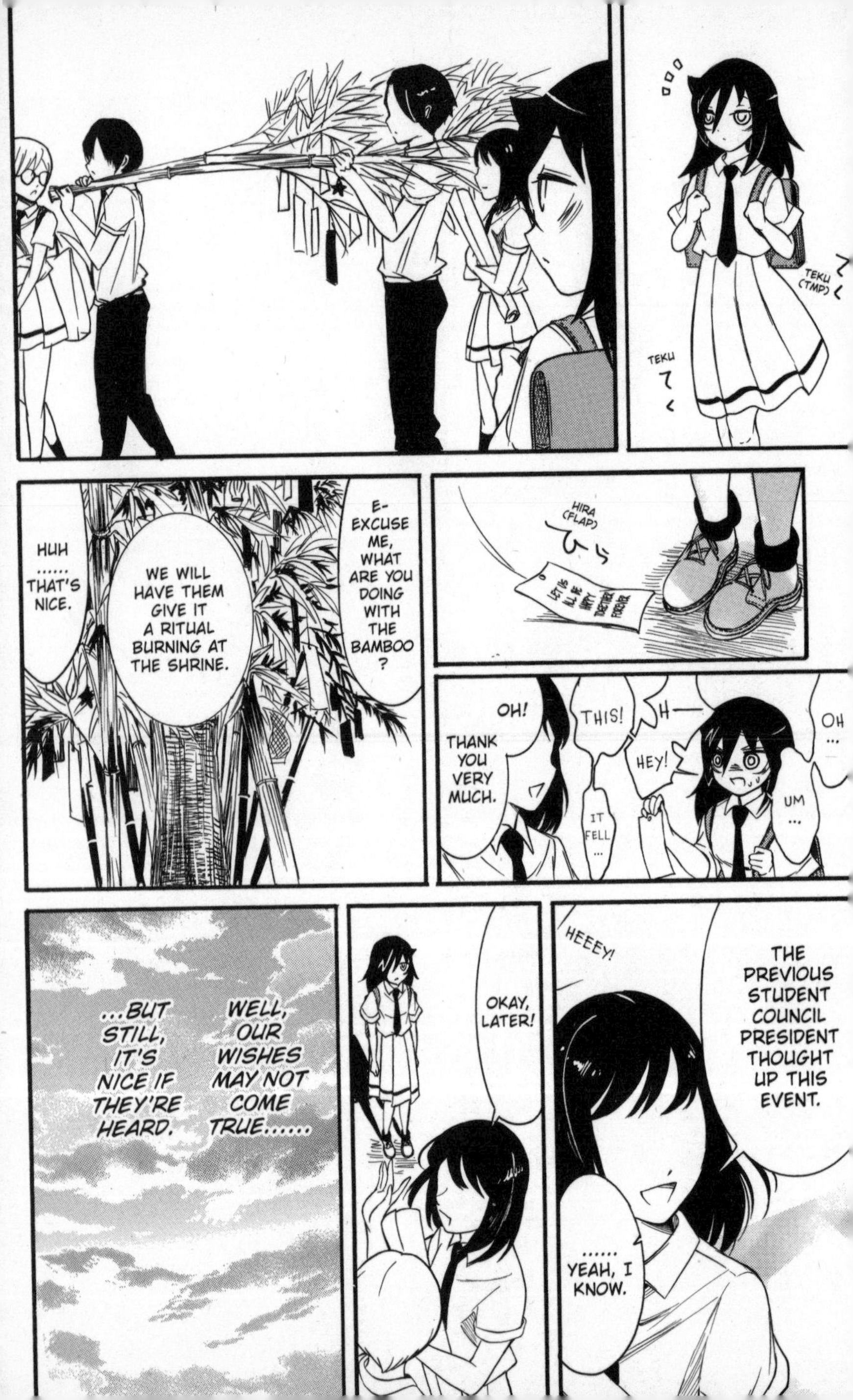
TEKU (TMP)
TEKU
HIRA (FLAP)
LET US ALL BE HAPPY TOGETHER FOREVER
OH...
UM...
H— HEY!
THIS! IT FELL...
OH! THANK YOU VERY MUCH.
E-EXCUSE ME, WHAT ARE YOU DOING WITH THE BAMBOO?
WE WILL HAVE THEM GIVE IT A RITUAL BURNING AT THE SHRINE.
HUH...... THAT'S NICE.
THE PREVIOUS STUDENT COUNCIL PRESIDENT THOUGHT UP THIS EVENT.
HEEEY!
......YEAH, I KNOW.
OKAY, LATER!
WELL, OUR WISHES MAY NOT COME TRUE......
...BUT STILL, IT'S NICE IF THEY'RE HEARD.

No Matter How I Look at It, It's You Guys' Fault I'm Not Popular!

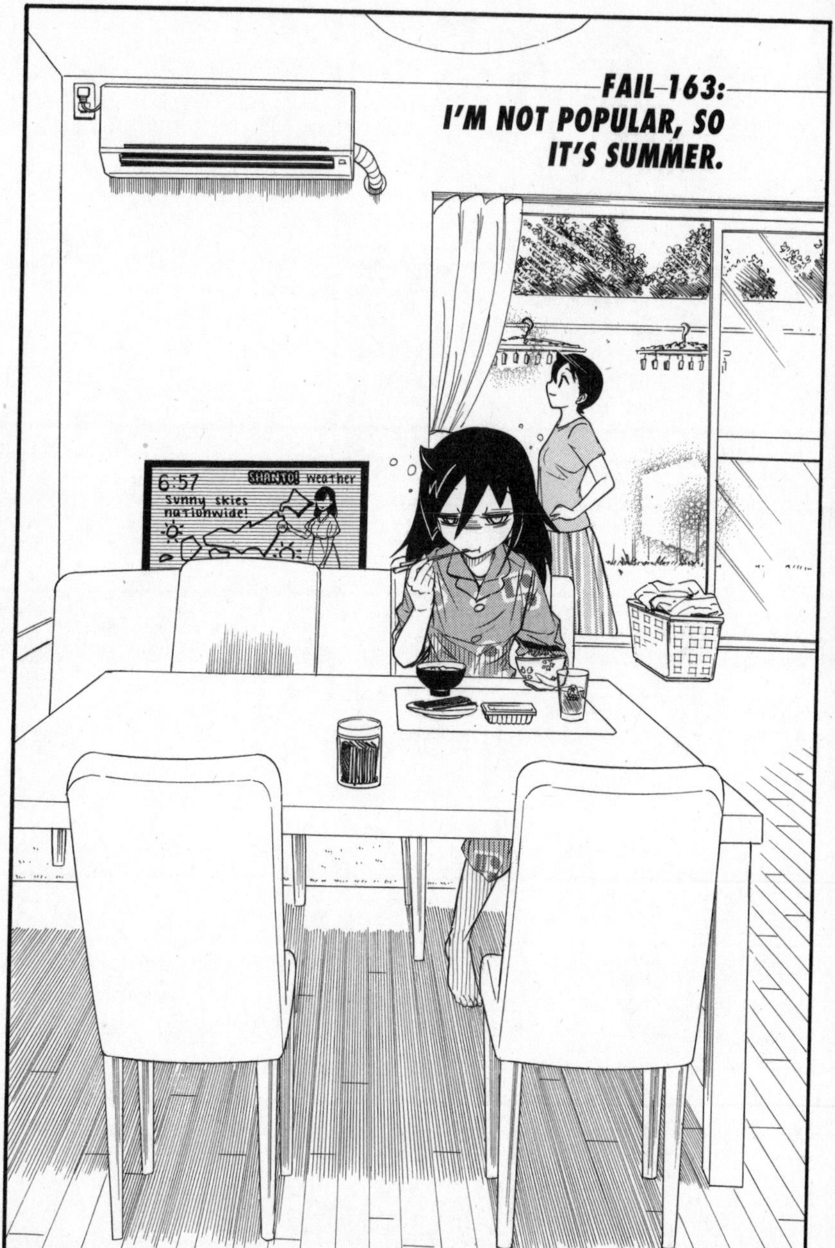
FAIL 163:
I'M NOT POPULAR, SO IT'S SUMMER.
6:57
SHANTO! weather
sunny skies nationwide!

SUNTANS

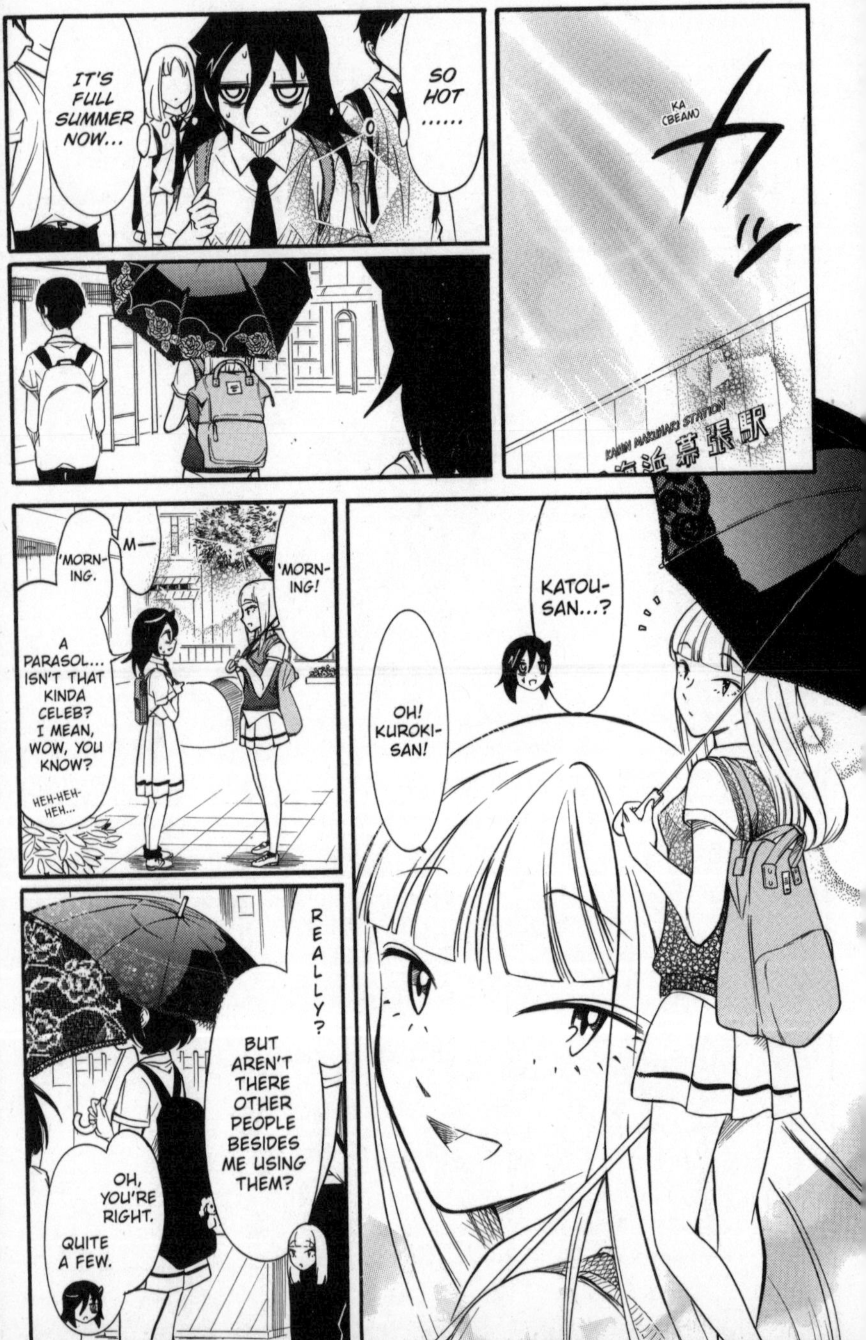
KA (BEAM)
KAIHIN MAKUHARI STATION
海浜幕張駅
SO HOT ......
IT'S FULL SUMMER NOW...
KATOU-SAN...?
OH! KUROKI-SAN!
'MORNING!
M— 'MORNING.
A PARASOL... ISN'T THAT KINDA CELEB? I MEAN, WOW, YOU KNOW?
HEH-HEH-HEH...
REALLY?
BUT AREN'T THERE OTHER PEOPLE BESIDES ME USING THEM?
OH, YOU'RE RIGHT.
QUITE A FEW.

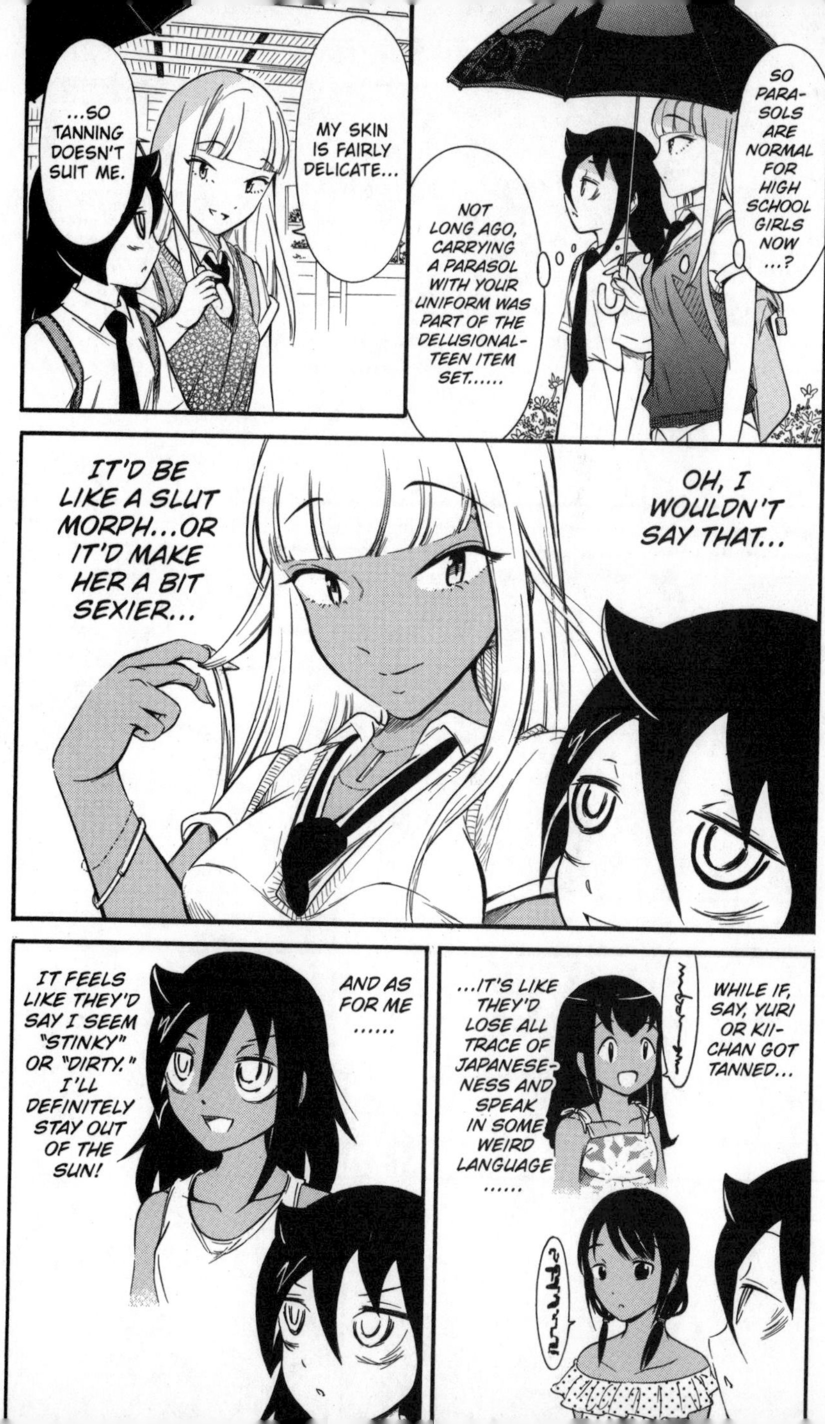
SO PARASOLS ARE NORMAL FOR HIGH SCHOOL GIRLS NOW ...?
NOT LONG AGO, CARRYING A PARASOL WITH YOUR UNIFORM WAS PART OF THE DELUSIONAL-TEEN ITEM SET......
MY SKIN IS FAIRLY DELICATE...
...SO TANNING DOESN'T SUIT ME.
OH, I WOULDN'T SAY THAT...
IT'D BE LIKE A SLUT MORPH...OR IT'D MAKE HER A BIT SEXIER...
WHILE IF, SAY, YURI OR KII-CHAN GOT TANNED...
...IT'S LIKE THEY'D LOSE ALL TRACE OF JAPANESE-NESS AND SPEAK IN SOME WEIRD LANGUAGE ......
AND AS FOR ME ......
IT FEELS LIKE THEY'D SAY I SEEM "STINKY" OR "DIRTY." I'LL DEFINITELY STAY OUT OF THE SUN!

HARAMAKU'S BIG FOUR

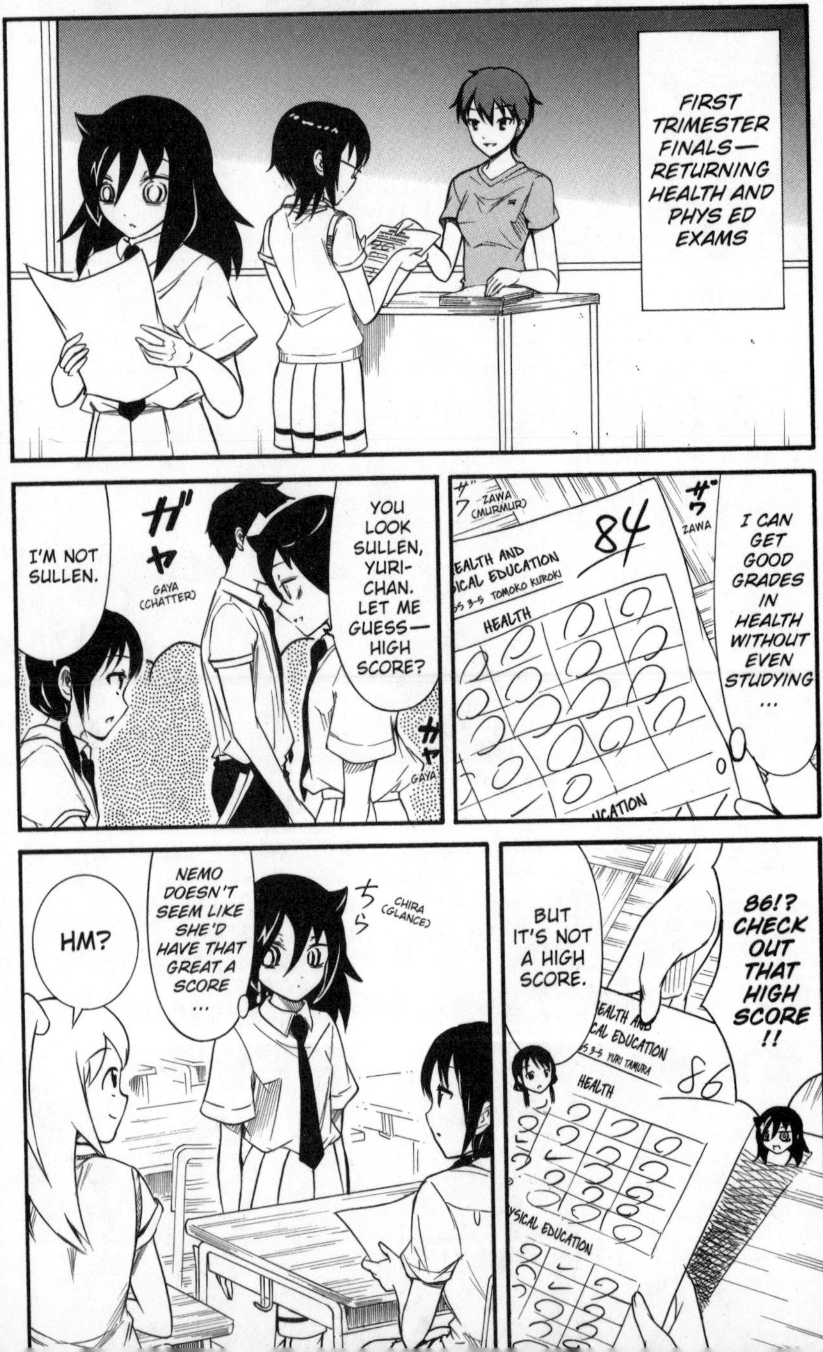
FIRST TRIMESTER FINALS—RETURNING HEALTH AND PHYS ED EXAMS
ザワ
ZAWA (MURMUR)
ザワ
ZAWA
84
TOMOKO KUROKI
HEALTH
I CAN GET GOOD GRADES IN HEALTH WITHOUT EVEN STUDYING ...
YOU LOOK SULLEN, YURI-CHAN. LET ME GUESS—HIGH SCORE?
ガヤ
GAYA (CHATTER)
ガヤ
GAYA
I'M NOT SULLEN.
86!? CHECK OUT THAT HIGH SCORE!!
BUT IT'S NOT A HIGH SCORE.
YURI TAMURA
86
HEALTH
ちら
CHIRA (GLANCE)
NEMO DOESN'T SEEM LIKE SHE'D HAVE THAT GREAT A SCORE ...
HM?

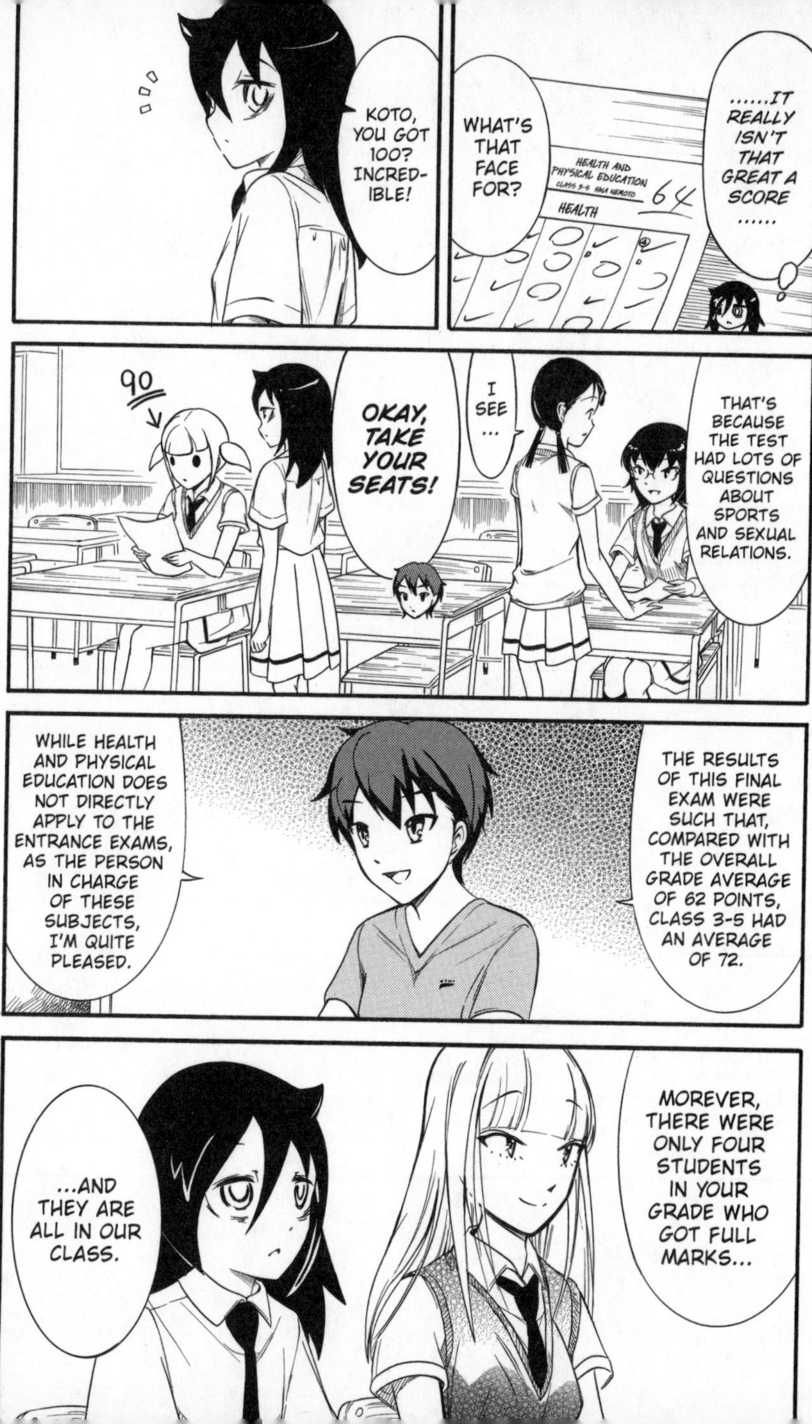
......IT REALLY ISN'T THAT GREAT A SCORE......
HEALTH AND PHYSICAL EDUCATION CLASS 3-5 HINA NEMOTO
64
HEALTH
WHAT'S THAT FACE FOR?
KOTO, YOU GOT 100? INCREDIBLE!
THAT'S BECAUSE THE TEST HAD LOTS OF QUESTIONS ABOUT SPORTS AND SEXUAL RELATIONS.
I SEE ...
OKAY, TAKE YOUR SEATS!
90
THE RESULTS OF THIS FINAL EXAM WERE SUCH THAT, COMPARED WITH THE OVERALL GRADE AVERAGE OF 62 POINTS, CLASS 3-5 HAD AN AVERAGE OF 72.
WHILE HEALTH AND PHYSICAL EDUCATION DOES NOT DIRECTLY APPLY TO THE ENTRANCE EXAMS, AS THE PERSON IN CHARGE OF THESE SUBJECTS, I'M QUITE PLEASED.
MOREVER, THERE WERE ONLY FOUR STUDENTS IN YOUR GRADE WHO GOT FULL MARKS...
...AND THEY ARE ALL IN OUR CLASS.

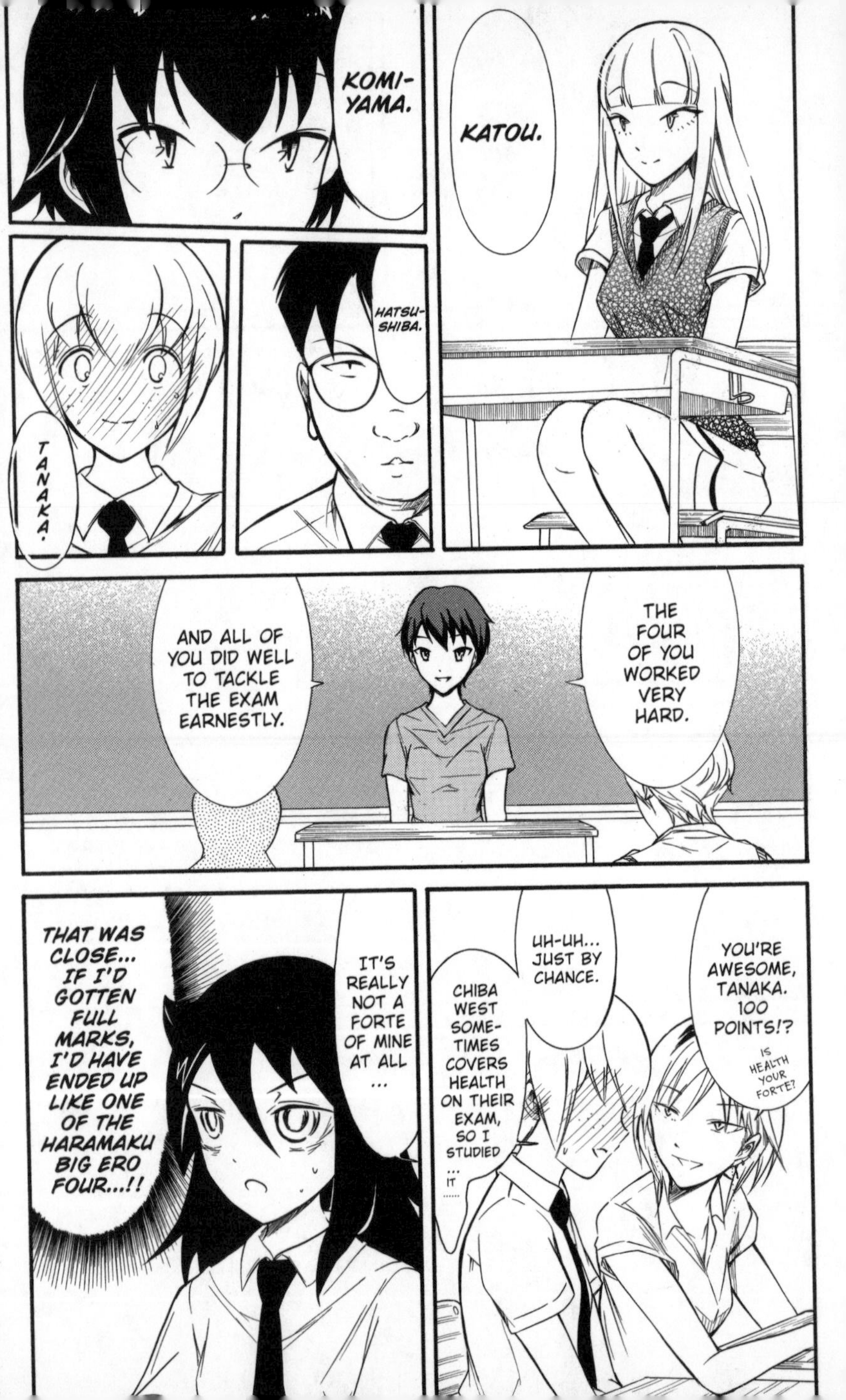
KATOU.
KOMI-YAMA.
HATSU-SHIBA.
TANAKA.
THE FOUR OF YOU WORKED VERY HARD.
AND ALL OF YOU DID WELL TO TACKLE THE EXAM EARNESTLY.
YOU'RE AWESOME, TANAKA. 100 POINTS!?
IS HEALTH YOUR FORTE?
UH-UH... JUST BY CHANCE.
CHIBA WEST SOME-TIMES COVERS HEALTH ON THEIR EXAM, SO I STUDIED ... IT ......
IT'S REALLY NOT A FORTE OF MINE AT ALL ...
THAT WAS CLOSE... IF I'D GOTTEN FULL MARKS, I'D HAVE ENDED UP LIKE ONE OF THE HARAMAKU BIG ERO FOUR...!!

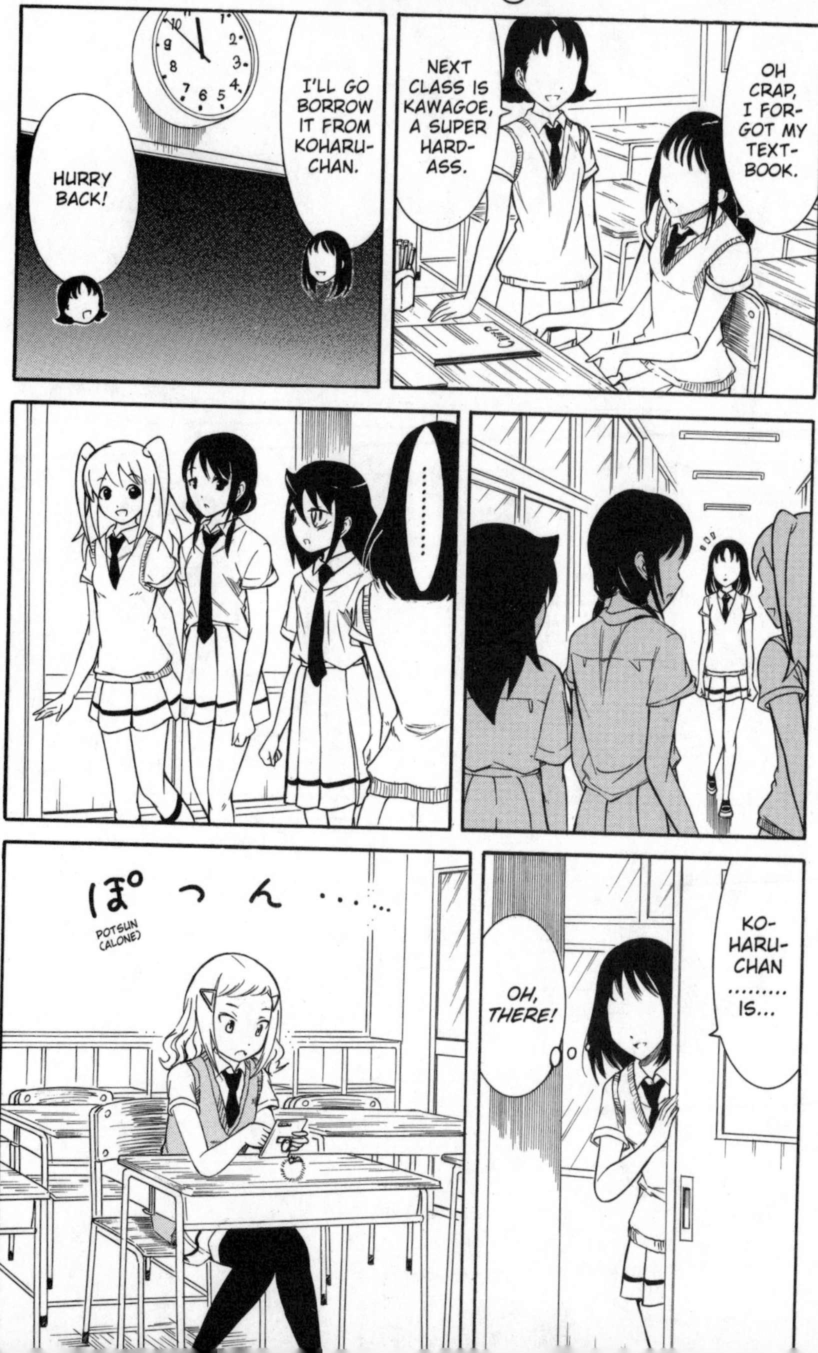
OH CRAP, I FORGOT MY TEXTBOOK.
NEXT CLASS IS KAWAGOE, A SUPER HARD-ASS.
I'LL GO BORROW IT FROM KOHARU-CHAN.
HURRY BACK!
....
KOHARU-CHAN .... IS...
OH, THERE!
ぽつん……
POTSUN (ALONE)

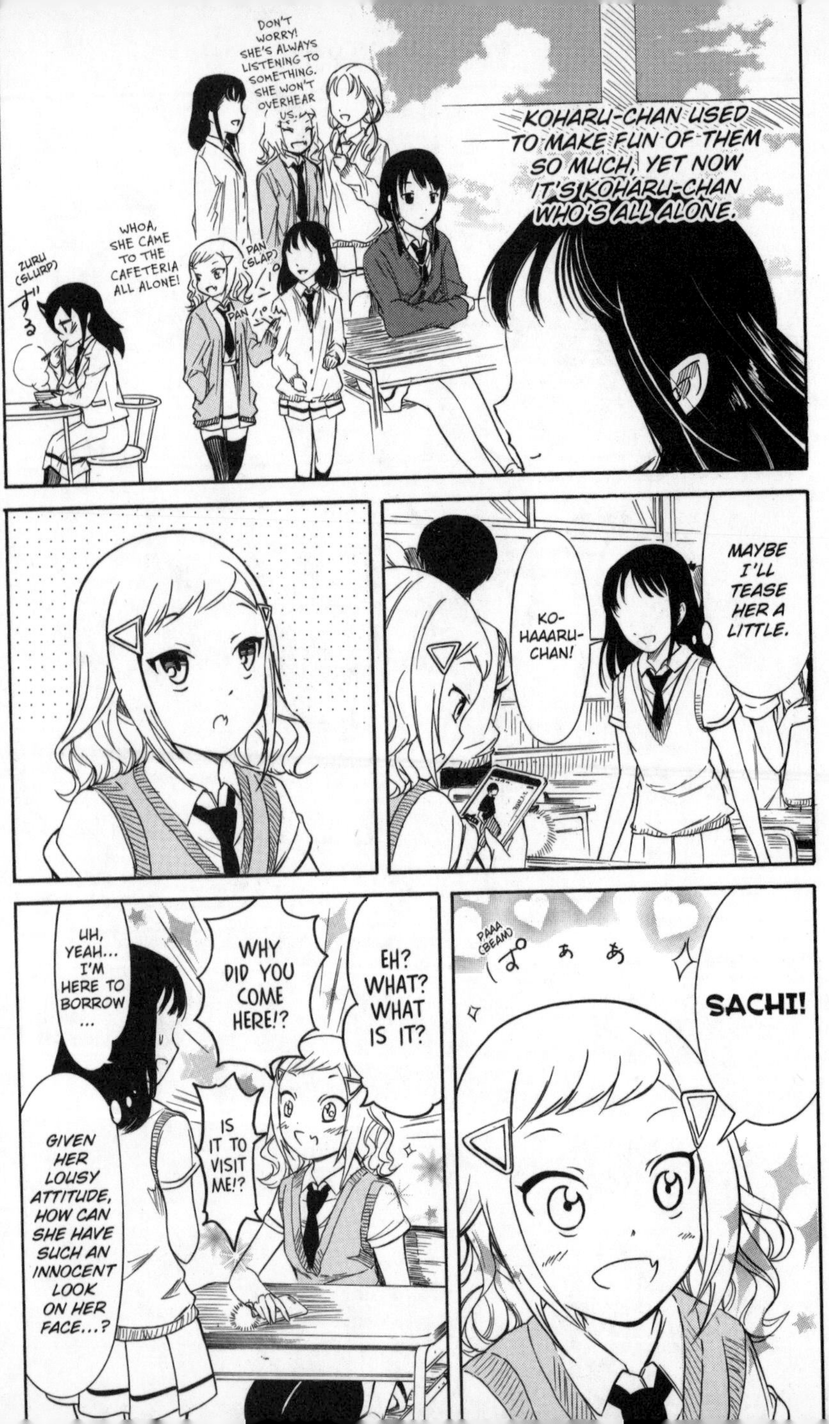
KOHARU-CHAN USED TO MAKE FUN OF THEM SO MUCH, YET NOW IT'S KOHARU-CHAN WHO'S ALL ALONE.
DON'T WORRY! SHE'S ALWAYS LISTENING TO SOMETHING. SHE WON'T OVERHEAR US.
PAN (SLAP)
PAN
WHOA, SHE CAME TO THE CAFETERIA ALL ALONE!
ZURU (SLURP)
する
MAYBE I'LL TEASE HER A LITTLE.
KO-HAAARU-CHAN!
SACHI!
PAAA (BEAM)
ぱああ
EH? WHAT? WHAT IS IT?
WHY DID YOU COME HERE!?
UH, YEAH... I'M HERE TO BORROW...
IS IT TO VISIT ME!?
GIVEN HER LOUSY ATTITUDE, HOW CAN SHE HAVE SUCH AN INNOCENT LOOK ON HER FACE...?

KOHARU-CHAN ②

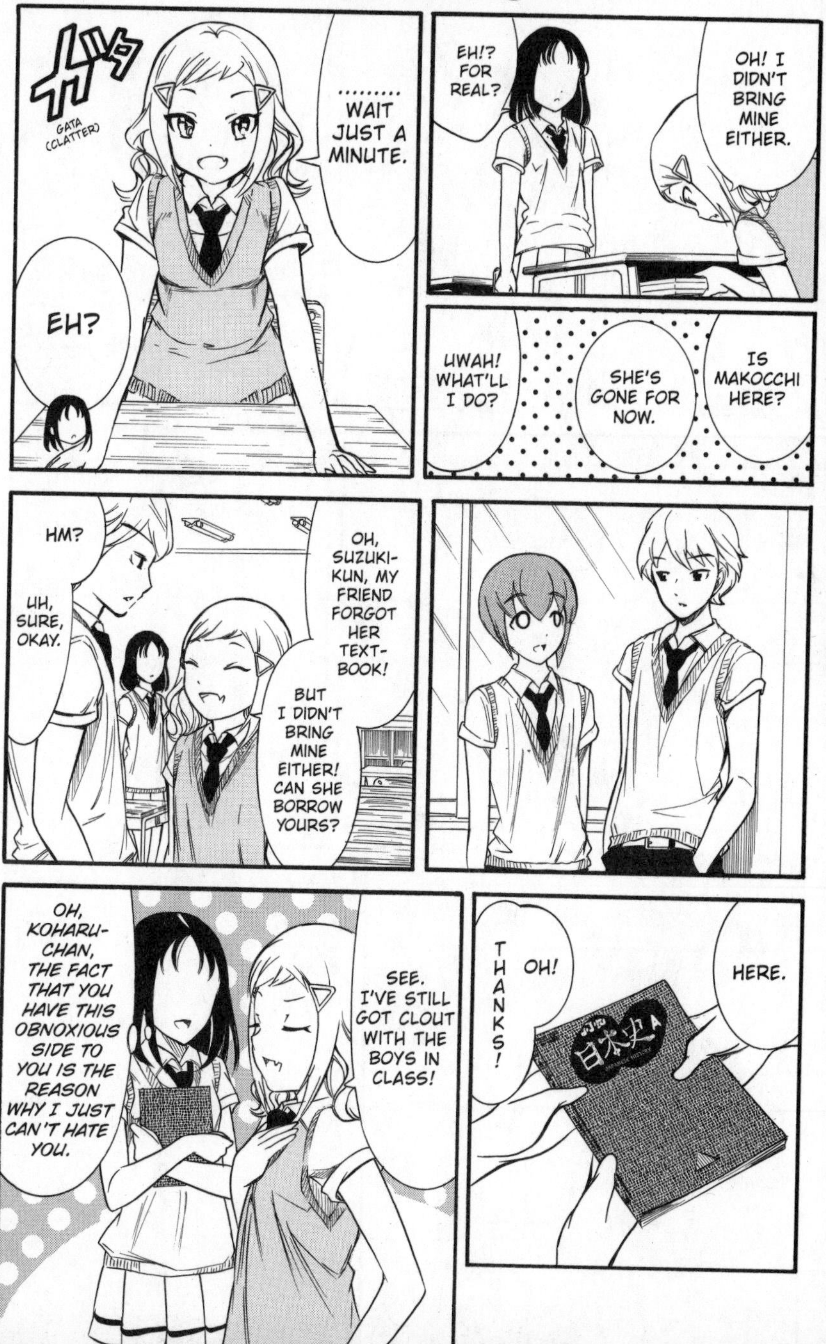
OH! I DIDN'T BRING MINE EITHER.
EH!? FOR REAL?
IS MAKOCCHI HERE?
SHE'S GONE FOR NOW.
UWAH! WHAT'LL I DO?
.... WAIT JUST A MINUTE.
GATA (CLATTER)
EH?
OH, SUZUKI-KUN, MY FRIEND FORGOT HER TEXT-BOOK!
BUT I DIDN'T BRING MINE EITHER! CAN SHE BORROW YOURS?
HM?
UH, SURE, OKAY.
HERE.
OH!
THANKS!
SEE. I'VE STILL GOT CLOUT WITH THE BOYS IN CLASS!
OH, KOHARU-CHAN, THE FACT THAT YOU HAVE THIS OBNOXIOUS SIDE TO YOU IS THE REASON WHY I JUST CAN'T HATE YOU.

STAY AWAY

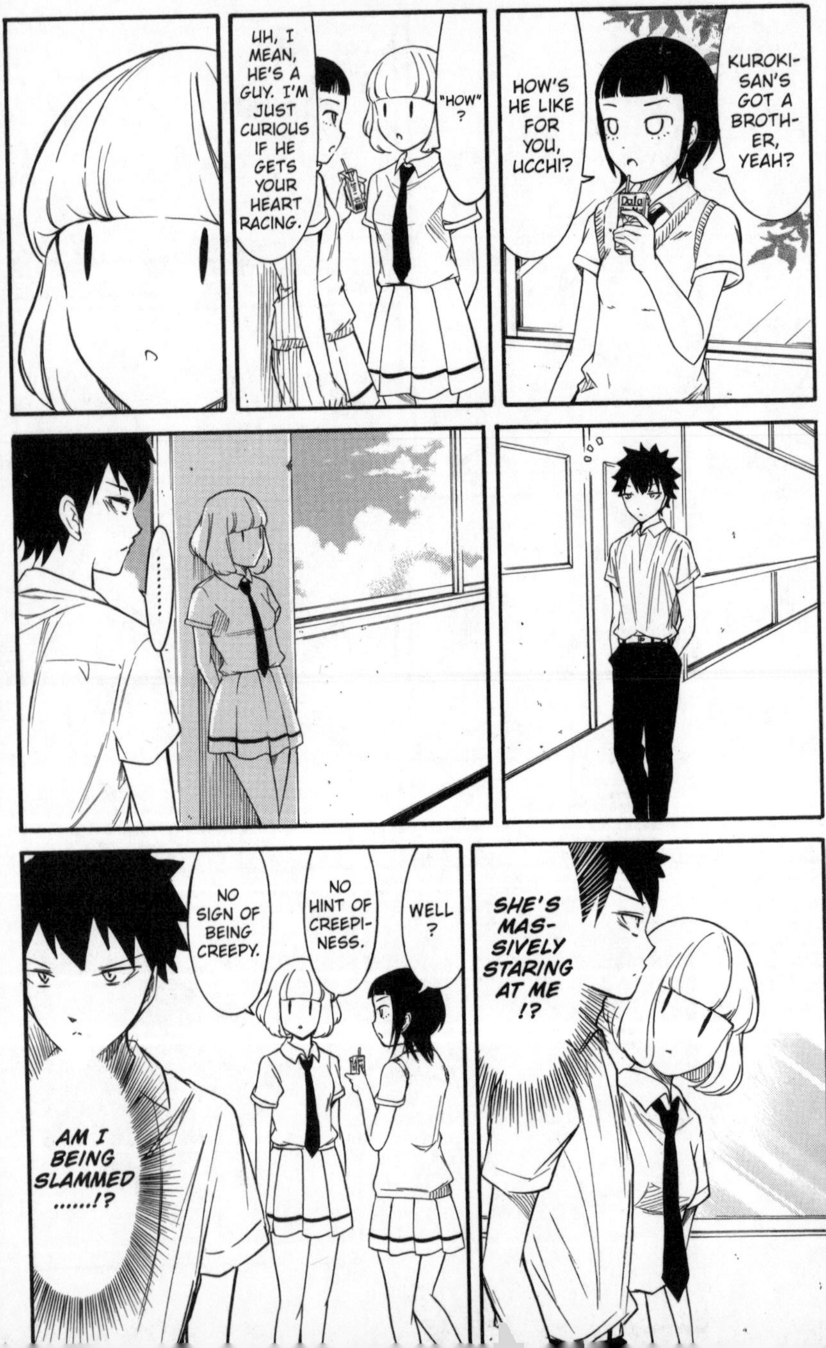
KUROKI-SAN'S GOT A BROTHER, YEAH?
HOW'S HE LIKE FOR YOU, UCCHI?
"HOW"?
UH, I MEAN, HE'S A GUY. I'M JUST CURIOUS IF HE GETS YOUR HEART RACING.
......
SHE'S MASSIVELY STARING AT ME !?
WELL?
NO HINT OF CREEPINESS.
NO SIGN OF BEING CREEPY.
AM I BEING SLAMMED ......!?

LOCKED UP

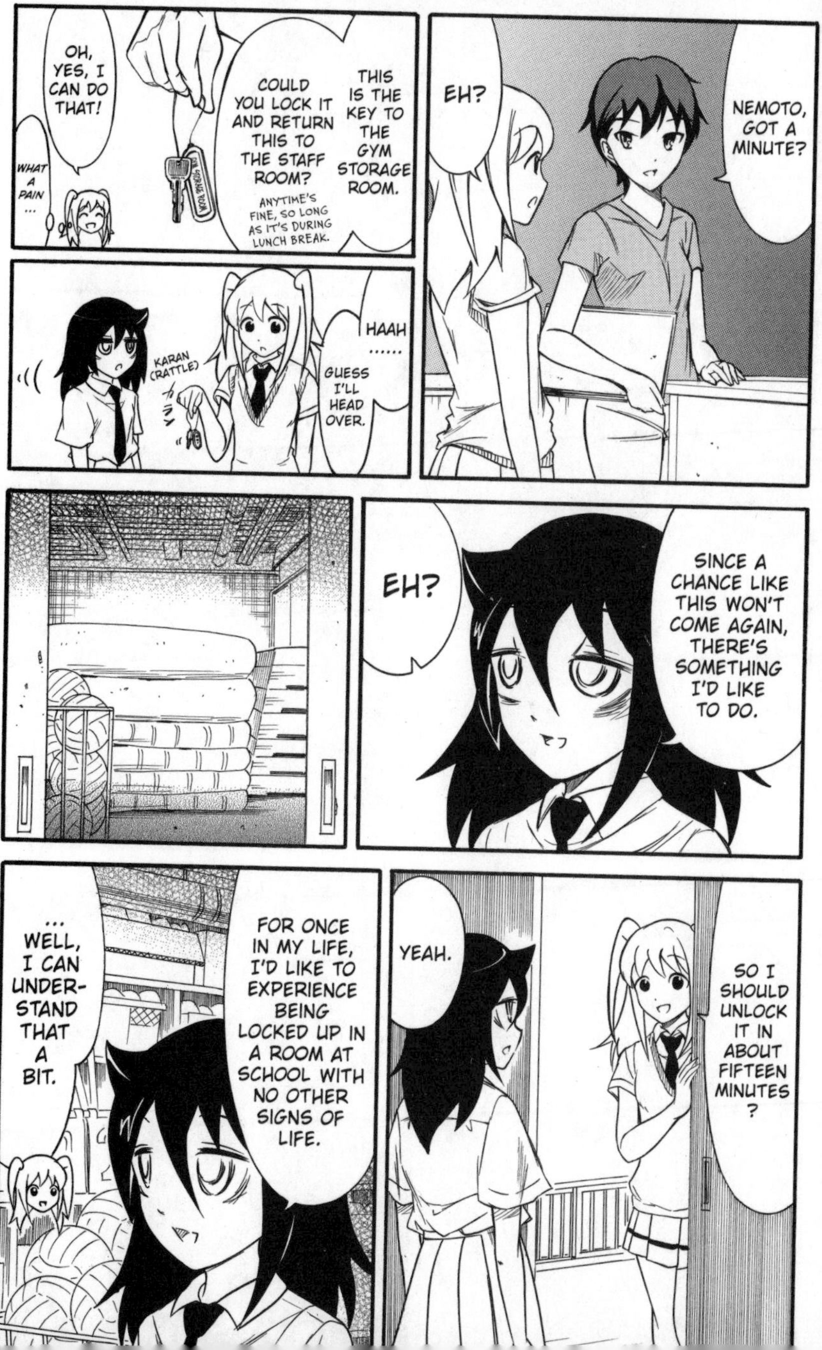
NEMOTO, GOT A MINUTE?
EH?
THIS IS THE KEY TO THE GYM STORAGE ROOM.
COULD YOU LOCK IT AND RETURN THIS TO THE STAFF ROOM?
ANYTIME'S FINE, SO LONG AS IT'S DURING LUNCH BREAK.
OH, YES, I CAN DO THAT!
WHAT A PAIN ...
HAAH ......
GUESS I'LL HEAD OVER.
KARAN (RATTLE)
SINCE A CHANCE LIKE THIS WON'T COME AGAIN, THERE'S SOMETHING I'D LIKE TO DO.
EH?
SO I SHOULD UNLOCK IT IN ABOUT FIFTEEN MINUTES?
YEAH.
FOR ONCE IN MY LIFE, I'D LIKE TO EXPERIENCE BEING LOCKED UP IN A ROOM AT SCHOOL WITH NO OTHER SIGNS OF LIFE.
... WELL, I CAN UNDERSTAND THAT A BIT.

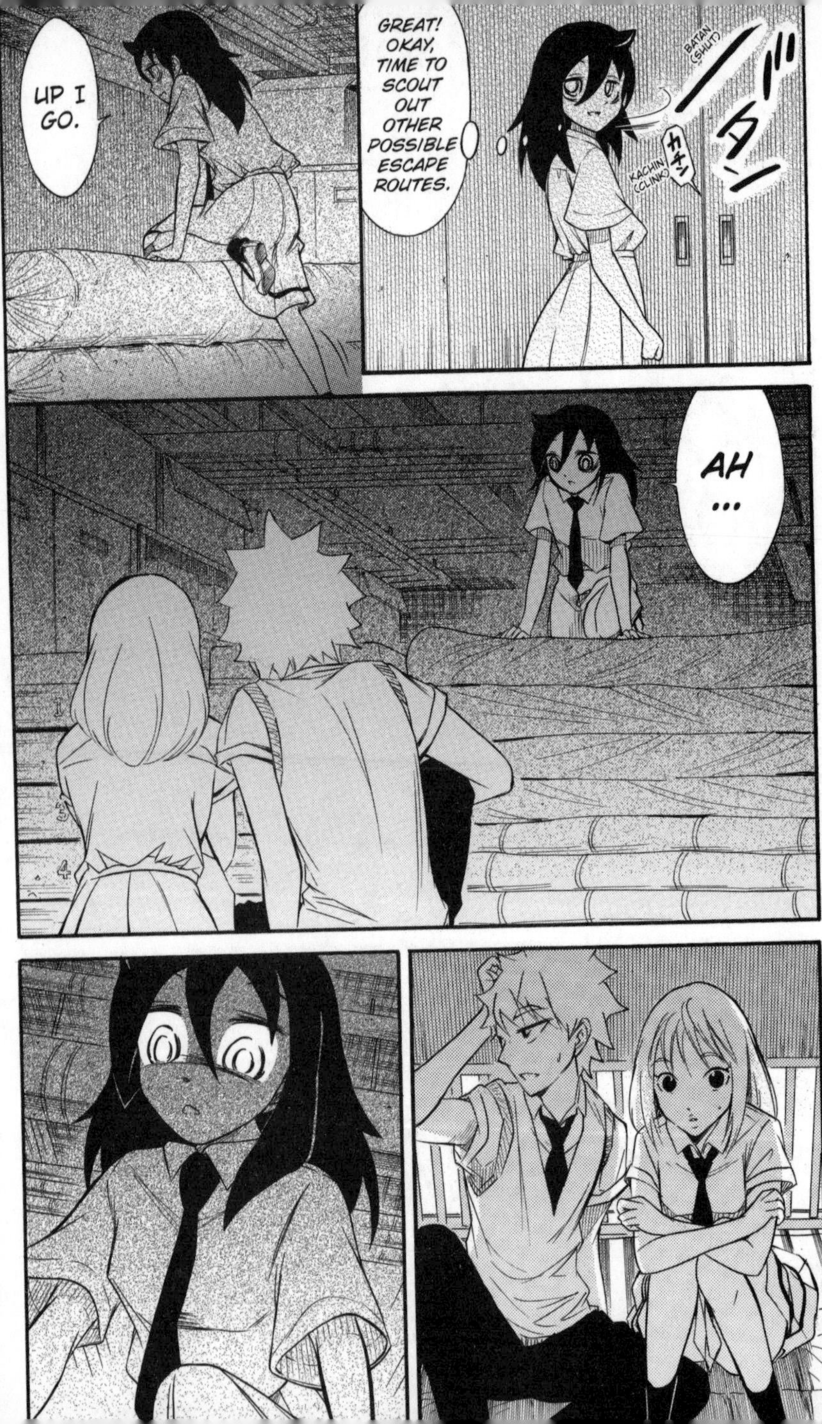
バタン
BATAN (SHUT)
カチン
KACHIN (CLINK)
GREAT! OKAY, TIME TO SCOUT OUT OTHER POSSIBLE ESCAPE ROUTES.
UP I GO.
AH ...

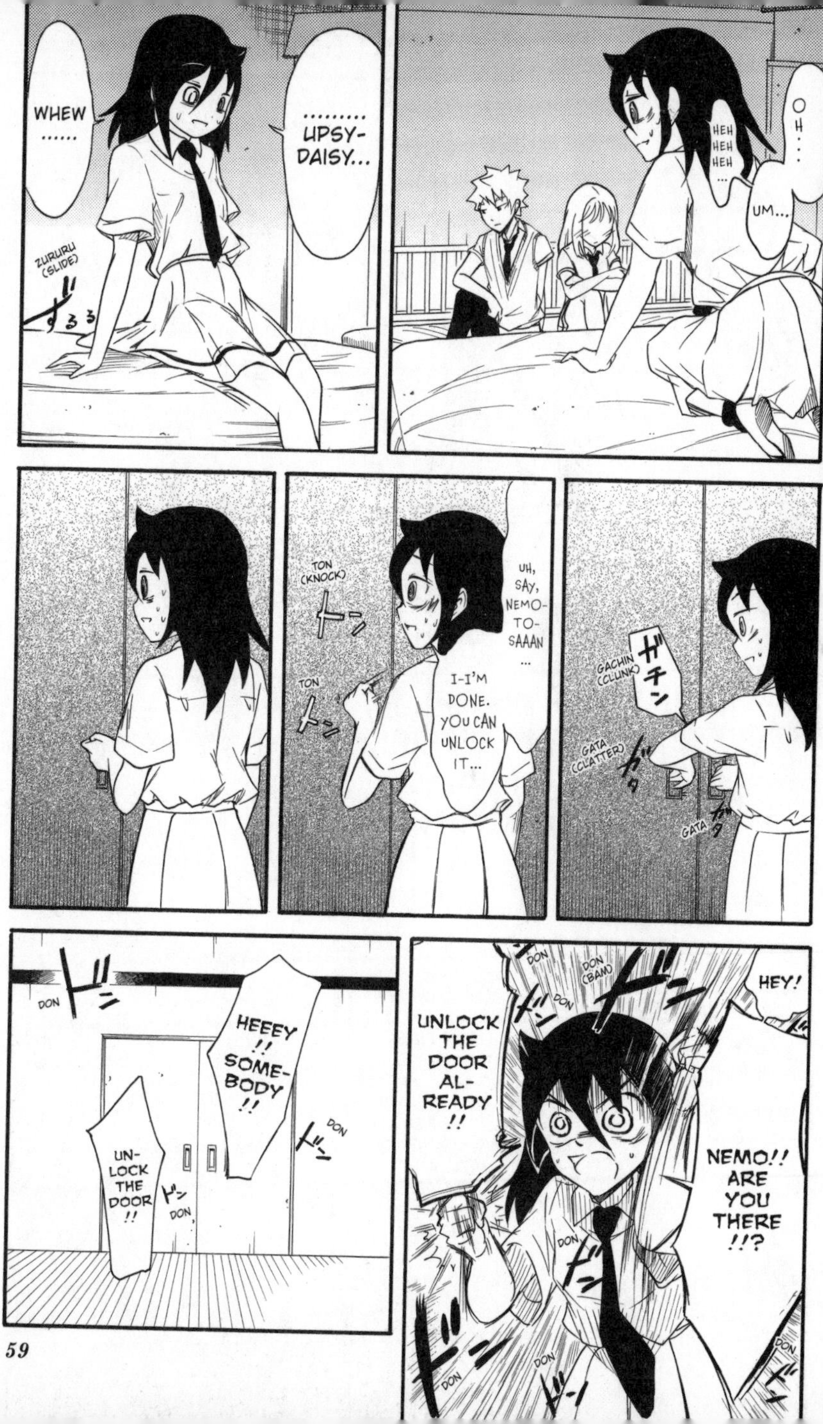
OH...
HEH HEH HEH...
UM...
.... UPSY-DAISY...
WHEW ......
ZURURU (SLIDE)
GACHIN (CLUNK)
GATA (CLATTER)
GATA
UH, SAY, NEMOTO-SAAAN...
TON (KNOCK)
I-I'M DONE. YOU CAN UNLOCK IT...
TON
HEY!
DON (BAM)
DON
DON
UNLOCK THE DOOR ALREADY!!
NEMO!! ARE YOU THERE!!?
DON
DON
DON
DON
HEEEY!! SOMEBODY!!
DON
DON
UNLOCK THE DOOR!!
DON

I'M NOT POPULAR, SO IT'S SUMMER.

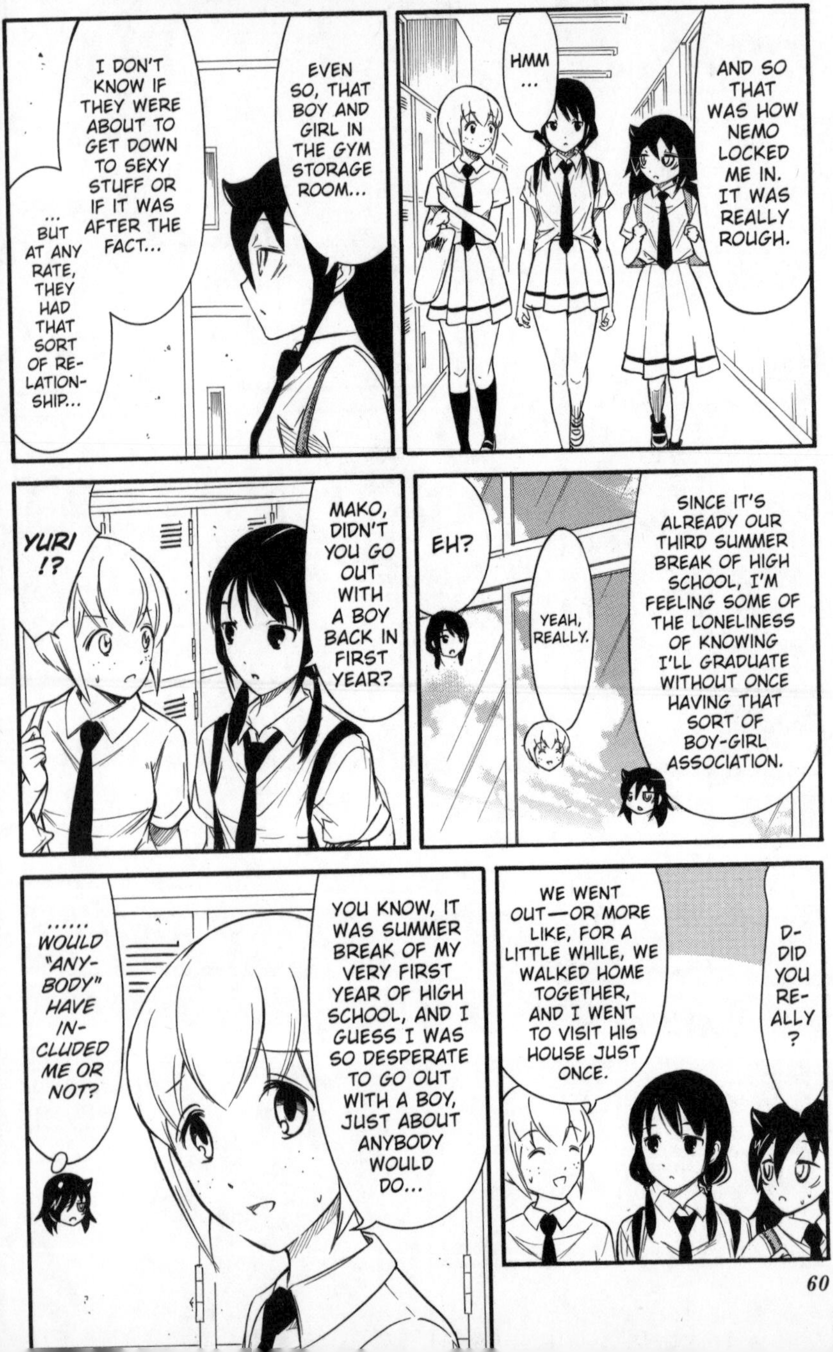

AND SO THAT WAS HOW NEMO LOCKED ME IN. IT WAS REALLY ROUGH.
HMM...
EVEN SO, THAT BOY AND GIRL IN THE GYM STORAGE ROOM...
I DON'T KNOW IF THEY WERE ABOUT TO GET DOWN TO SEXY STUFF OR IF IT WAS AFTER THE FACT...
...BUT AT ANY RATE, THEY HAD THAT SORT OF RE-LATION-SHIP...
SINCE IT'S ALREADY OUR THIRD SUMMER BREAK OF HIGH SCHOOL, I'M FEELING SOME OF THE LONELINESS OF KNOWING I'LL GRADUATE WITHOUT ONCE HAVING THAT SORT OF BOY-GIRL ASSOCIATION.
YEAH, REALLY.
EH?
MAKO, DIDN'T YOU GO OUT WITH A BOY BACK IN FIRST YEAR?
YURI!?
WE WENT OUT—OR MORE LIKE, FOR A LITTLE WHILE, WE WALKED HOME TOGETHER, AND I WENT TO VISIT HIS HOUSE JUST ONCE.
D-DID YOU RE-ALLY?
YOU KNOW, IT WAS SUMMER BREAK OF MY VERY FIRST YEAR OF HIGH SCHOOL, AND I GUESS I WAS SO DESPERATE TO GO OUT WITH A BOY, JUST ABOUT ANYBODY WOULD DO...
......WOULD "ANY-BODY" HAVE IN-CLUDED ME OR NOT?

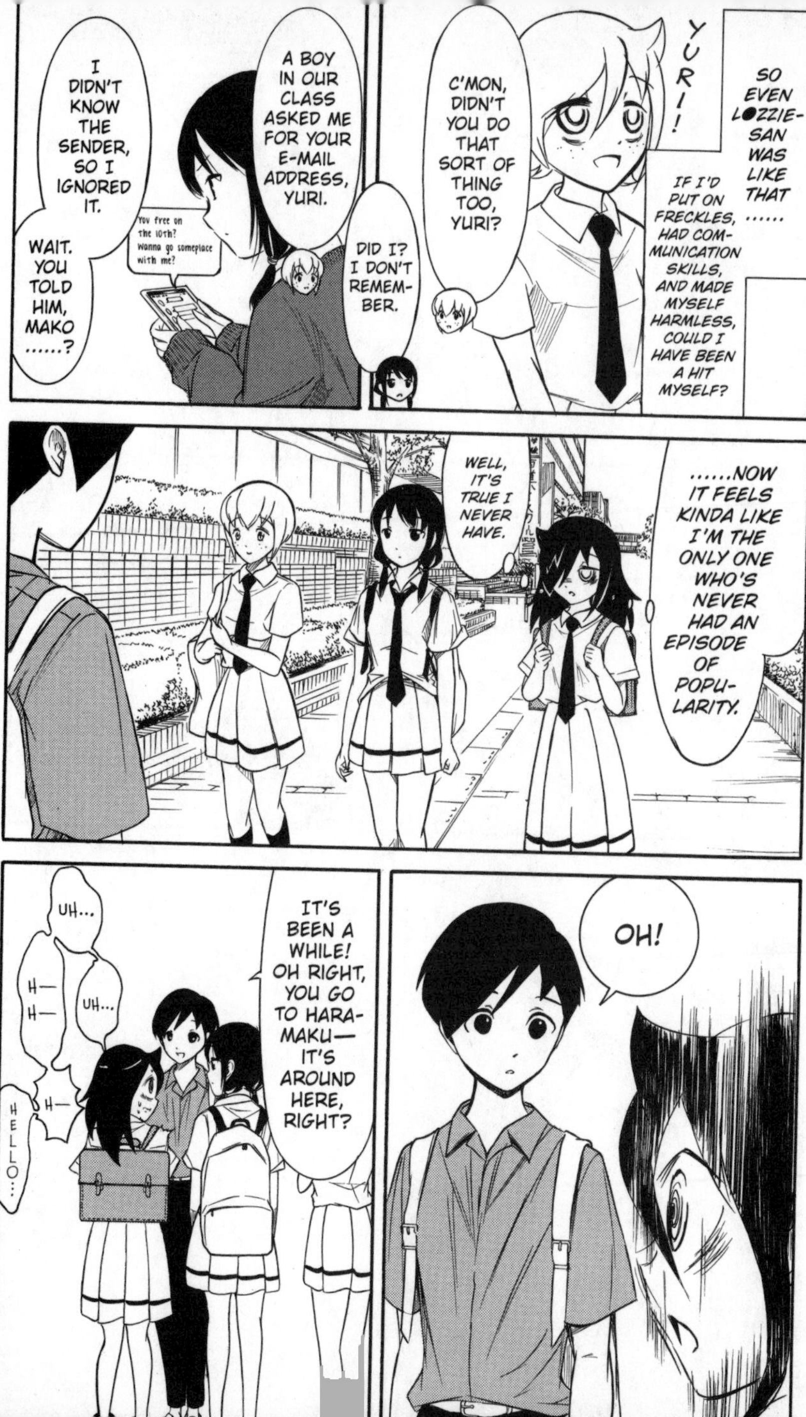
SO EVEN L●ZZIE-SAN WAS LIKE THAT ......
IF I'D PUT ON FRECKLES, HAD COMMUNICATION SKILLS, AND MADE MYSELF HARMLESS, COULD I HAVE BEEN A HIT MYSELF?
YURI!
C'MON, DIDN'T YOU DO THAT SORT OF THING TOO, YURI?
DID I? I DON'T REMEMBER.
A BOY IN OUR CLASS ASKED ME FOR YOUR E-MAIL ADDRESS, YURI.
You free on the 10th? Wanna go someplace with me?
I DIDN'T KNOW THE SENDER, SO I IGNORED IT.
WAIT. YOU TOLD HIM, MAKO ......?
......NOW IT FEELS KINDA LIKE I'M THE ONLY ONE WHO'S NEVER HAD AN EPISODE OF POPULARITY.
WELL, IT'S TRUE I NEVER HAVE.
OH!
IT'S BEEN A WHILE! OH RIGHT, YOU GO TO HARAMAKU— IT'S AROUND HERE, RIGHT?
UH...
H— H—
UH...
H—
HELLO...

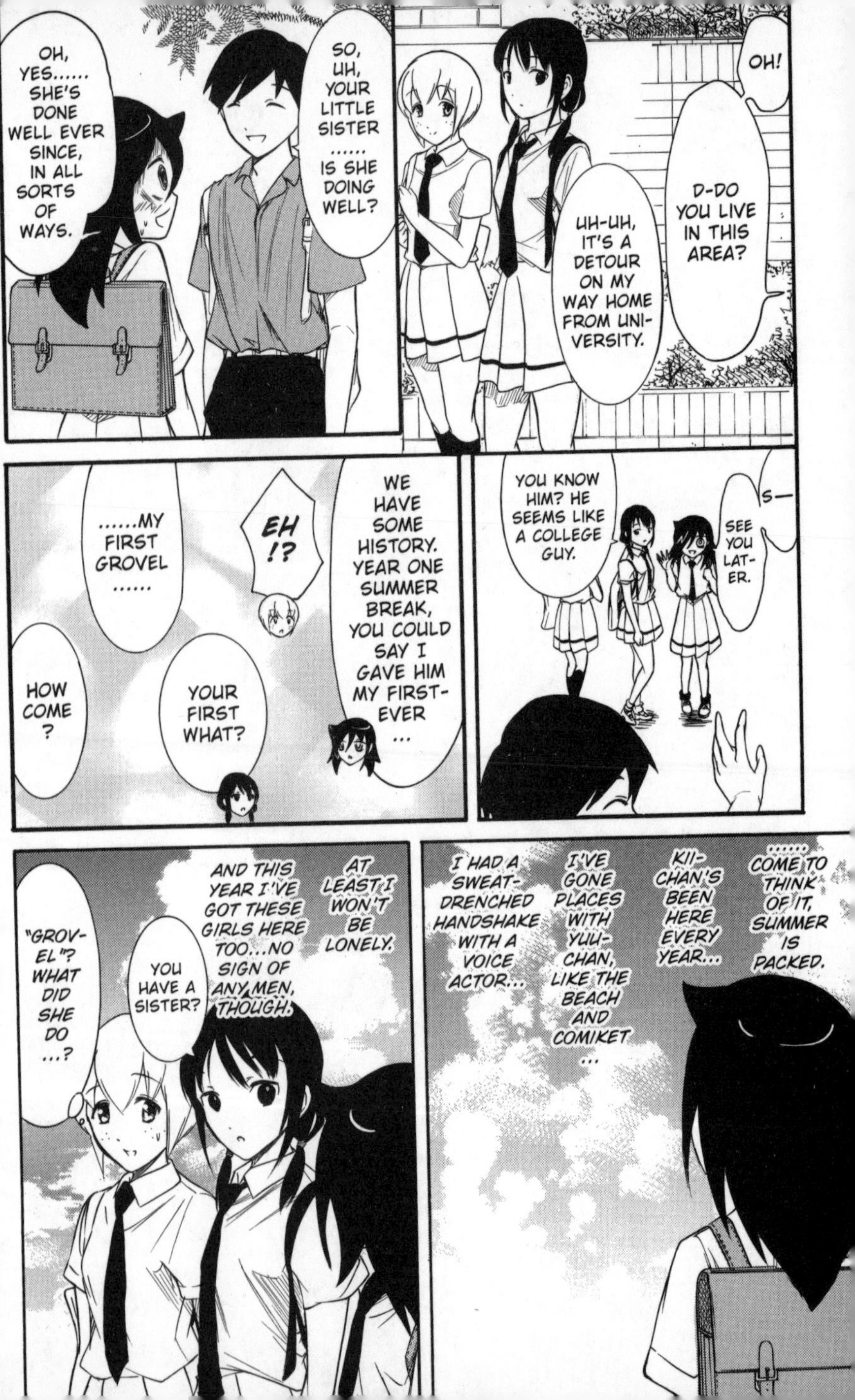
OH!
D-DO YOU LIVE IN THIS AREA?
UH-UH, IT'S A DETOUR ON MY WAY HOME FROM UNIVERSITY.
SO, UH, YOUR LITTLE SISTER ...... IS SHE DOING WELL?
OH, YES...... SHE'S DONE WELL EVER SINCE, IN ALL SORTS OF WAYS.
S— SEE YOU LATER.
YOU KNOW HIM? HE SEEMS LIKE A COLLEGE GUY.
WE HAVE SOME HISTORY. YEAR ONE SUMMER BREAK, YOU COULD SAY I GAVE HIM MY FIRST-EVER ...
EH !?
......MY FIRST GROVEL ......
YOUR FIRST WHAT?
HOW COME?
......COME TO THINK OF IT, SUMMER IS PACKED.
KII-CHAN'S BEEN HERE EVERY YEAR...
I'VE GONE PLACES WITH YUU-CHAN, LIKE THE BEACH AND COMIKET ...
I HAD A SWEAT-DRENCHED HANDSHAKE WITH A VOICE ACTOR...
AT LEAST I WON'T BE LONELY.
AND THIS YEAR I'VE GOT THESE GIRLS HERE TOO...NO SIGN OF ANY MEN, THOUGH.
YOU HAVE A SISTER?
"GROVEL"? WHAT DID SHE DO ...?

No Matter How I Look at It, It's You Guys' Fault I'm Not Popular!

FAIL 164:
I'M NOT POPULAR, SO I'LL WORK HARD OVER SUMMER BREAK.

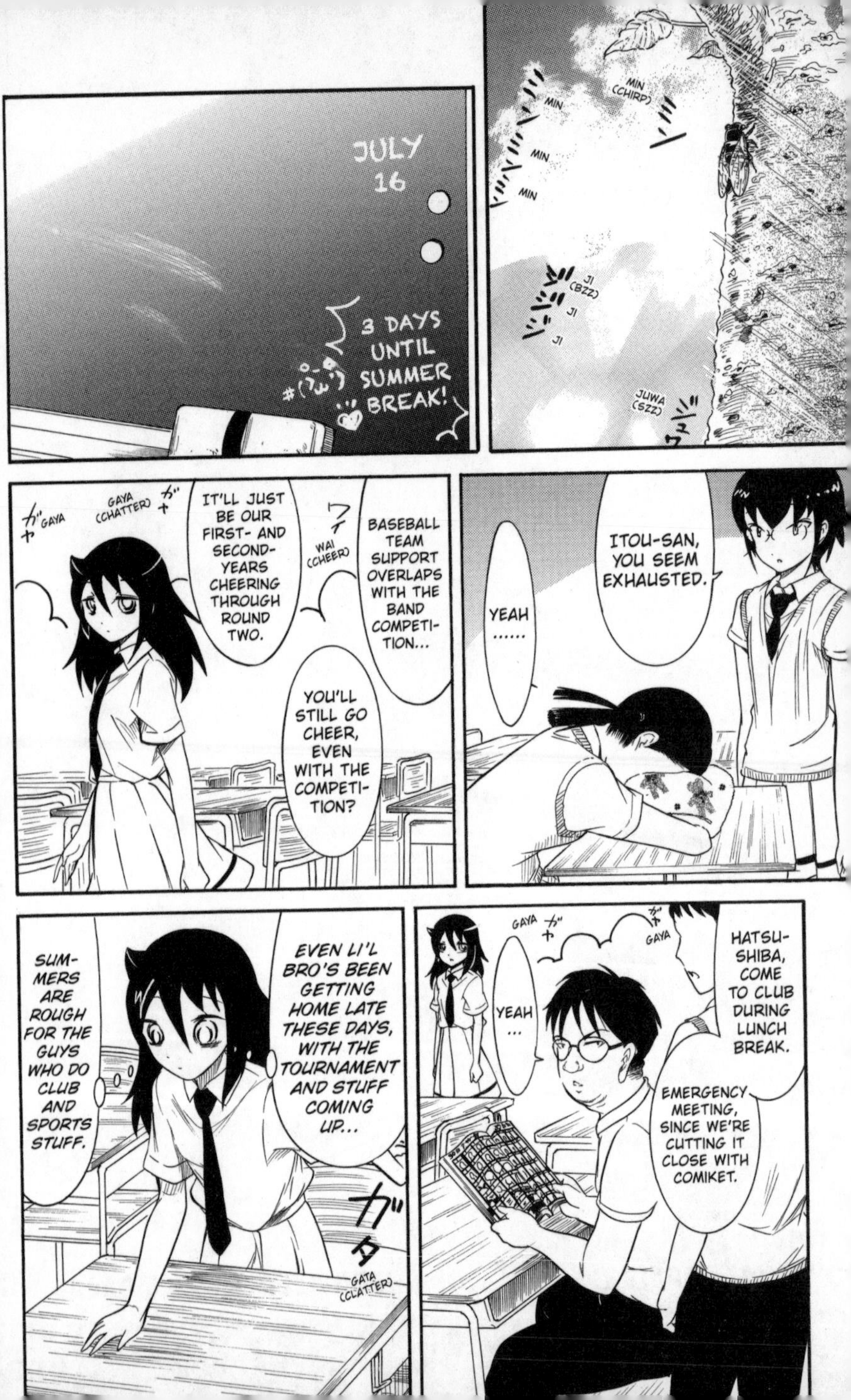
MIN (CHIRP)
MIN
MIN
MIN
JI (BZZ)
JI
JI
JUWA (SZZ)
JULY 16
3 DAYS UNTIL SUMMER BREAK!
ITOU-SAN, YOU SEEM EXHAUSTED.
YEAH ......
BASEBALL TEAM SUPPORT OVERLAPS WITH THE BAND COMPETITION...
WAI (CHEER)
IT'LL JUST BE OUR FIRST- AND SECOND-YEARS CHEERING THROUGH ROUND TWO.
GAYA (CHATTER)
GAYA
YOU'LL STILL GO CHEER, EVEN WITH THE COMPETITION?
HATSUSHIBA, COME TO CLUB DURING LUNCH BREAK.
GAYA
GAYA
YEAH ...
EMERGENCY MEETING, SINCE WE'RE CUTTING IT CLOSE WITH COMIKET.
EVEN LI'L BRO'S BEEN GETTING HOME LATE THESE DAYS, WITH THE TOURNAMENT AND STUFF COMING UP...
SUMMERS ARE ROUGH FOR THE GUYS WHO DO CLUB AND SPORTS STUFF.
GATA (CLATTER)

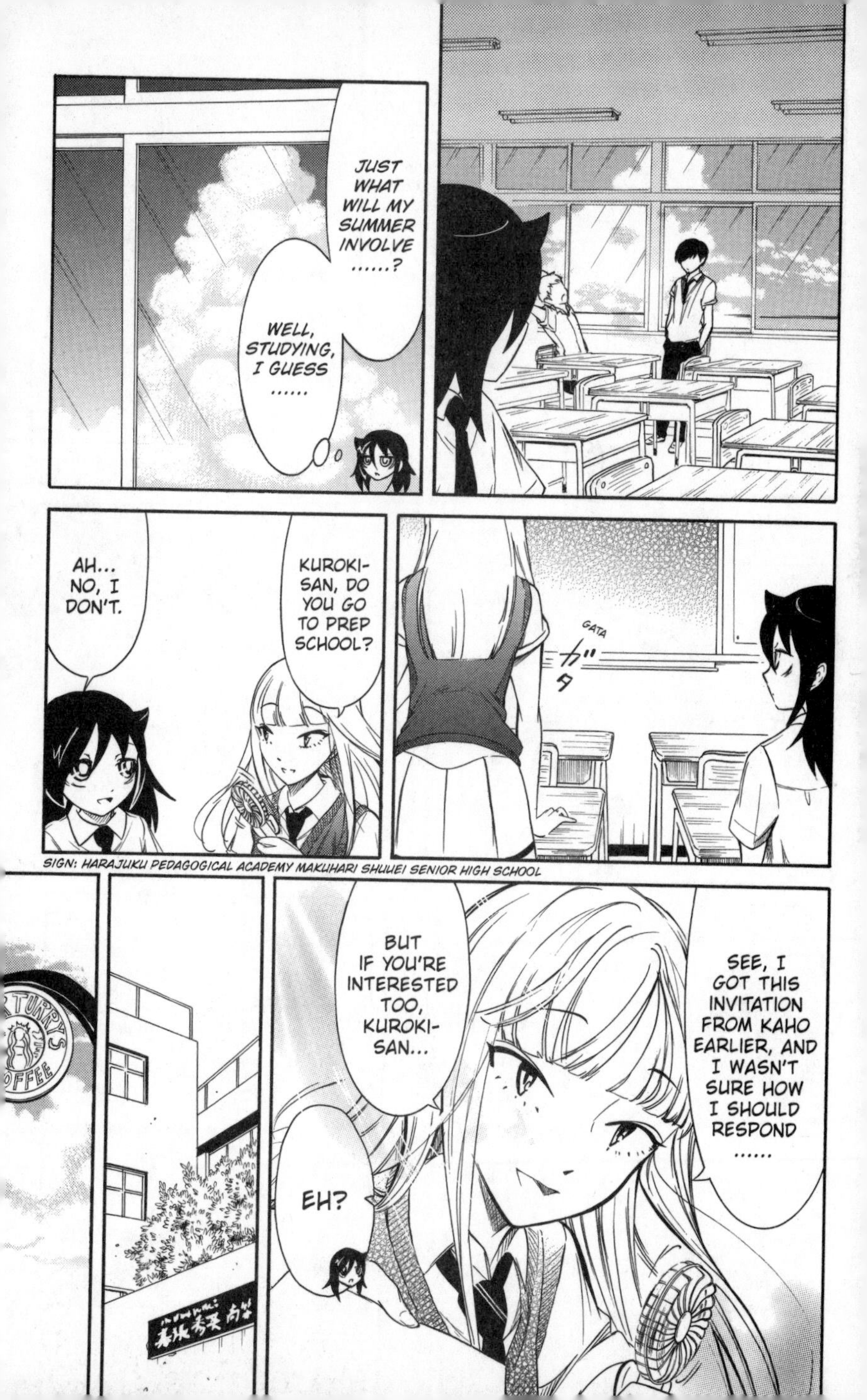
JUST WHAT WILL MY SUMMER INVOLVE ......?
WELL, STUDYING, I GUESS ......
GATA
ガタ
KUROKI-SAN, DO YOU GO TO PREP SCHOOL?
AH... NO, I DON'T.
SEE, I GOT THIS INVITATION FROM KAHO EARLIER, AND I WASN'T SURE HOW I SHOULD RESPOND ......
BUT IF YOU'RE INTERESTED TOO, KUROKI-SAN...
EH?
SIGN: HARAJUKU PEDAGOGICAL ACADEMY MAKUHARI SHUUEI SENIOR HIGH SCHOOL

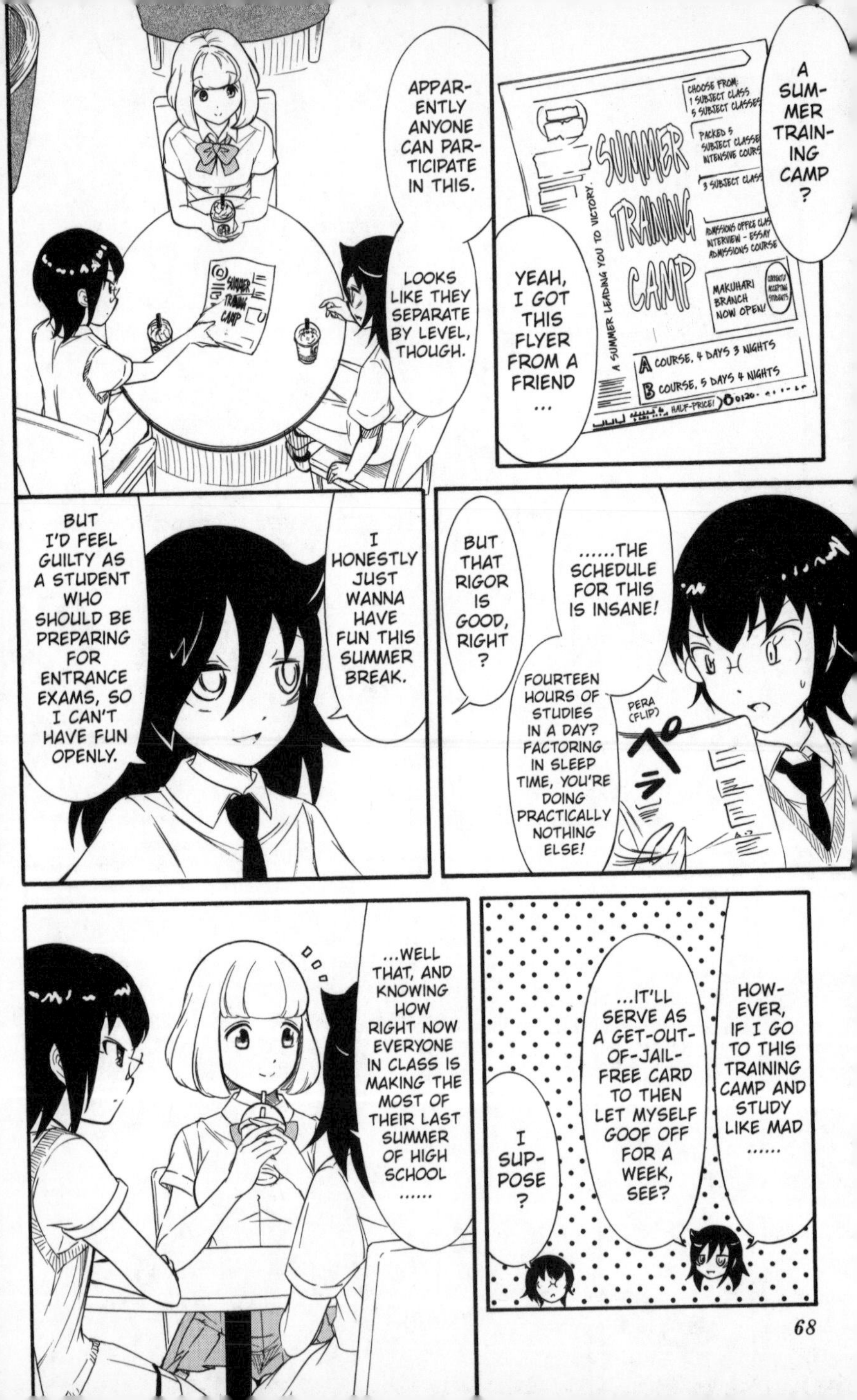
A SUMMER TRAINING CAMP?
SUMMER TRAINING CAMP
A SUMMER LEADING YOU TO VICTORY.
CHOOSE FROM: 1 SUBJECT CLASS 5 SUBJECT CLASSES
PACKED 5 SUBJECT CLASSES INTENSIVE COURSE
3 SUBJECT CLASS
ADMISSIONS OFFICE CLASS INTERVIEW - ESSAY ADMISSIONS COURSE
MAKUHARI BRANCH NOW OPEN!
CURRENTLY ACCEPTING STUDENTS
A COURSE, 4 DAYS 3 NIGHTS
B COURSE, 5 DAYS 4 NIGHTS
HALF-PRICE!
YEAH, I GOT THIS FLYER FROM A FRIEND...
APPARENTLY ANYONE CAN PARTICIPATE IN THIS.
LOOKS LIKE THEY SEPARATE BY LEVEL, THOUGH.
......THE SCHEDULE FOR THIS IS INSANE!
FOURTEEN HOURS OF STUDIES IN A DAY? FACTORING IN SLEEP TIME, YOU'RE DOING PRACTICALLY NOTHING ELSE!
PERA (FLIP)
BUT THAT RIGOR IS GOOD, RIGHT?
I HONESTLY JUST WANNA HAVE FUN THIS SUMMER BREAK.
BUT I'D FEEL GUILTY AS A STUDENT WHO SHOULD BE PREPARING FOR ENTRANCE EXAMS, SO I CAN'T HAVE FUN OPENLY.
HOWEVER, IF I GO TO THIS TRAINING CAMP AND STUDY LIKE MAD......
...IT'LL SERVE AS A GET-OUT-OF-JAIL-FREE CARD TO THEN LET MYSELF GOOF OFF FOR A WEEK, SEE?
I SUPPOSE?
...WELL THAT, AND KNOWING HOW RIGHT NOW EVERYONE IN CLASS IS MAKING THE MOST OF THEIR LAST SUMMER OF HIGH SCHOOL......

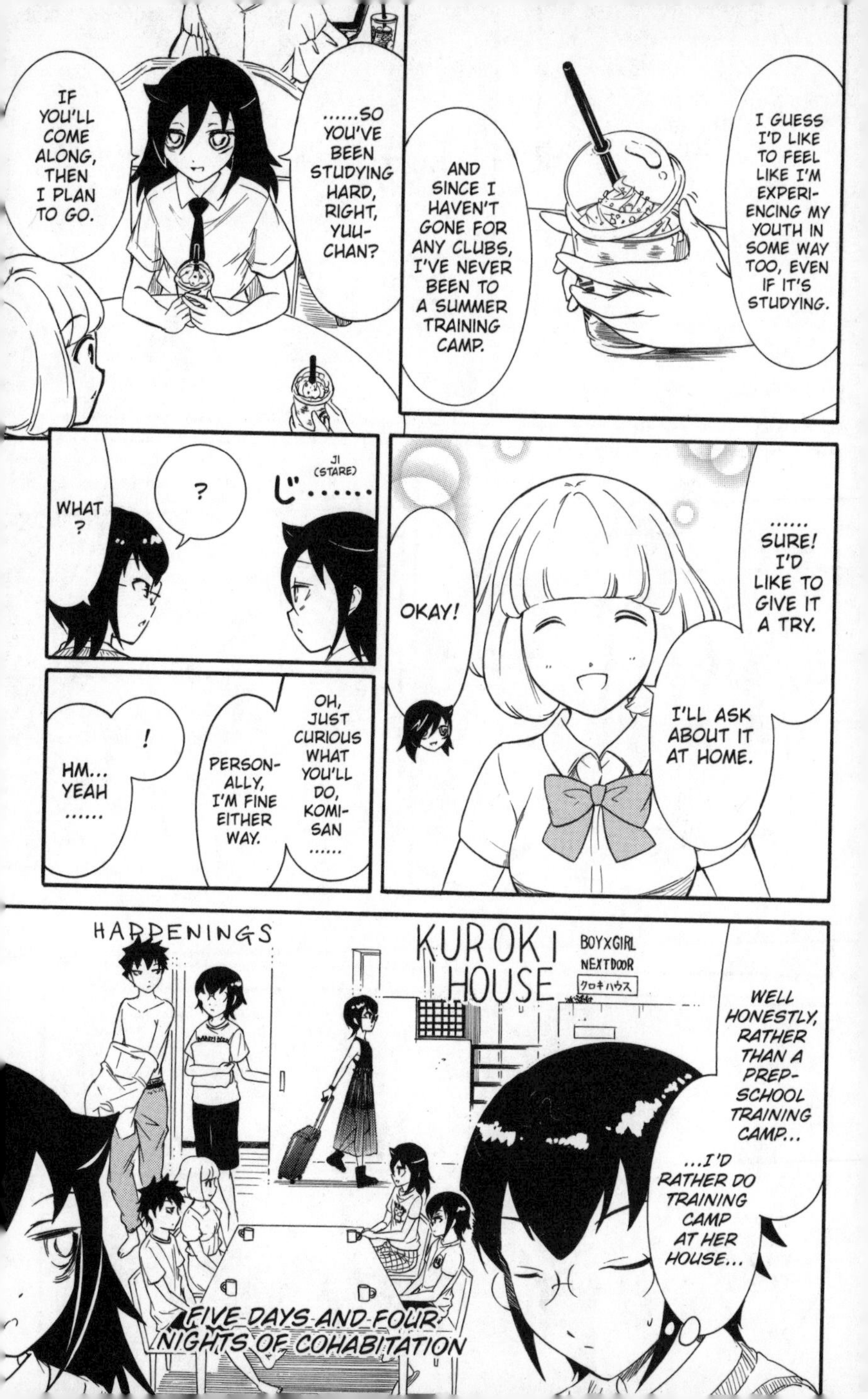
I GUESS I'D LIKE TO FEEL LIKE I'M EXPERI-ENCING MY YOUTH IN SOME WAY TOO, EVEN IF IT'S STUDYING.
AND SINCE I HAVEN'T GONE FOR ANY CLUBS, I'VE NEVER BEEN TO A SUMMER TRAINING CAMP.
......SO YOU'VE BEEN STUDYING HARD, RIGHT, YUU-CHAN?
IF YOU'LL COME ALONG, THEN I PLAN TO GO.
......SURE! I'D LIKE TO GIVE IT A TRY.
OKAY!
I'LL ASK ABOUT IT AT HOME.
JI (STARE)
じ......
?
WHAT?
OH, JUST CURIOUS WHAT YOU'LL DO, KOMI-SAN......
PERSON-ALLY, I'M FINE EITHER WAY.
!
HM... YEAH......
WELL HONESTLY, RATHER THAN A PREP-SCHOOL TRAINING CAMP...
...I'D RATHER DO TRAINING CAMP AT HER HOUSE...
KUROKI HOUSE
BOYXGIRL NEXTDOOR
クロキハウス
HAPPENINGS
FIVE DAYS AND FOUR NIGHTS OF COHABITATION

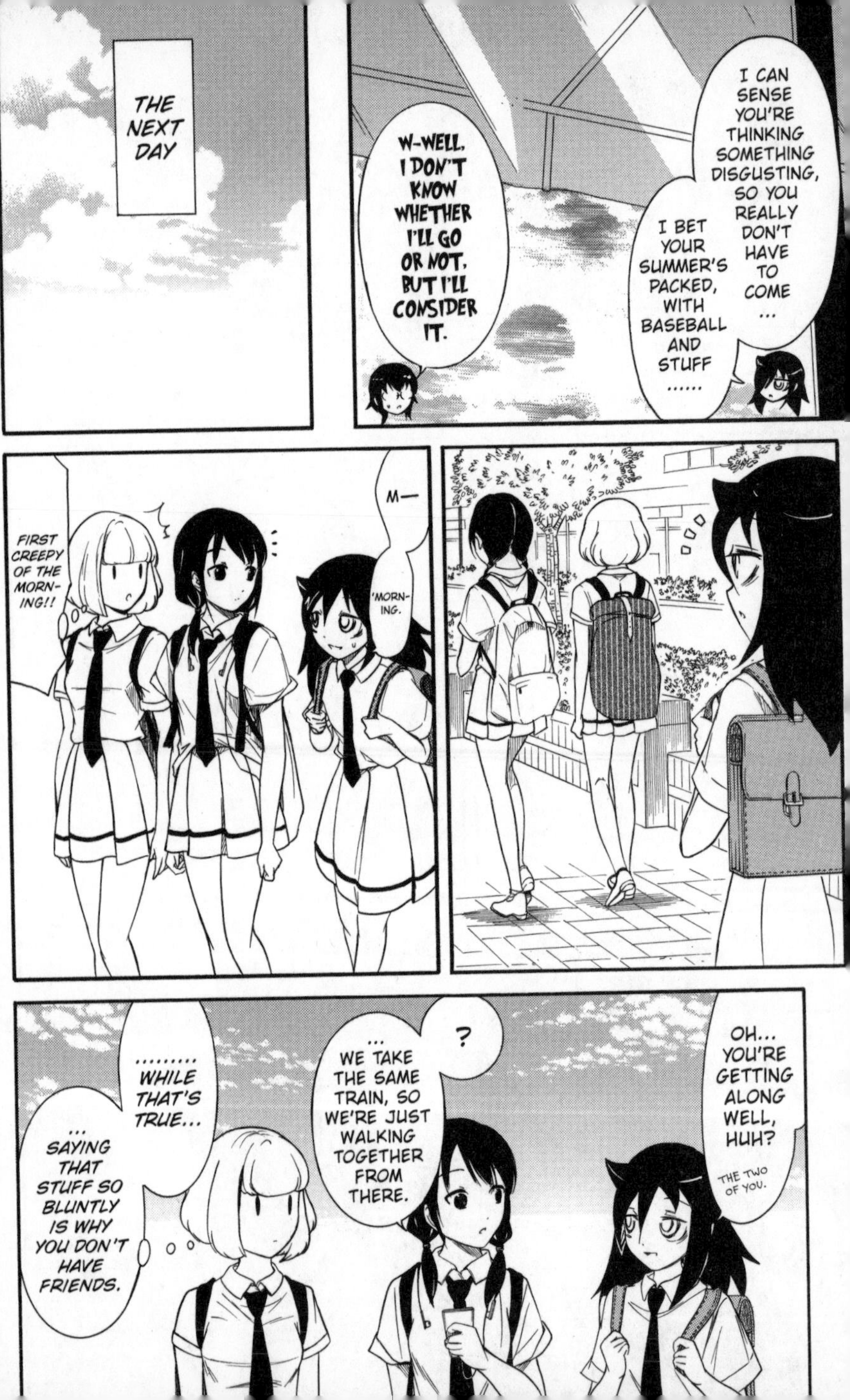
I CAN SENSE YOU'RE THINKING SOMETHING DISGUSTING, SO YOU REALLY DON'T HAVE TO COME ...
I BET YOUR SUMMER'S PACKED, WITH BASEBALL AND STUFF ......
W-WELL, I DON'T KNOW WHETHER I'LL GO OR NOT, BUT I'LL CONSIDER IT.
THE NEXT DAY
M—
'MORNING.
FIRST CREEPY OF THE MORNING!!
OH... YOU'RE GETTING ALONG WELL, HUH?
THE TWO OF YOU.
?
... WE TAKE THE SAME TRAIN, SO WE'RE JUST WALKING TOGETHER FROM THERE.
.... WHILE THAT'S TRUE...
... SAYING THAT STUFF SO BLUNTLY IS WHY YOU DON'T HAVE FRIENDS.

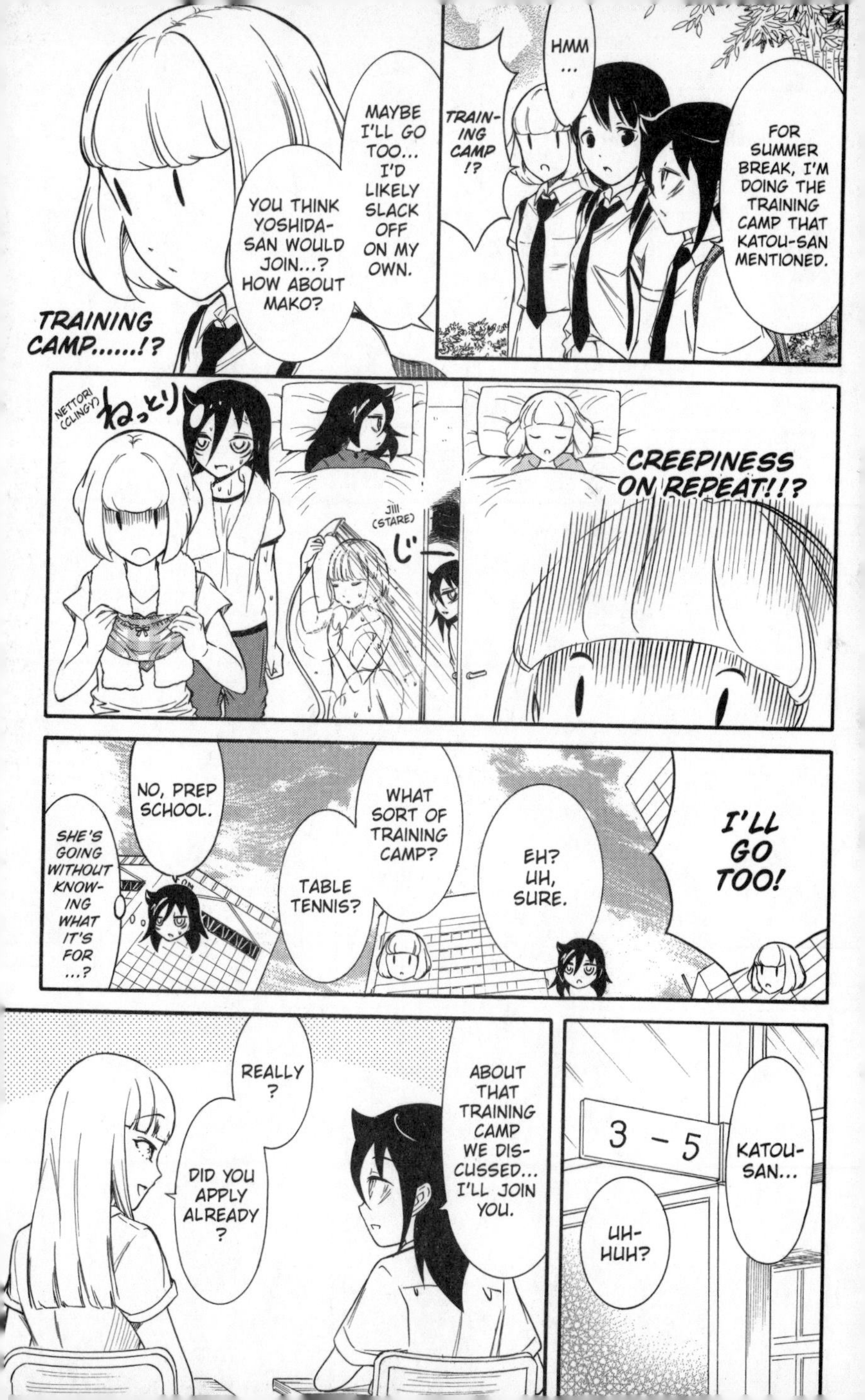

FOR SUMMER BREAK, I'M DOING THE TRAINING CAMP THAT KATOU-SAN MENTIONED.
HMM ...
TRAIN-ING CAMP !?
MAYBE I'LL GO TOO... I'D LIKELY SLACK OFF ON MY OWN.
YOU THINK YOSHIDA-SAN WOULD JOIN...? HOW ABOUT MAKO?
TRAINING CAMP......!?
CREEPINESS ON REPEAT!!?
じー
JIII (STARE)
ねっとり
NETTORI (CLINGY)
I'LL GO TOO!
EH? UH, SURE.
WHAT SORT OF TRAINING CAMP?
TABLE TENNIS?
NO, PREP SCHOOL.
SHE'S GOING WITHOUT KNOWING WHAT IT'S FOR ...?
3 - 5
KATOU-SAN...
UH-HUH?
ABOUT THAT TRAINING CAMP WE DISCUSSED... I'LL JOIN YOU.
REALLY?
DID YOU APPLY ALREADY?

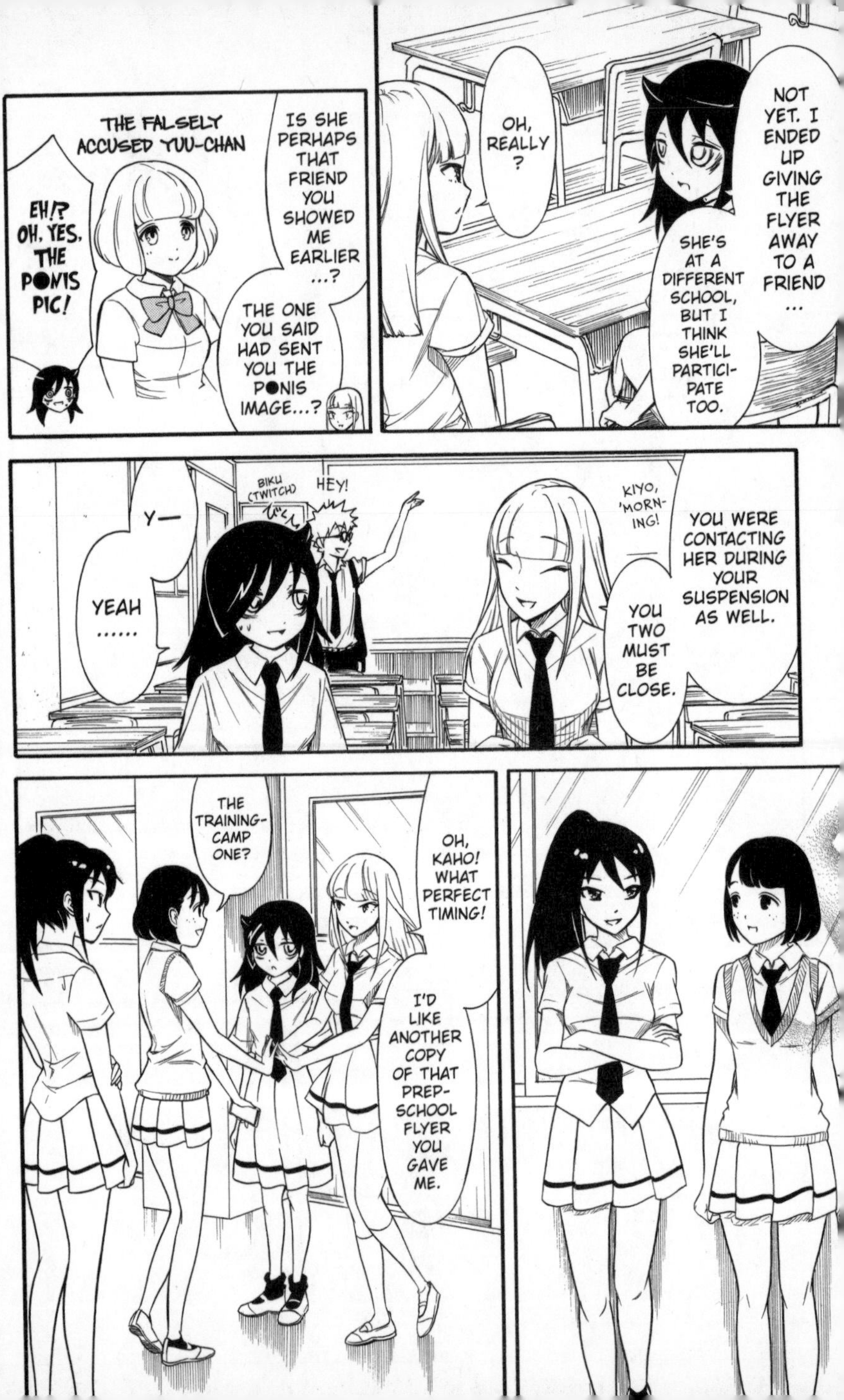
NOT YET. I ENDED UP GIVING THE FLYER AWAY TO A FRIEND...
OH, REALLY?
SHE'S AT A DIFFERENT SCHOOL, BUT I THINK SHE'LL PARTICI-PATE TOO.
IS SHE PERHAPS THAT FRIEND YOU SHOWED ME EARLIER...?
THE ONE YOU SAID HAD SENT YOU THE P●NIS IMAGE...?
THE FALSELY ACCUSED YUU-CHAN
EH!? OH, YES, THE P●NIS PIC!
YOU WERE CONTACTING HER DURING YOUR SUSPENSION AS WELL.
YOU TWO MUST BE CLOSE.
KIYO, 'MORNING!
HEY!
BIKU (TWITCH)
びくん
Y—
YEAH......
OH, KAHO! WHAT PERFECT TIMING!
I'D LIKE ANOTHER COPY OF THAT PREP-SCHOOL FLYER YOU GAVE ME.
THE TRAINING-CAMP ONE?

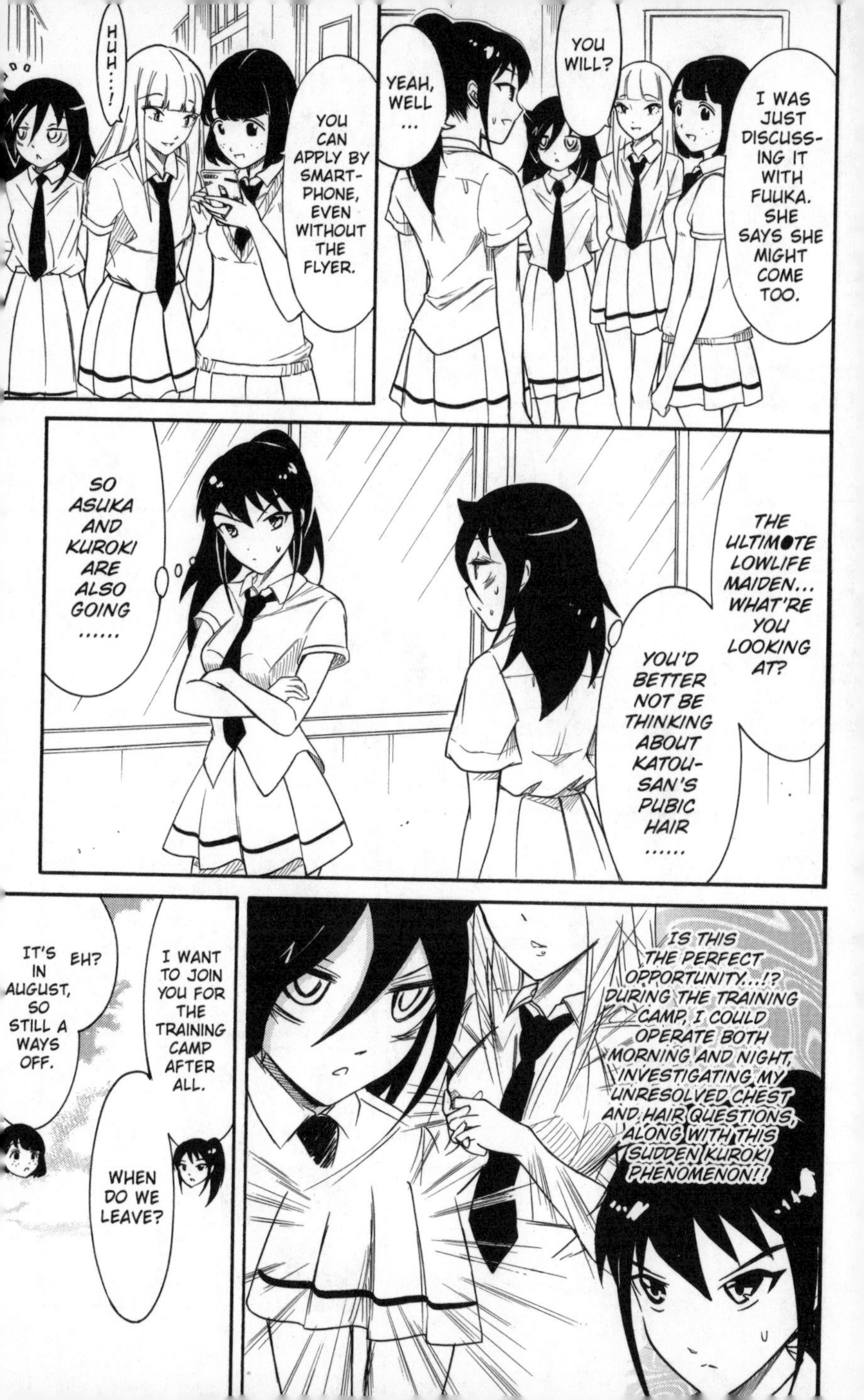
I WAS JUST DISCUSSING IT WITH FUUKA. SHE SAYS SHE MIGHT COME TOO.
YOU WILL?
YEAH, WELL...
YOU CAN APPLY BY SMARTPHONE, EVEN WITHOUT THE FLYER.
HUH...!
THE ULTIMATE LOWLIFE MAIDEN... WHAT'RE YOU LOOKING AT?
YOU'D BETTER NOT BE THINKING ABOUT KATOU-SAN'S PUBIC HAIR......
SO ASUKA AND KUROKI ARE ALSO GOING......
IS THIS THE PERFECT OPPORTUNITY...!? DURING THE TRAINING CAMP, I COULD OPERATE BOTH MORNING AND NIGHT, INVESTIGATING MY UNRESOLVED CHEST AND HAIR QUESTIONS, ALONG WITH THIS SUDDEN KUROKI PHENOMENON!!
I WANT TO JOIN YOU FOR THE TRAINING CAMP AFTER ALL.
EH?
IT'S IN AUGUST, SO STILL A WAYS OFF.
WHEN DO WE LEAVE?

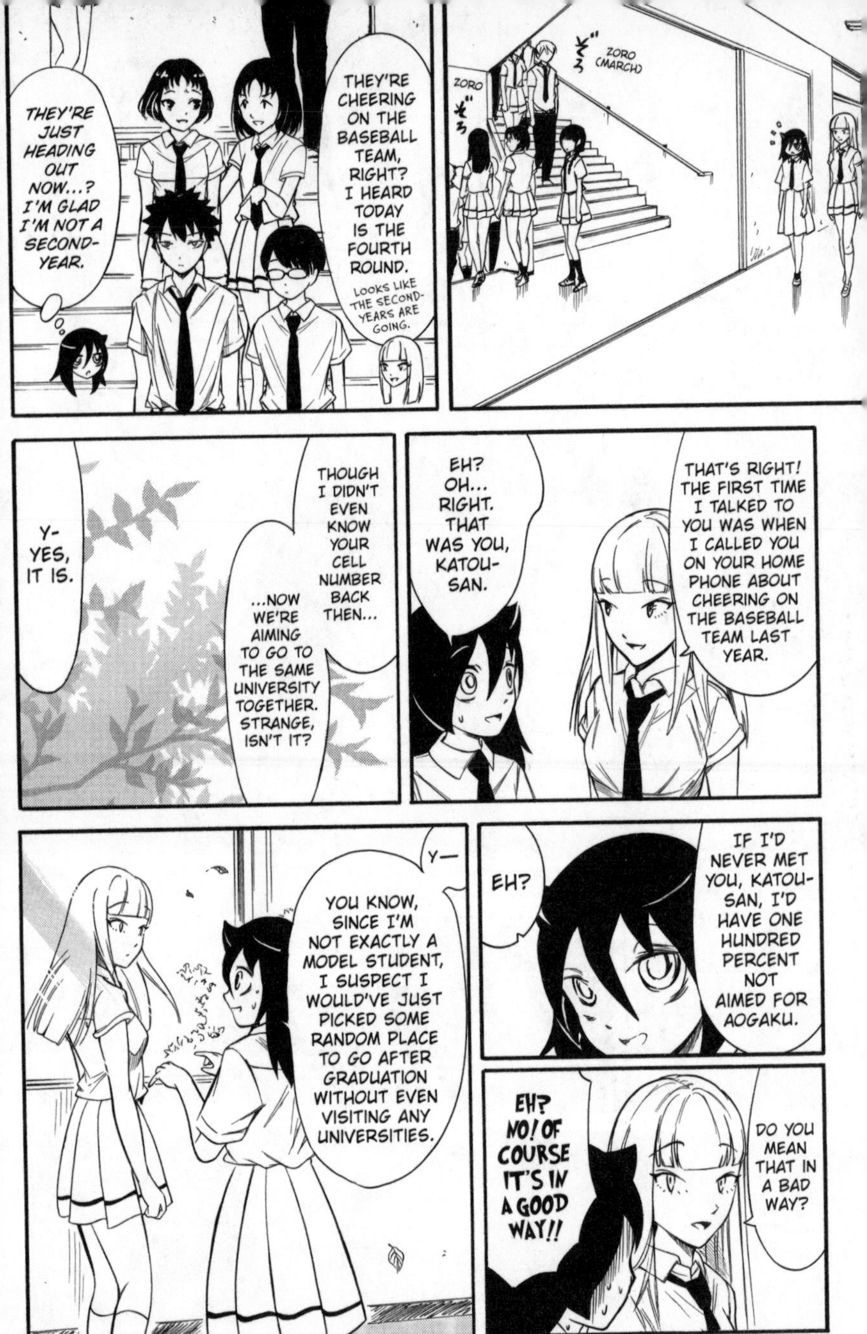
ZORO (MARCH)
ZORO
THEY'RE CHEERING ON THE BASEBALL TEAM, RIGHT? I HEARD TODAY IS THE FOURTH ROUND.
LOOKS LIKE THE SECOND-YEARS ARE GOING.
THEY'RE JUST HEADING OUT NOW...? I'M GLAD I'M NOT A SECOND-YEAR.
THAT'S RIGHT! THE FIRST TIME I TALKED TO YOU WAS WHEN I CALLED YOU ON YOUR HOME PHONE ABOUT CHEERING ON THE BASEBALL TEAM LAST YEAR.
EH? OH... RIGHT. THAT WAS YOU, KATOU-SAN.
THOUGH I DIDN'T EVEN KNOW YOUR CELL NUMBER BACK THEN...
...NOW WE'RE AIMING TO GO TO THE SAME UNIVERSITY TOGETHER. STRANGE, ISN'T IT?
Y- YES, IT IS.
IF I'D NEVER MET YOU, KATOU-SAN, I'D HAVE ONE HUNDRED PERCENT NOT AIMED FOR AOGAKU.
EH?
DO YOU MEAN THAT IN A BAD WAY?
EH? NO! OF COURSE IT'S IN A GOOD WAY!!
Y—
YOU KNOW, SINCE I'M NOT EXACTLY A MODEL STUDENT, I SUSPECT I WOULD'VE JUST PICKED SOME RANDOM PLACE TO GO AFTER GRADUATION WITHOUT EVEN VISITING ANY UNIVERSITIES.

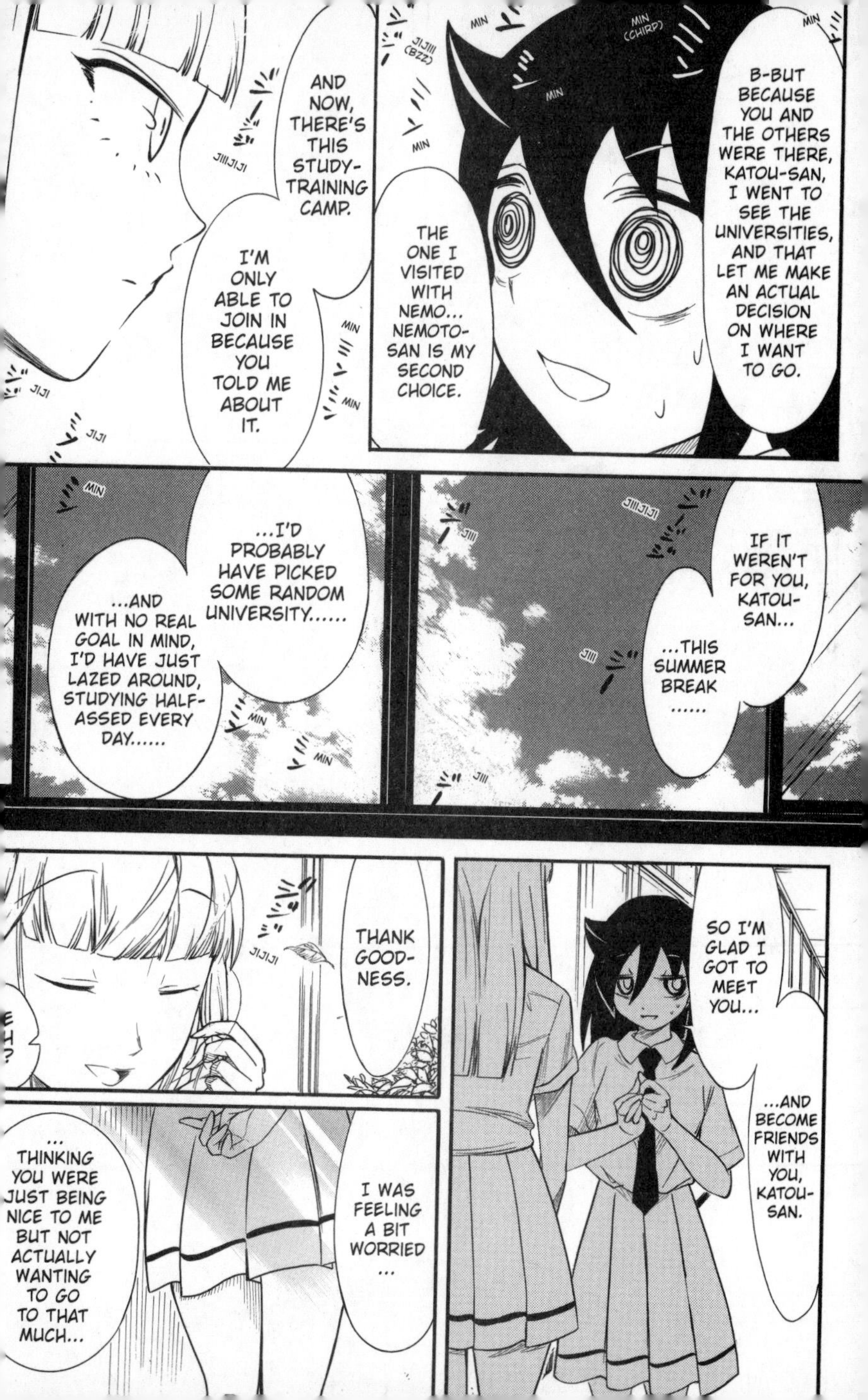
MIN (CHIRP)
MIN
MIN
MIN
B-BUT BECAUSE YOU AND THE OTHERS WERE THERE, KATOU-SAN, I WENT TO SEE THE UNIVERSITIES, AND THAT LET ME MAKE AN ACTUAL DECISION ON WHERE I WANT TO GO.
THE ONE I VISITED WITH NEMO... NEMOTO-SAN IS MY SECOND CHOICE.
JIJIII (BZZ)
MIN
AND NOW, THERE'S THIS STUDY-TRAINING CAMP.
JIIIJIJI
I'M ONLY ABLE TO JOIN IN BECAUSE YOU TOLD ME ABOUT IT.
MIN
MIN
JIJI
JIJI
JIIIJIJI
IF IT WEREN'T FOR YOU, KATOU-SAN...
JIII
...THIS SUMMER BREAK......
JIII
JIII
MIN
...I'D PROBABLY HAVE PICKED SOME RANDOM UNIVERSITY......
...AND WITH NO REAL GOAL IN MIND, I'D HAVE JUST LAZED AROUND, STUDYING HALF-ASSED EVERY DAY......
MIN
MIN
SO I'M GLAD I GOT TO MEET YOU...
...AND BECOME FRIENDS WITH YOU, KATOU-SAN.
JIJIJI
THANK GOODNESS.
I WAS FEELING A BIT WORRIED...
...THINKING YOU WERE JUST BEING NICE TO ME BUT NOT ACTUALLY WANTING TO GO TO THAT MUCH...

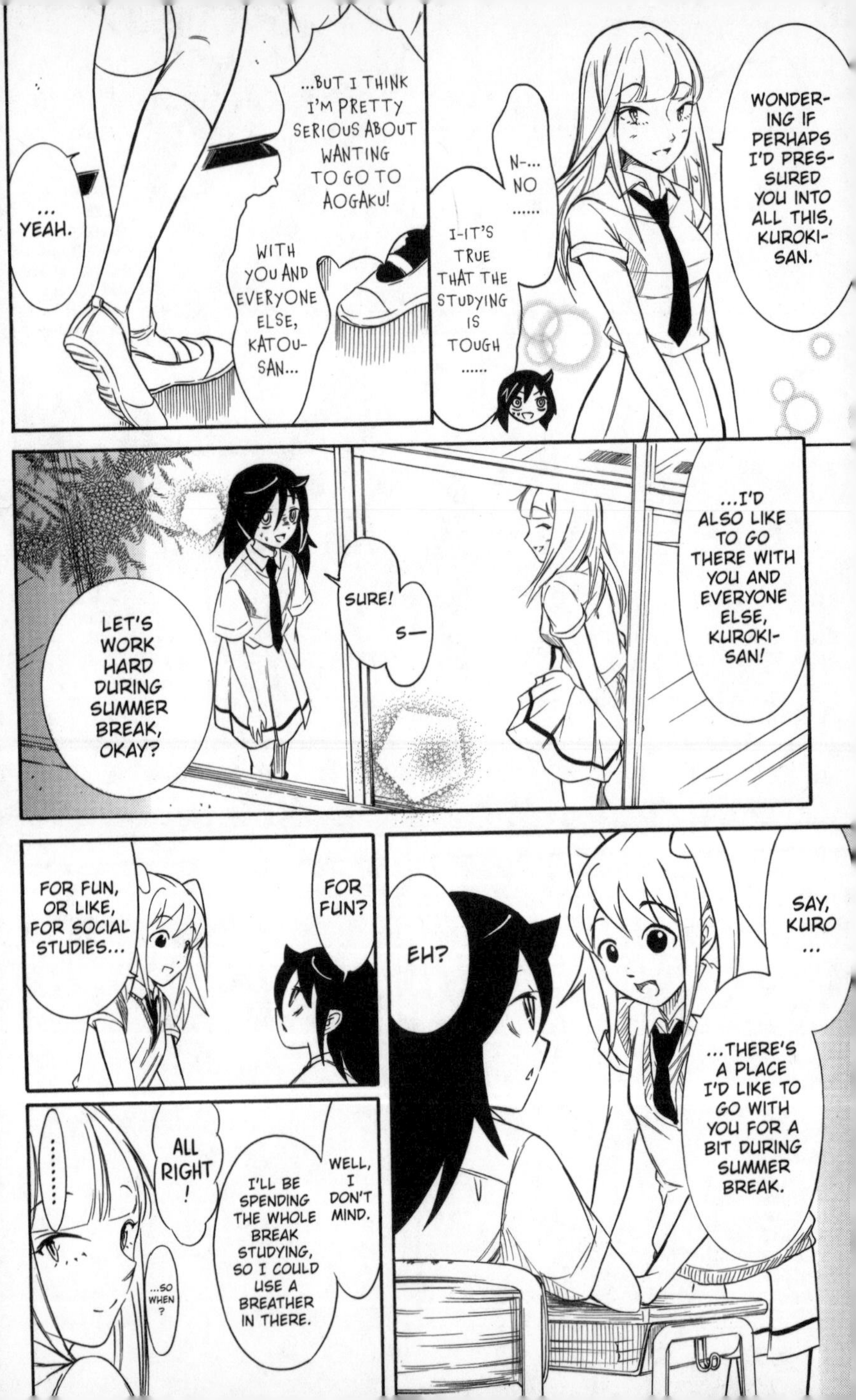
WONDERING IF PERHAPS I'D PRESSURED YOU INTO ALL THIS, KUROKI-SAN.
N-... NO ......
I-IT'S TRUE THAT THE STUDYING IS TOUGH ......
...BUT I THINK I'M PRETTY SERIOUS ABOUT WANTING TO GO TO AOGAKU!
WITH YOU AND EVERYONE ELSE, KATOU-SAN...
... YEAH.
...I'D ALSO LIKE TO GO THERE WITH YOU AND EVERYONE ELSE, KUROKI-SAN!
SURE!
S—
LET'S WORK HARD DURING SUMMER BREAK, OKAY?
SAY, KURO ...
...THERE'S A PLACE I'D LIKE TO GO WITH YOU FOR A BIT DURING SUMMER BREAK.
EH?
FOR FUN?
FOR FUN, OR LIKE, FOR SOCIAL STUDIES...
WELL, I DON'T MIND.
I'LL BE SPENDING THE WHOLE BREAK STUDYING, SO I COULD USE A BREATHER IN THERE.
ALL RIGHT!
....
...SO WHEN?

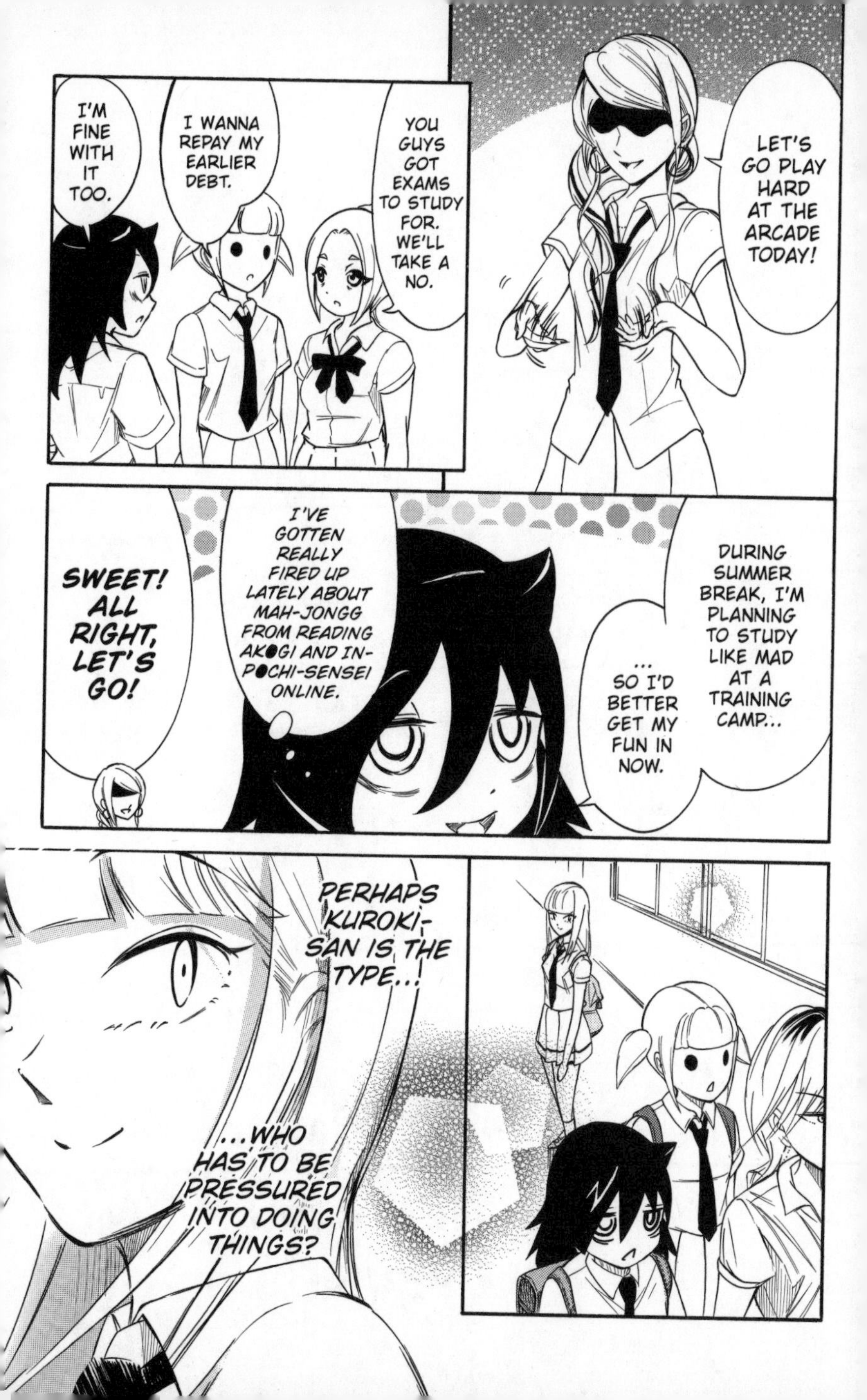
LET'S GO PLAY HARD AT THE ARCADE TODAY!
YOU GUYS GOT EXAMS TO STUDY FOR. WE'LL TAKE A NO.
I WANNA REPAY MY EARLIER DEBT.
I'M FINE WITH IT TOO.
DURING SUMMER BREAK, I'M PLANNING TO STUDY LIKE MAD AT A TRAINING CAMP...
...SO I'D BETTER GET MY FUN IN NOW.
I'VE GOTTEN REALLY FIRED UP LATELY ABOUT MAH-JONGG FROM READING AKOGI AND IN-POCHI-SENSEI ONLINE.
SWEET! ALL RIGHT, LET'S GO!
PERHAPS KUROKI-SAN IS THE TYPE...
...WHO HAS TO BE PRESSURED INTO DOING THINGS?

No Matter How I Look at It, It's You Guys' Fault I'm Not Popular!

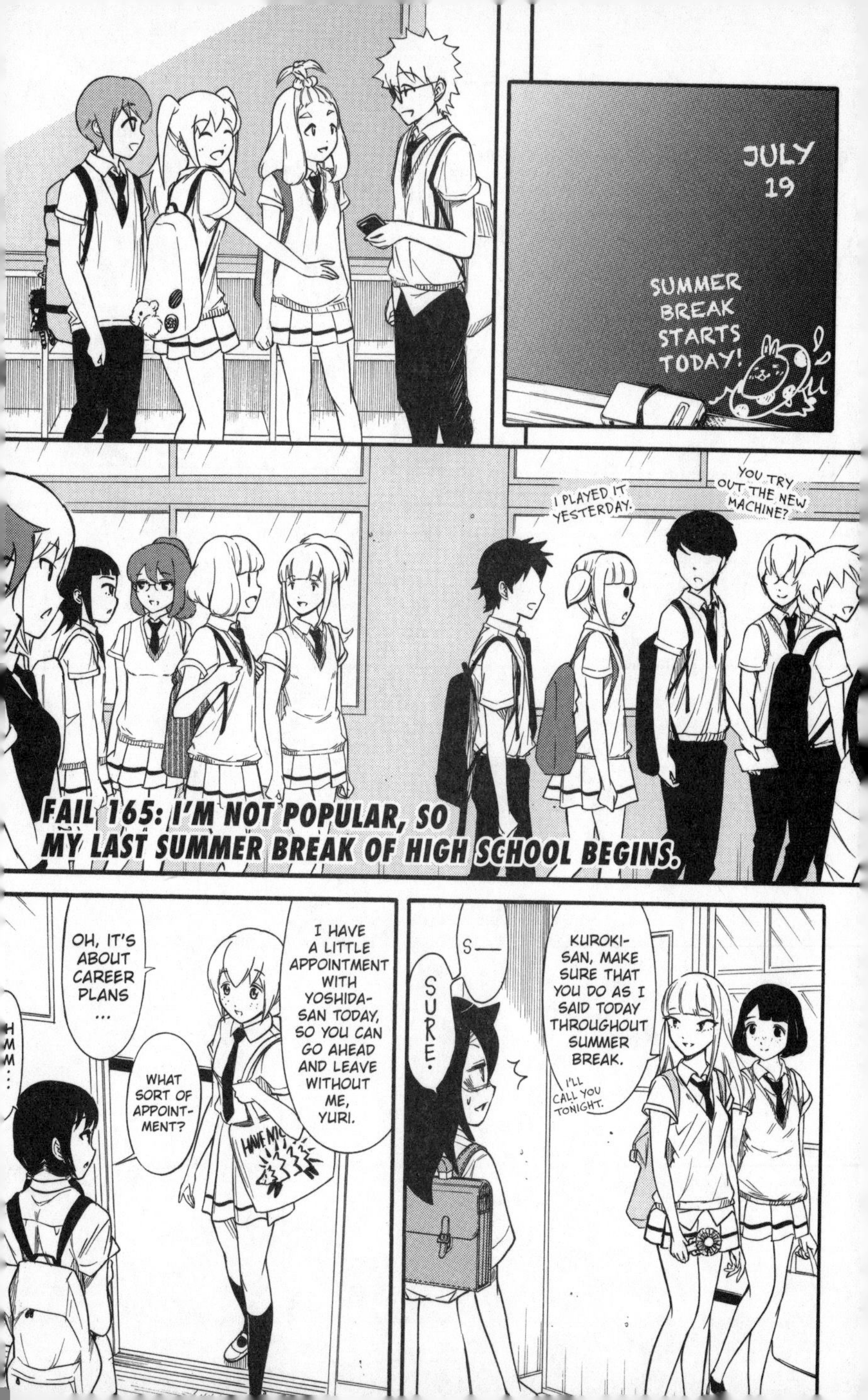
JULY 19
SUMMER BREAK STARTS TODAY!
YOU TRY OUT THE NEW MACHINE?
I PLAYED IT YESTERDAY.
FAIL 165: I'M NOT POPULAR, SO MY LAST SUMMER BREAK OF HIGH SCHOOL BEGINS.
KUROKI-SAN, MAKE SURE THAT YOU DO AS I SAID TODAY THROUGHOUT SUMMER BREAK.
I'LL CALL YOU TONIGHT.
S—
SURE.
I HAVE A LITTLE APPOINTMENT WITH YOSHIDA-SAN TODAY, SO YOU CAN GO AHEAD AND LEAVE WITHOUT ME, YURI.
WHAT SORT OF APPOINTMENT?
OH, IT'S ABOUT CAREER PLANS...
HMM...

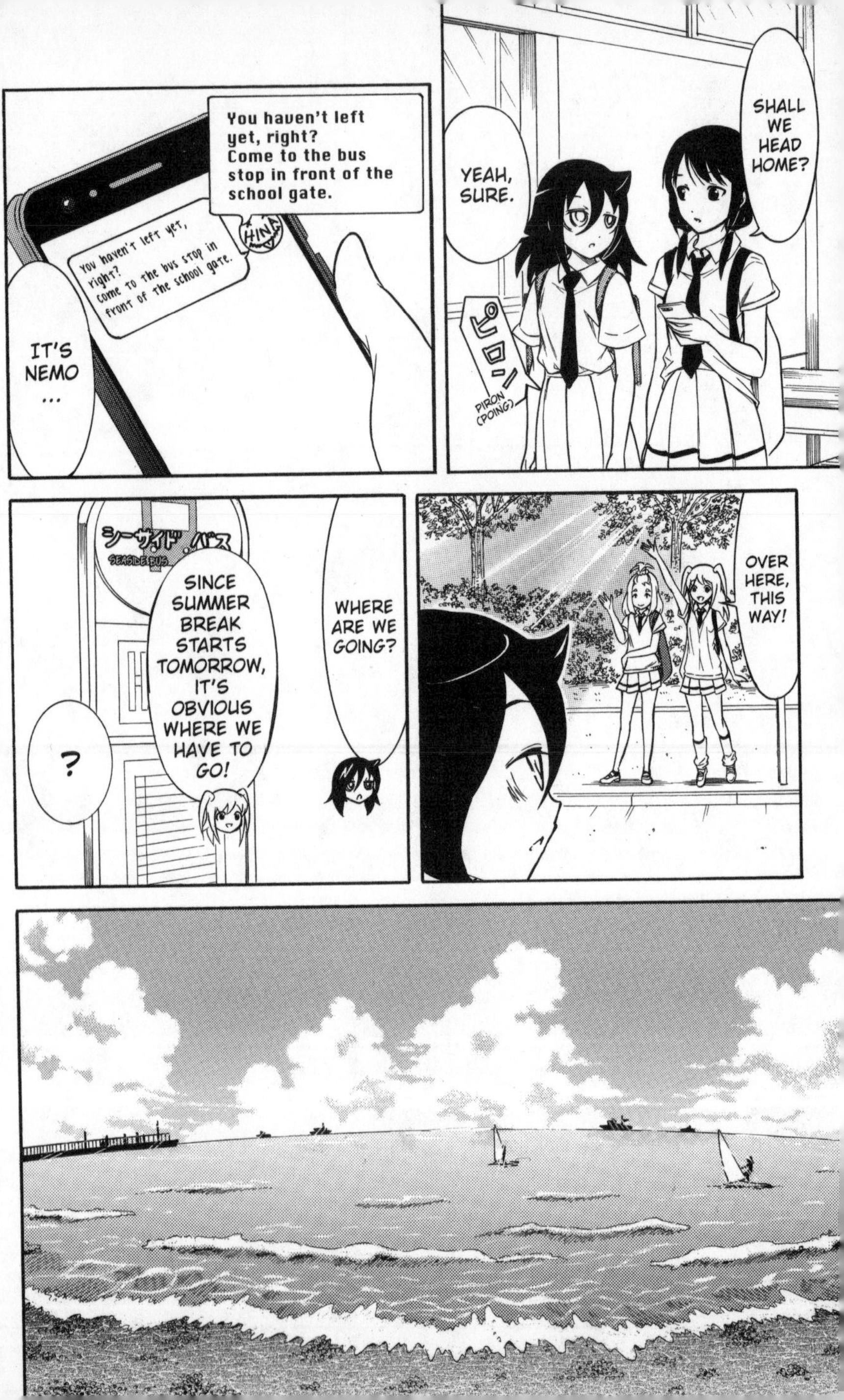
SHALL WE HEAD HOME?
YEAH, SURE.
ピロン
PIRON (POING)
You haven't left yet, right? Come to the bus stop in front of the school gate.
HINA
You haven't left yet, right? Come to the bus stop in front of the school gate.
IT'S NEMO...
OVER HERE, THIS WAY!
WHERE ARE WE GOING?
シーサイド・バス
SEASIDE BUS
SINCE SUMMER BREAK STARTS TOMORROW, IT'S OBVIOUS WHERE WE HAVE TO GO!
?

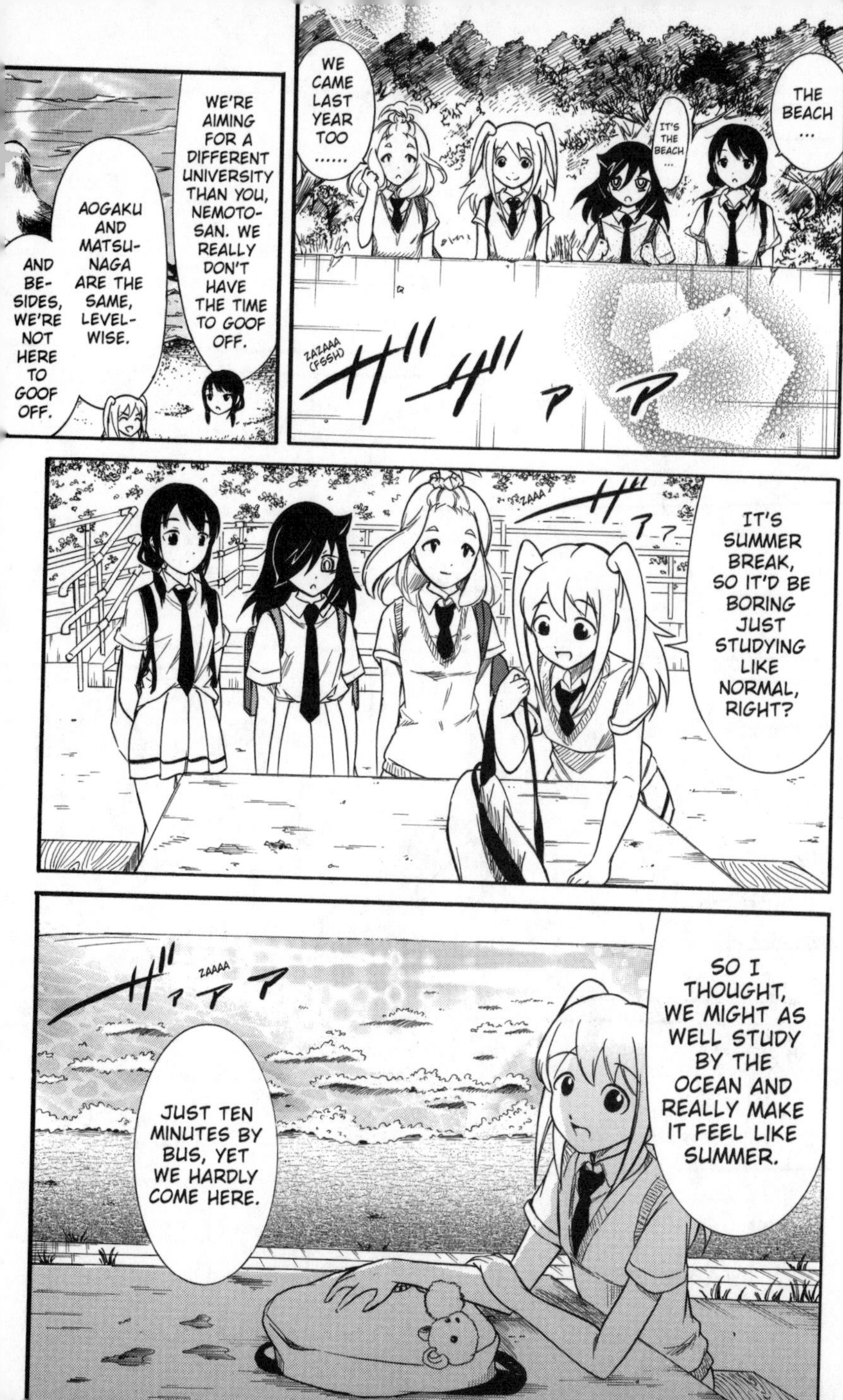
THE BEACH ...
IT'S THE BEACH ...
WE CAME LAST YEAR TOO ......
ZAZAAA (FSSH)
WE'RE AIMING FOR A DIFFERENT UNIVERSITY THAN YOU, NEMOTO-SAN. WE REALLY DON'T HAVE THE TIME TO GOOF OFF.
AOGAKU AND MATSU-NAGA ARE THE SAME, LEVEL-WISE.
AND BE-SIDES, WE'RE NOT HERE TO GOOF OFF.
ZAAAA
IT'S SUMMER BREAK, SO IT'D BE BORING JUST STUDYING LIKE NORMAL, RIGHT?
ZAAAA
SO I THOUGHT, WE MIGHT AS WELL STUDY BY THE OCEAN AND REALLY MAKE IT FEEL LIKE SUMMER.
JUST TEN MINUTES BY BUS, YET WE HARDLY COME HERE.

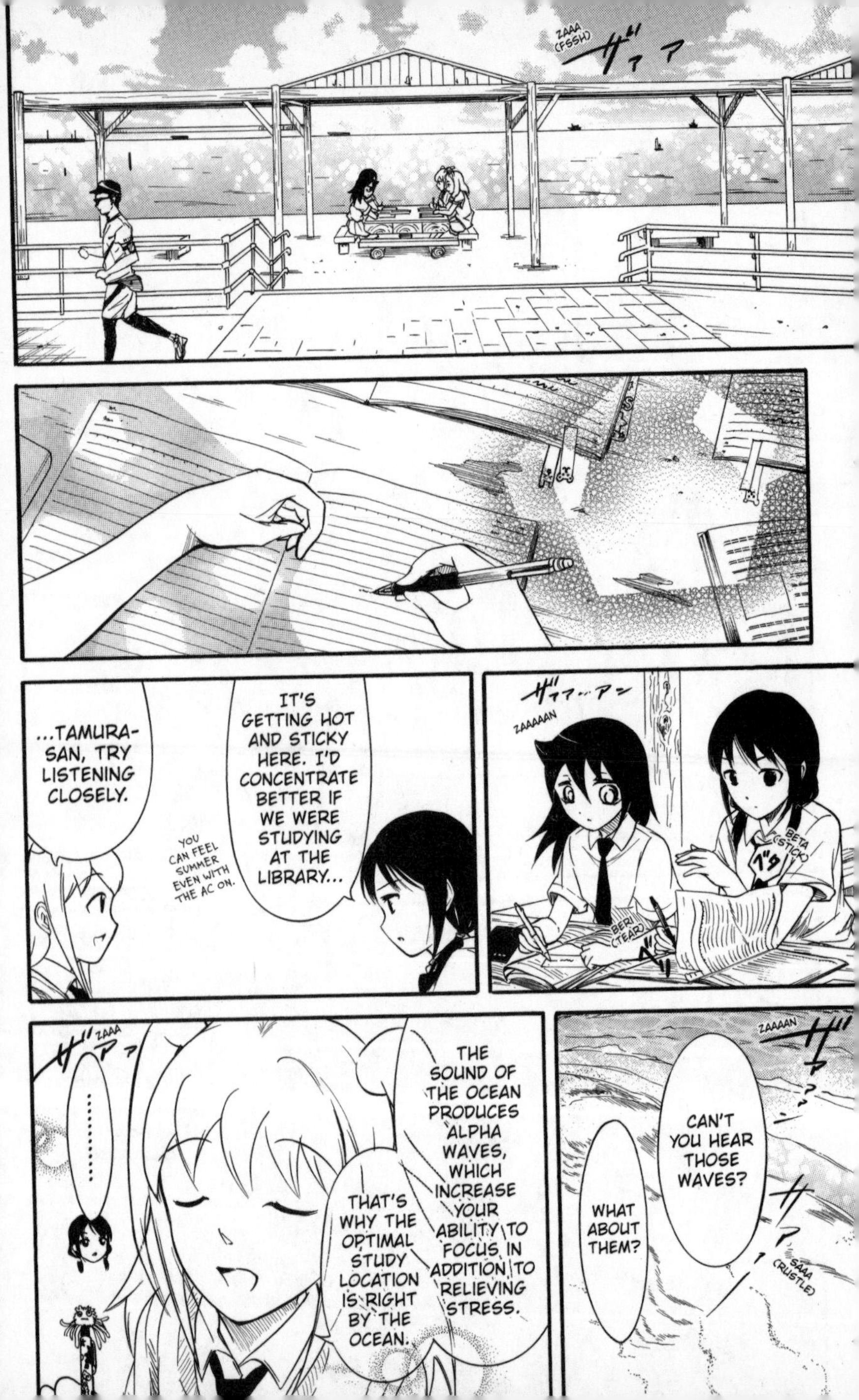
ZAAA (FSSH)
ザァア
ザァア…アン
ZAAAAAN
BETA (STICK)
ベタ
BERI (TEAR)
ベリ
IT'S GETTING HOT AND STICKY HERE. I'D CONCENTRATE BETTER IF WE WERE STUDYING AT THE LIBRARY...
YOU CAN FEEL SUMMER EVEN WITH THE AC ON.
...TAMURA-SAN, TRY LISTENING CLOSELY.
ZAAAAN
ザァ
CAN'T YOU HEAR THOSE WAVES?
WHAT ABOUT THEM?
SAAA (RUSTLE)
THE SOUND OF THE OCEAN PRODUCES ALPHA WAVES, WHICH INCREASE YOUR ABILITY TO FOCUS IN ADDITION TO RELIEVING STRESS.
THAT'S WHY THE OPTIMAL STUDY LOCATION IS RIGHT BY THE OCEAN.
ZAAA
ザァ
....

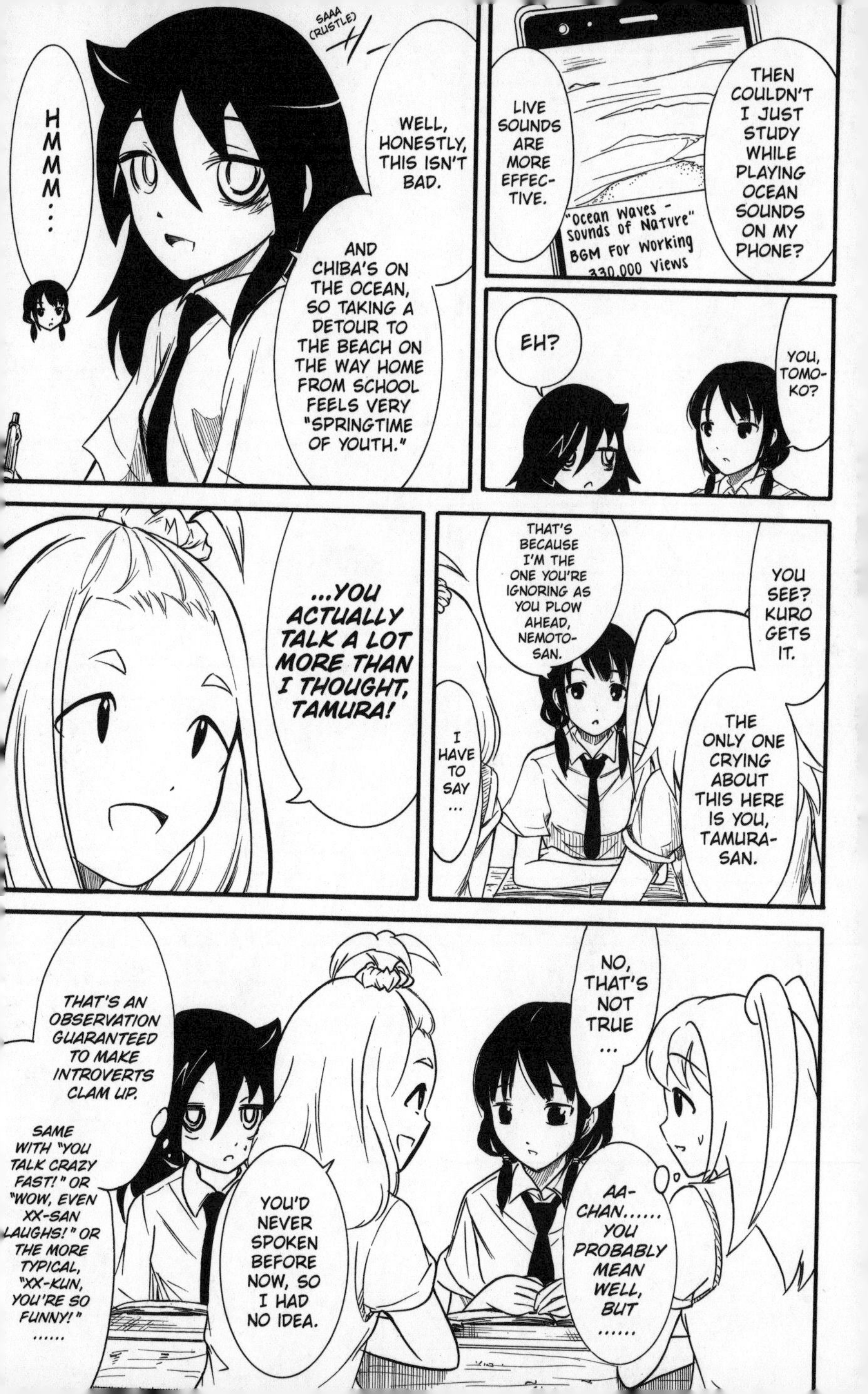
THEN COULDN'T I JUST STUDY WHILE PLAYING OCEAN SOUNDS ON MY PHONE?
LIVE SOUNDS ARE MORE EFFEC-TIVE.
"Ocean Waves - Sounds of Nature" BGM For Working 330,000 Views
YOU, TOMO-KO?
EH?
SAAA (RUSTLE)
WELL, HONESTLY, THIS ISN'T BAD.
AND CHIBA'S ON THE OCEAN, SO TAKING A DETOUR TO THE BEACH ON THE WAY HOME FROM SCHOOL FEELS VERY "SPRINGTIME OF YOUTH."
HMMM...
YOU SEE? KURO GETS IT.
THAT'S BECAUSE I'M THE ONE YOU'RE IGNORING AS YOU PLOW AHEAD, NEMOTO-SAN.
THE ONLY ONE CRYING ABOUT THIS HERE IS YOU, TAMURA-SAN.
I HAVE TO SAY...
...YOU ACTUALLY TALK A LOT MORE THAN I THOUGHT, TAMURA!
NO, THAT'S NOT TRUE...
AA-CHAN...... YOU PROBABLY MEAN WELL, BUT......
YOU'D NEVER SPOKEN BEFORE NOW, SO I HAD NO IDEA.
THAT'S AN OBSERVATION GUARANTEED TO MAKE INTROVERTS CLAM UP.
SAME WITH "YOU TALK CRAZY FAST!" OR "WOW, EVEN XX-SAN LAUGHS!" OR THE MORE TYPICAL, "XX-KUN, YOU'RE SO FUNNY!"......

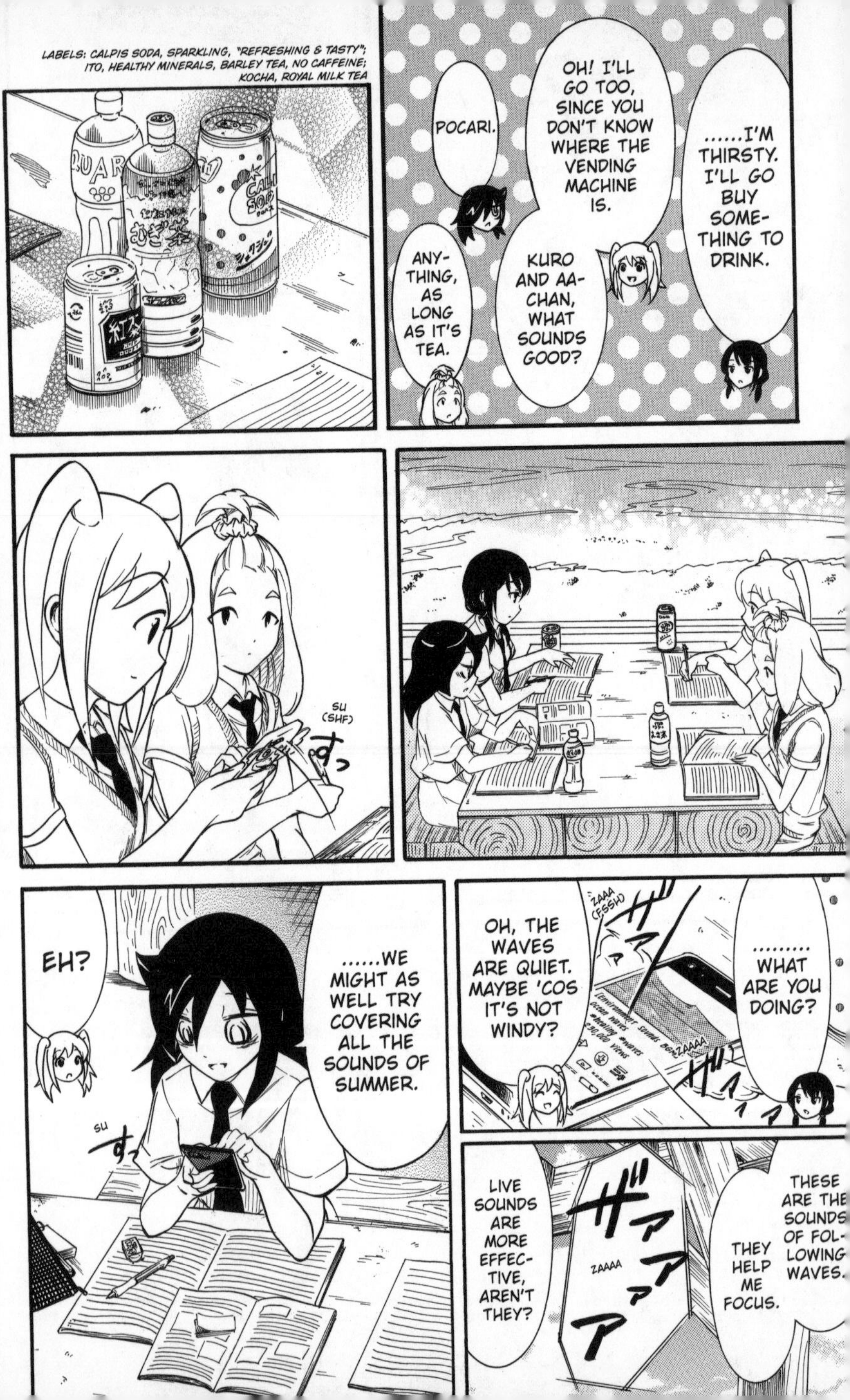
......I'M THIRSTY. I'LL GO BUY SOME-THING TO DRINK.
OH! I'LL GO TOO, SINCE YOU DON'T KNOW WHERE THE VENDING MACHINE IS.
KURO AND AA-CHAN, WHAT SOUNDS GOOD?
POCARI.
ANY-THING, AS LONG AS IT'S TEA.
LABELS: CALPIS SODA, SPARKLING, "REFRESHING & TASTY"; ITO, HEALTHY MINERALS, BARLEY TEA, NO CAFFEINE; KOCHA, ROYAL MILK TEA
SU (SHF)
すっ
ZAAA (FSSSH)
.........WHAT ARE YOU DOING?
OH, THE WAVES ARE QUIET. MAYBE 'COS IT'S NOT WINDY?
ZAAAA
THESE ARE THE SOUNDS OF FOL-LOWING WAVES.
THEY HELP ME FOCUS.
LIVE SOUNDS ARE MORE EFFEC-TIVE, AREN'T THEY?
ZAAAA
......WE MIGHT AS WELL TRY COVERING ALL THE SOUNDS OF SUMMER.
EH?
SU
すっ

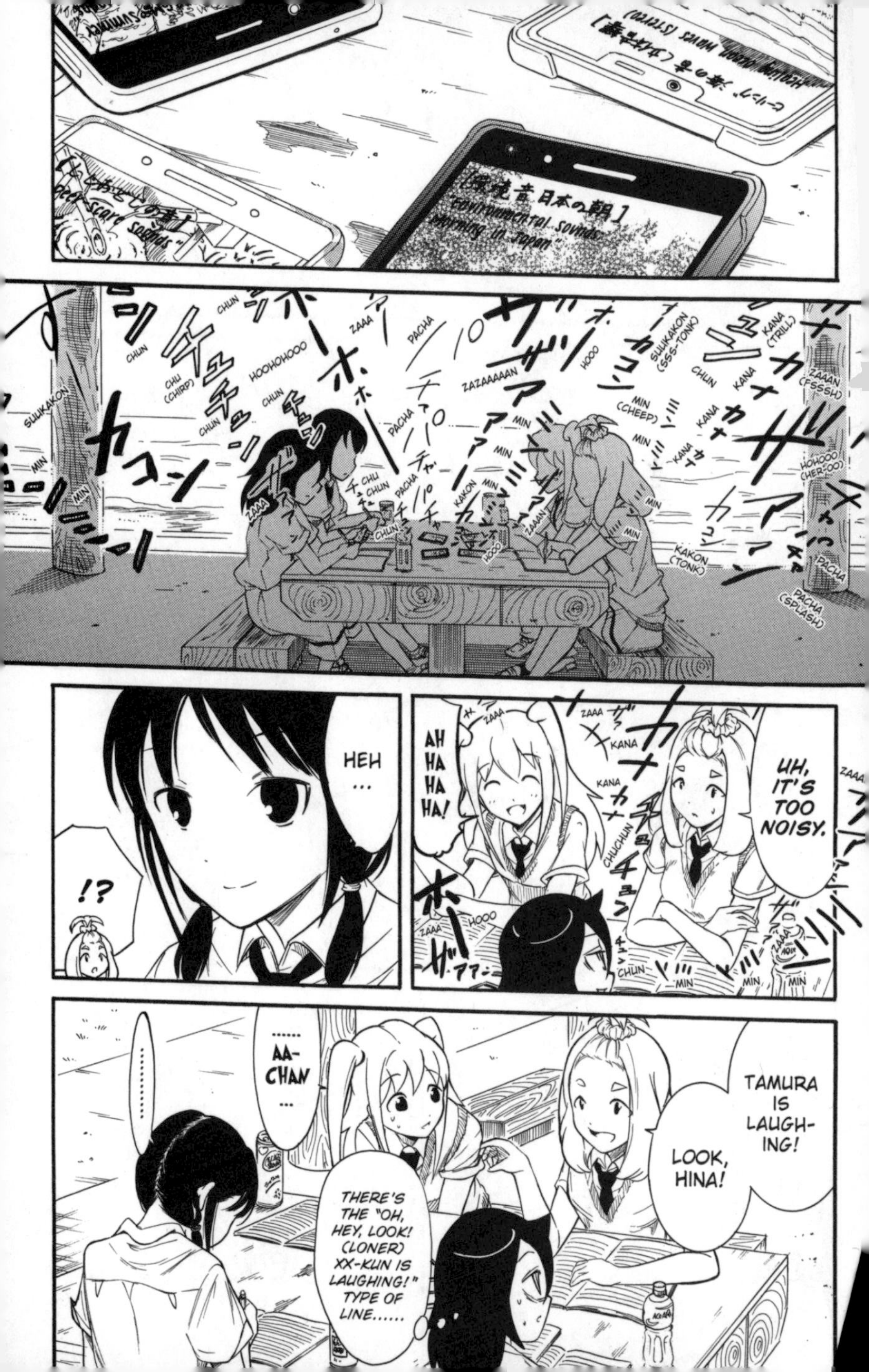

Healing ocean waves (Stereo)
【環境音 日本の朝】
"Environmental sounds: Morning in Japan"
"Deer-scare sounds"
ZAAAN (FSSSH)
KANA (TRILL)
SUIKAKON (SSS-TONK)
HOO
ZAZAAAAAN
PACHA
ZAAA
CHUN
HOOHOHOOO
CHU (CHIRP)
CHUN
CHUN
SUIKAKON
KANA
CHUN
MIN (CHEEP)
MIN
KANA
MIN
KANA
HOHOOO (HER-OO)
MIN
MIN
KAKON (TONK)
PACHA
PACHA (SPLASH)
ZAAAN
HOOO
KAKON
PACHA
CHU CHUN
CHUN
ZAAA
MIN
MIN
ZAAA
KANA
KANA
UH, IT'S TOO NOISY.
AH HA HA HA HA!
CHUCHUN
HOOO
ZAAA
CHUN
MIN
MIN
MIN
HEH ...
!?
TAMURA IS LAUGHING!
LOOK, HINA!
THERE'S THE "OH, HEY, LOOK! (LONER) XX-KUN IS LAUGHING!" TYPE OF LINE......
.... AA-CHAN ...
....

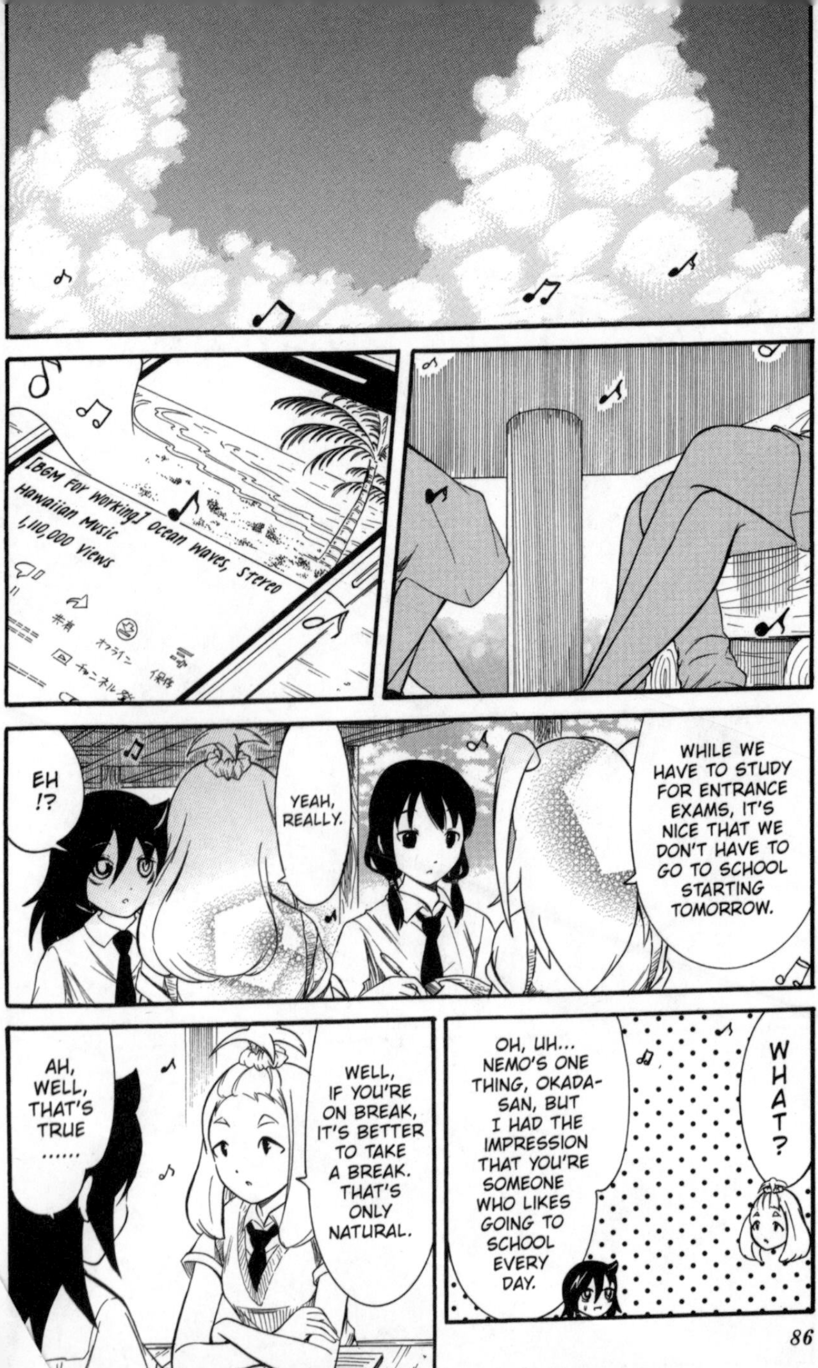
[BGM for working] Ocean waves, Stereo Hawaiian Music
1,110,000 Views
共有
オフライン
保存
WHILE WE HAVE TO STUDY FOR ENTRANCE EXAMS, IT'S NICE THAT WE DON'T HAVE TO GO TO SCHOOL STARTING TOMORROW.
YEAH, REALLY.
EH !?
WHAT?
OH, UH... NEMO'S ONE THING, OKADA-SAN, BUT I HAD THE IMPRESSION THAT YOU'RE SOMEONE WHO LIKES GOING TO SCHOOL EVERY DAY.
WELL, IF YOU'RE ON BREAK, IT'S BETTER TO TAKE A BREAK. THAT'S ONLY NATURAL.
AH, WELL, THAT'S TRUE ......

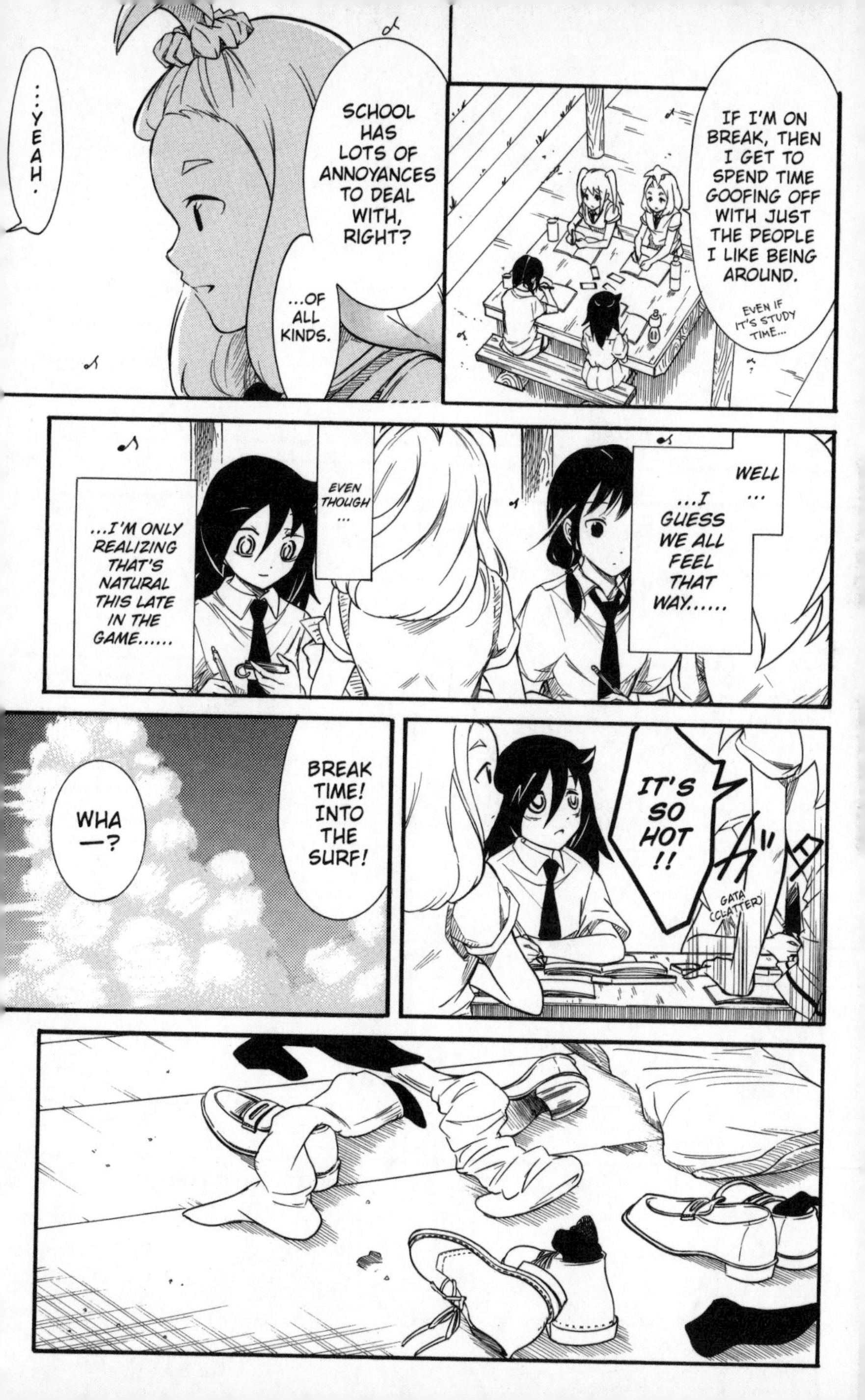
IF I'M ON BREAK, THEN I GET TO SPEND TIME GOOFING OFF WITH JUST THE PEOPLE I LIKE BEING AROUND.
EVEN IF IT'S STUDY TIME...
SCHOOL HAS LOTS OF ANNOYANCES TO DEAL WITH, RIGHT?
...OF ALL KINDS.
...YEAH.
WELL...
...I GUESS WE ALL FEEL THAT WAY......
EVEN THOUGH...
...I'M ONLY REALIZING THAT'S NATURAL THIS LATE IN THE GAME......
IT'S SO HOT!!
ガタ
GATA (CLATTER)
BREAK TIME! INTO THE SURF!
WHA—?

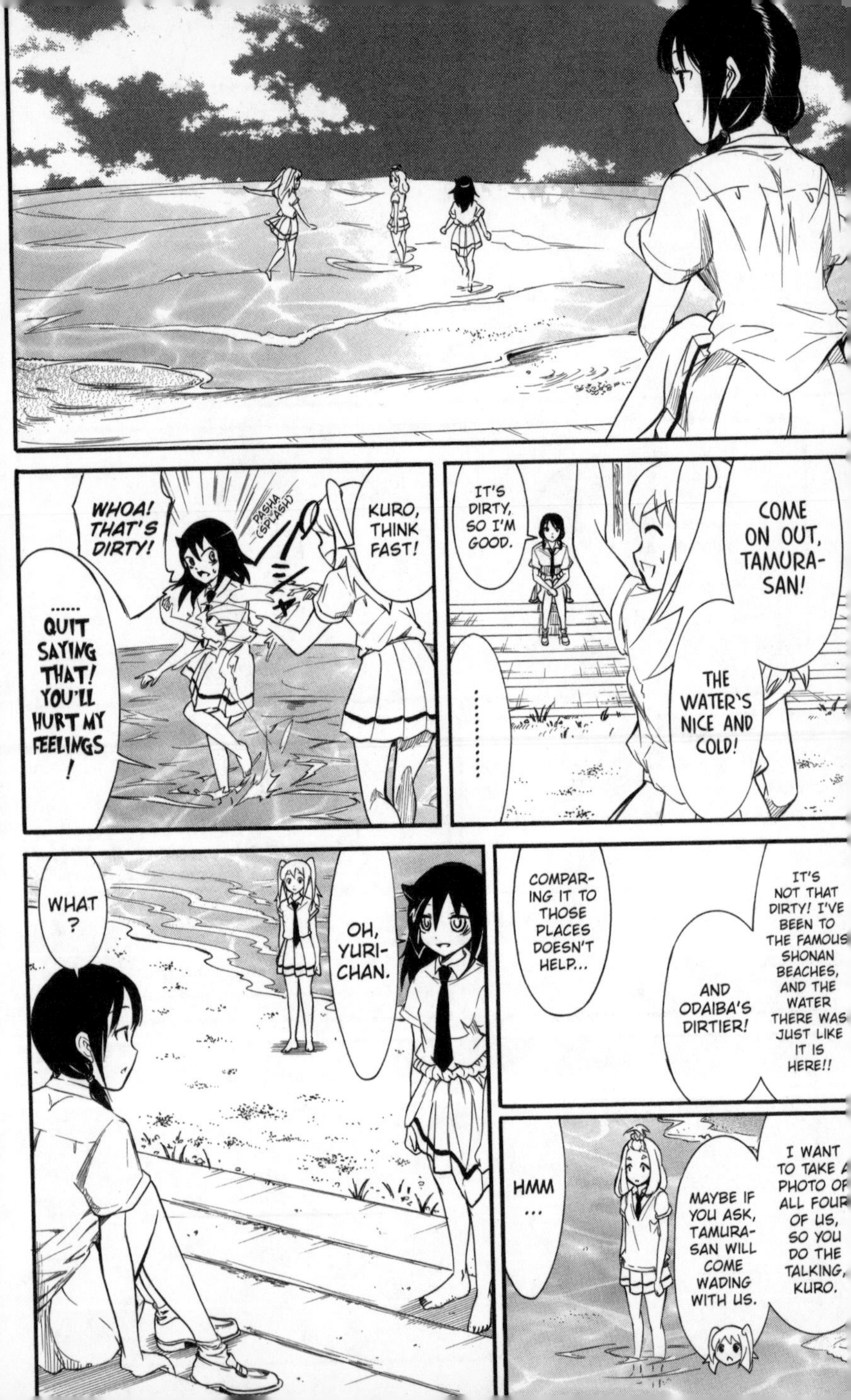
COME ON OUT, TAMURA-SAN!
THE WATER'S NICE AND COLD!
....
IT'S DIRTY, SO I'M GOOD.
KURO, THINK FAST!
PASHA (SPLASH)
WHOA! THAT'S DIRTY!
...... QUIT SAYING THAT! YOU'LL HURT MY FEELINGS!
IT'S NOT THAT DIRTY! I'VE BEEN TO THE FAMOUS SHONAN BEACHES, AND THE WATER THERE WAS JUST LIKE IT IS HERE!!
AND ODAIBA'S DIRTIER!
COMPARING IT TO THOSE PLACES DOESN'T HELP...
I WANT TO TAKE A PHOTO OF ALL FOUR OF US, SO YOU DO THE TALKING, KURO.
MAYBE IF YOU ASK, TAMURA-SAN WILL COME WADING WITH US.
HMM...
OH, YURI-CHAN.
WHAT?

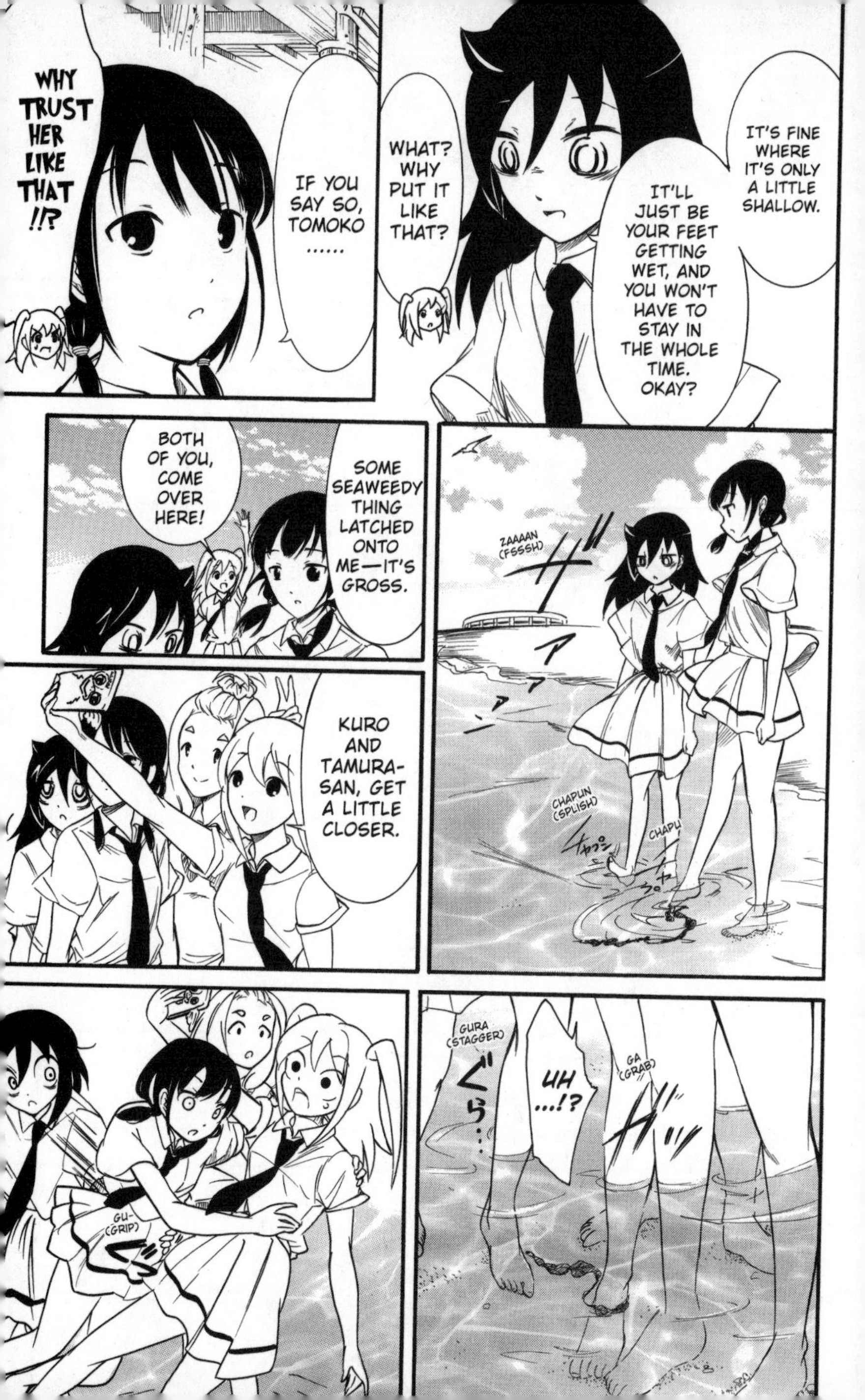
IT'S FINE WHERE IT'S ONLY A LITTLE SHALLOW.
IT'LL JUST BE YOUR FEET GETTING WET, AND YOU WON'T HAVE TO STAY IN THE WHOLE TIME. OKAY?
WHAT? WHY PUT IT LIKE THAT?
IF YOU SAY SO, TOMOKO ......
WHY TRUST HER LIKE THAT!!?
ZAAAAN (FSSSH)
CHAPUN (SPLISH)
CHAPU
SOME SEAWEEDY THING LATCHED ONTO ME—IT'S GROSS.
BOTH OF YOU, COME OVER HERE!
KURO AND TAMURA-SAN, GET A LITTLE CLOSER.
GURA (STAGGER)
UH ...!?
GA (GRAB)
GU- (GRIP)

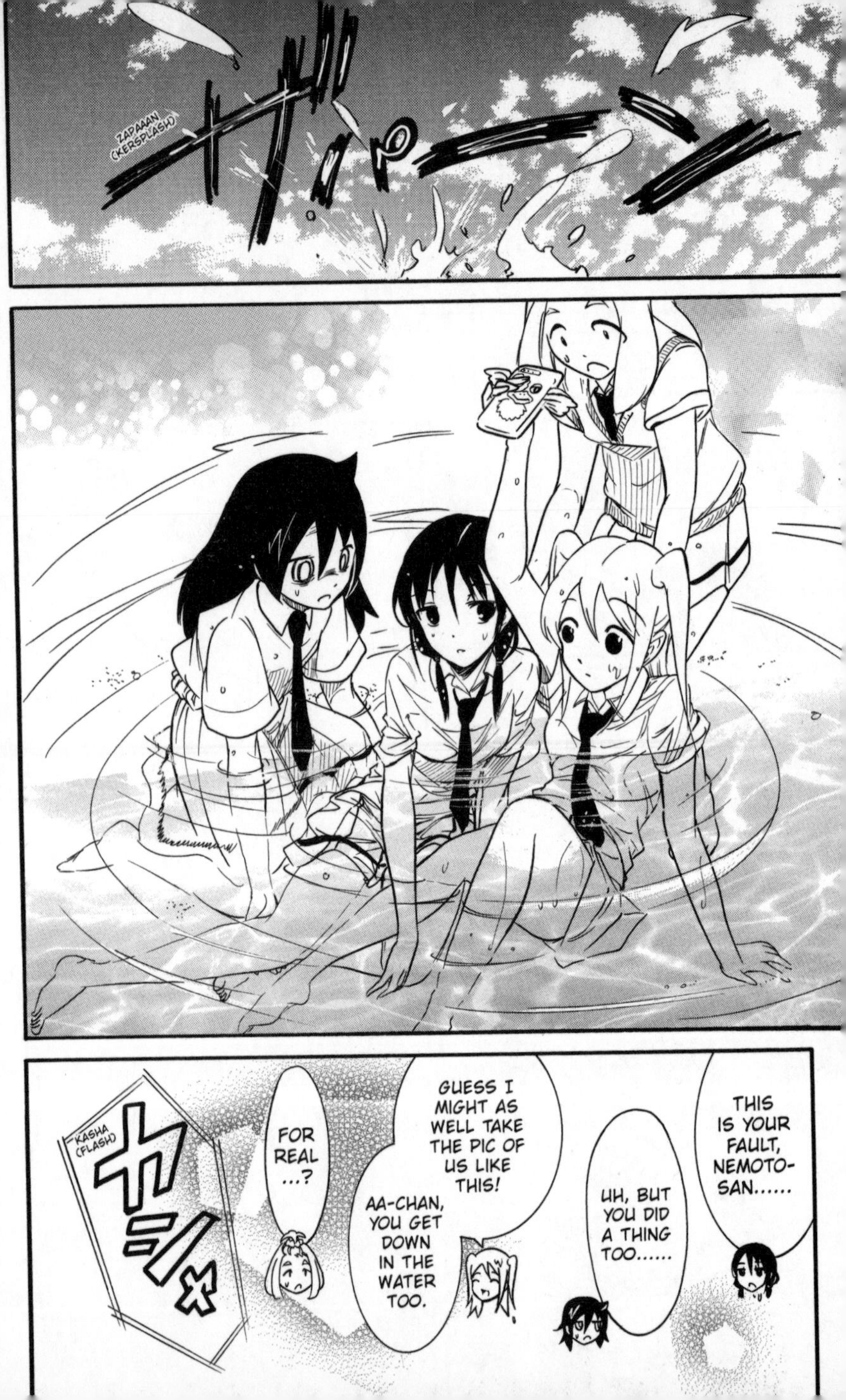
ZAPAAAN (KERSPLASH)
THIS IS YOUR FAULT, NEMOTO-SAN......
UH, BUT YOU DID A THING TOO......
GUESS I MIGHT AS WELL TAKE THE PIC OF US LIKE THIS!
AA-CHAN, YOU GET DOWN IN THE WATER TOO.
FOR REAL ...?
KASHA (FLASH)

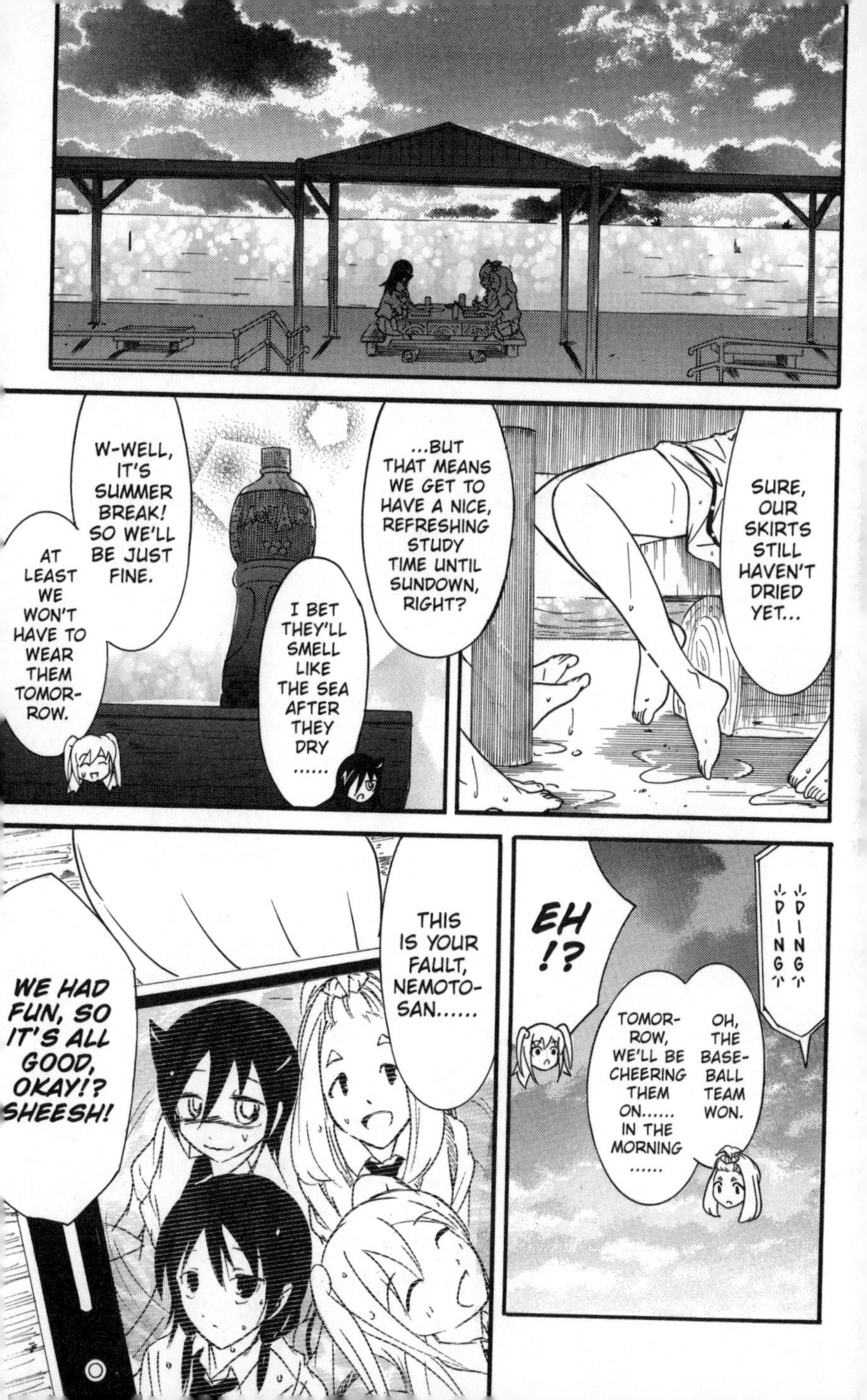
SURE, OUR SKIRTS STILL HAVEN'T DRIED YET...
...BUT THAT MEANS WE GET TO HAVE A NICE, REFRESHING STUDY TIME UNTIL SUNDOWN, RIGHT?
W-WELL, IT'S SUMMER BREAK! SO WE'LL BE JUST FINE.
I BET THEY'LL SMELL LIKE THE SEA AFTER THEY DRY ......
AT LEAST WE WON'T HAVE TO WEAR THEM TOMORROW.
DING DING
OH, THE BASEBALL TEAM WON.
TOMORROW, WE'LL BE CHEERING THEM ON...... IN THE MORNING ......
EH!?
THIS IS YOUR FAULT, NEMOTO-SAN......
WE HAD FUN, SO IT'S ALL GOOD, OKAY!? SHEESH!

No Matter How I Look at It, It's You Guys' Fault I'm Not Popular!

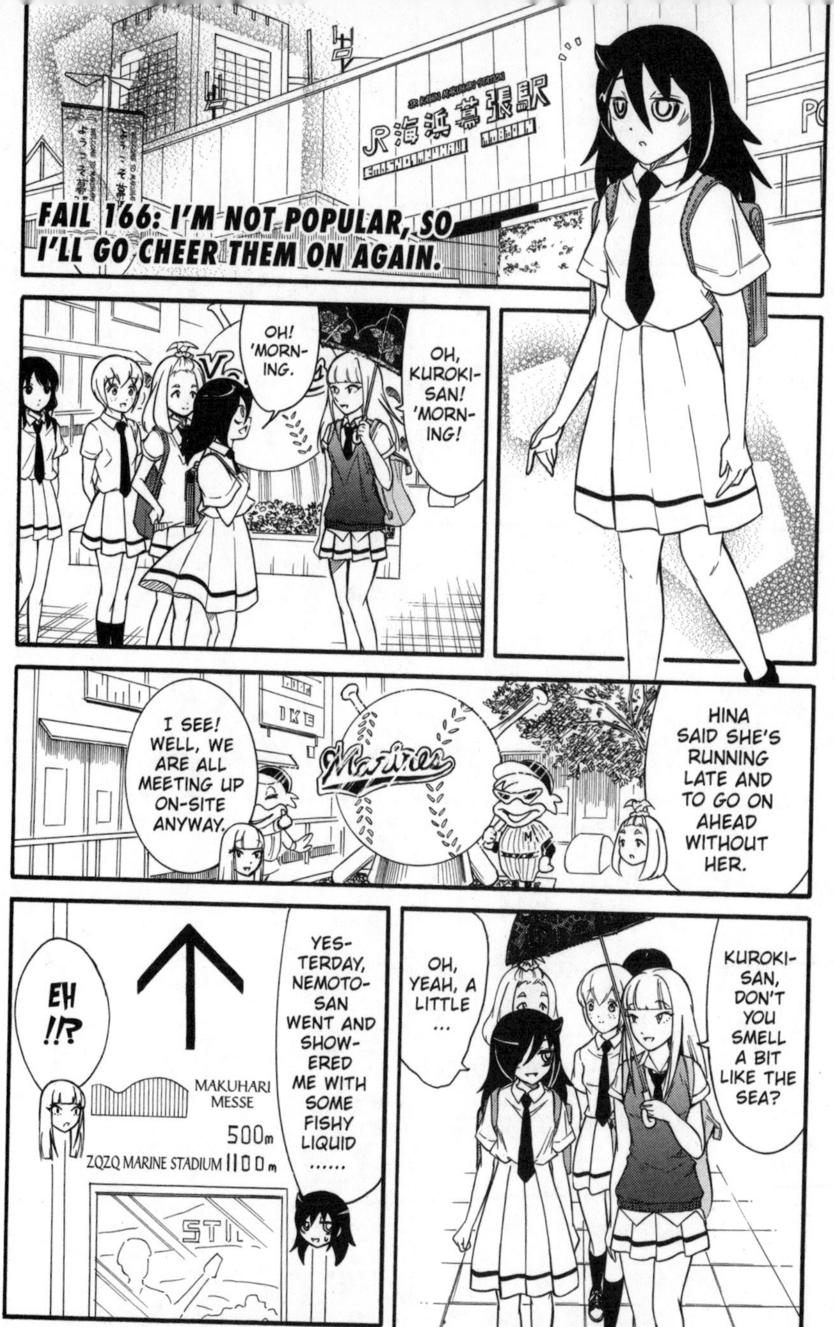
FAIL 166: I'M NOT POPULAR, SO I'LL GO CHEER THEM ON AGAIN.
JR海浜幕張駅
OH, KUROKI-SAN! 'MORNING!
OH! 'MORNING.
HINA SAID SHE'S RUNNING LATE AND TO GO ON AHEAD WITHOUT HER.
I SEE! WELL, WE ARE ALL MEETING UP ON-SITE ANYWAY.
KUROKI-SAN, DON'T YOU SMELL A BIT LIKE THE SEA?
OH, YEAH, A LITTLE ...
YESTERDAY, NEMOTO-SAN WENT AND SHOWERED ME WITH SOME FISHY LIQUID ......
EH !!?
MAKUHARI MESSE 500m
ZQZQ MARINE STADIUM 1100m

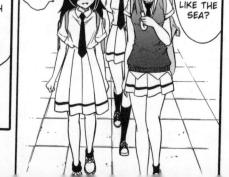

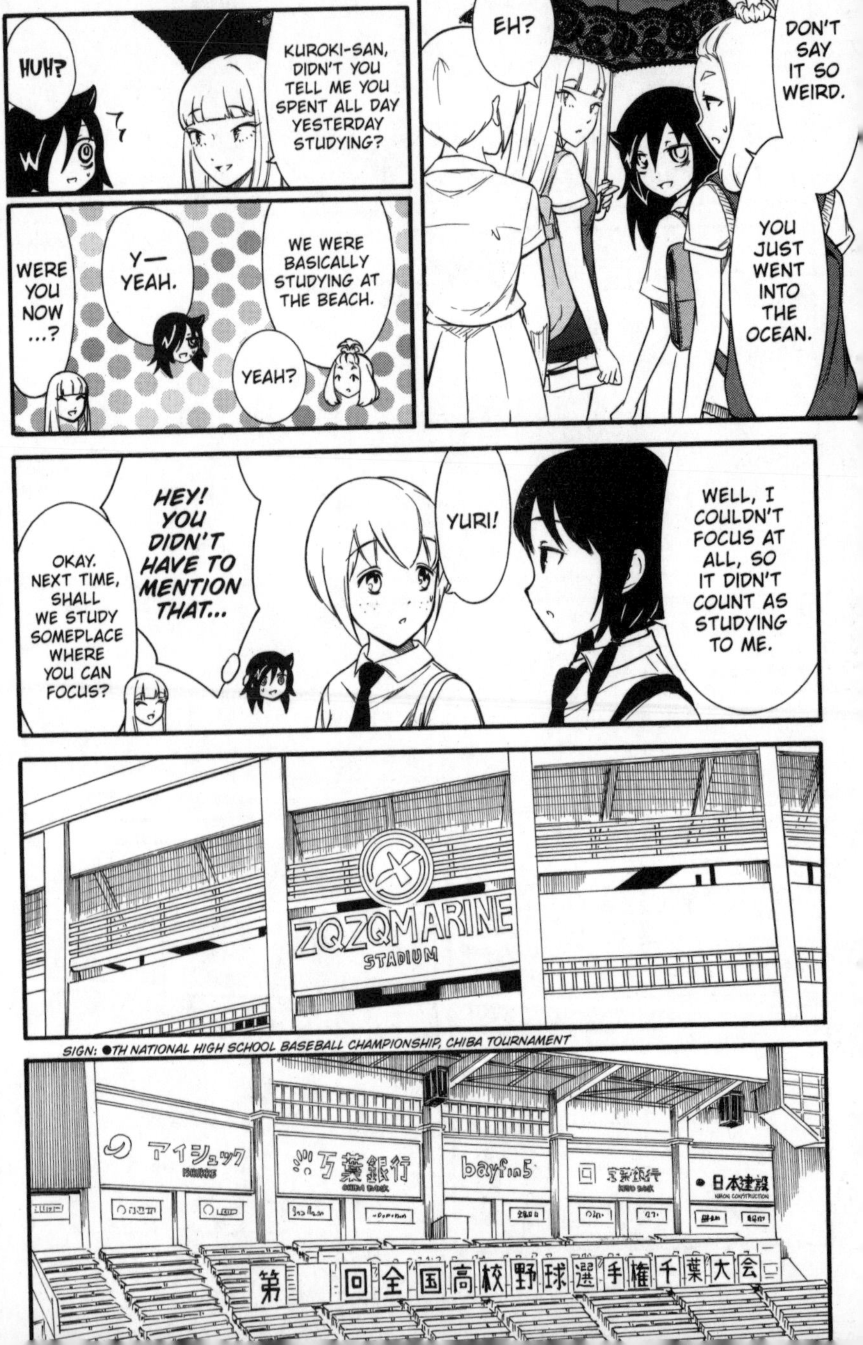
EH?
DON'T SAY IT SO WEIRD.
YOU JUST WENT INTO THE OCEAN.
KUROKI-SAN, DIDN'T YOU TELL ME YOU SPENT ALL DAY YESTERDAY STUDYING?
HUH?
WE WERE BASICALLY STUDYING AT THE BEACH.
YEAH?
Y— YEAH.
WERE YOU NOW ...?
WELL, I COULDN'T FOCUS AT ALL, SO IT DIDN'T COUNT AS STUDYING TO ME.
YURI!
HEY! YOU DIDN'T HAVE TO MENTION THAT...
OKAY. NEXT TIME, SHALL WE STUDY SOMEPLACE WHERE YOU CAN FOCUS?
ZQZQMARINE
STADIUM
SIGN: ●TH NATIONAL HIGH SCHOOL BASEBALL CHAMPIONSHIP, CHIBA TOURNAMENT
アイシュック
bayfm
日本建設
NIHON CONSTRUCTION
第　回全国高校野球選手権千葉大会

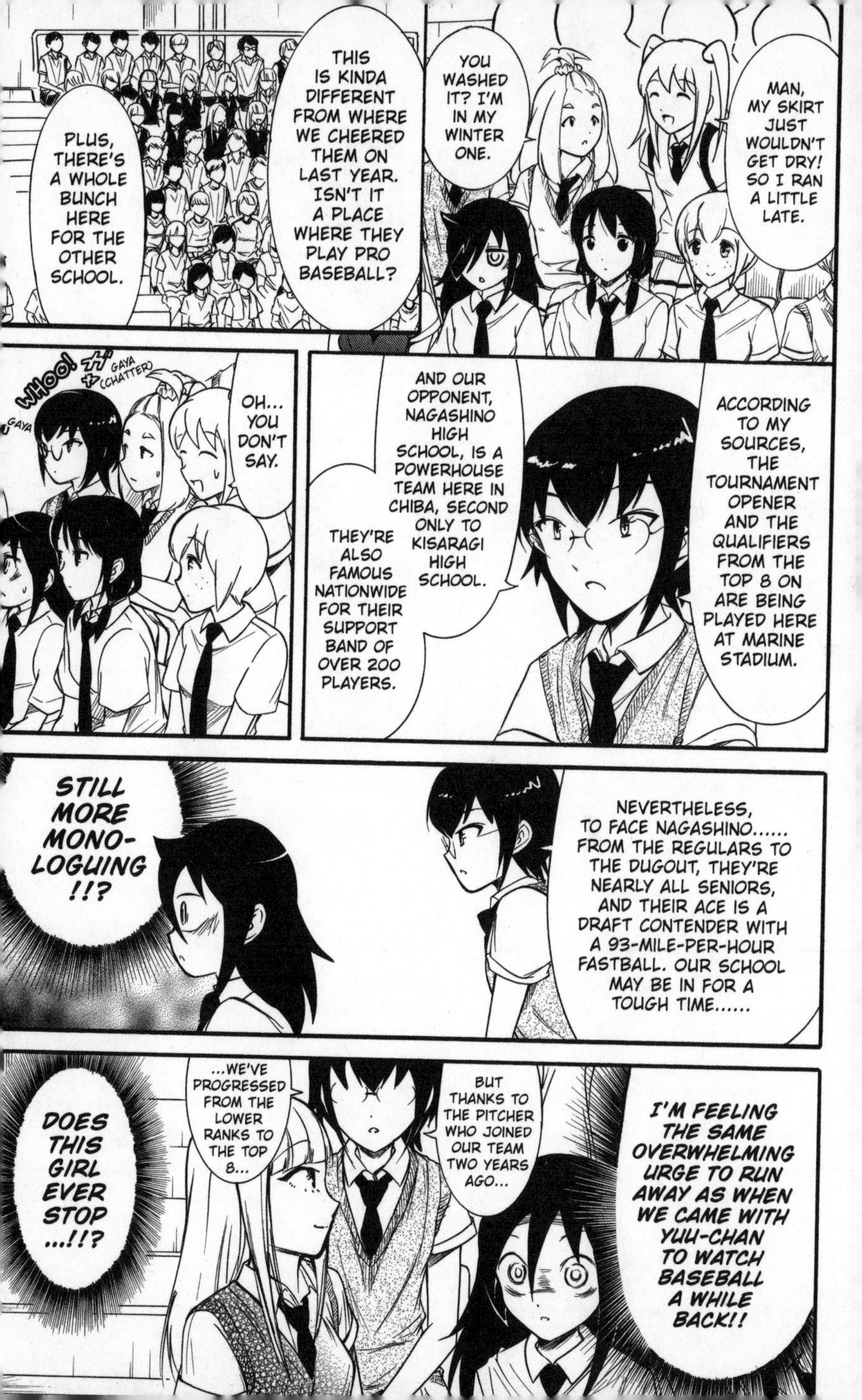
MAN, MY SKIRT JUST WOULDN'T GET DRY! SO I RAN A LITTLE LATE.
YOU WASHED IT? I'M IN MY WINTER ONE.
THIS IS KINDA DIFFERENT FROM WHERE WE CHEERED THEM ON LAST YEAR. ISN'T IT A PLACE WHERE THEY PLAY PRO BASEBALL?
PLUS, THERE'S A WHOLE BUNCH HERE FOR THE OTHER SCHOOL.
ACCORDING TO MY SOURCES, THE TOURNAMENT OPENER AND THE QUALIFIERS FROM THE TOP 8 ON ARE BEING PLAYED HERE AT MARINE STADIUM.
AND OUR OPPONENT, NAGASHINO HIGH SCHOOL, IS A POWERHOUSE TEAM HERE IN CHIBA, SECOND ONLY TO KISARAGI HIGH SCHOOL.
THEY'RE ALSO FAMOUS NATIONWIDE FOR THEIR SUPPORT BAND OF OVER 200 PLAYERS.
OH... YOU DON'T SAY.
WHOO!
GAYA (CHATTER)
GAYA
NEVERTHELESS, TO FACE NAGASHINO...... FROM THE REGULARS TO THE DUGOUT, THEY'RE NEARLY ALL SENIORS, AND THEIR ACE IS A DRAFT CONTENDER WITH A 93-MILE-PER-HOUR FASTBALL. OUR SCHOOL MAY BE IN FOR A TOUGH TIME......
STILL MORE MONO-LOGUING!!?
I'M FEELING THE SAME OVERWHELMING URGE TO RUN AWAY AS WHEN WE CAME WITH YUU-CHAN TO WATCH BASEBALL A WHILE BACK!!
BUT THANKS TO THE PITCHER WHO JOINED OUR TEAM TWO YEARS AGO...
...WE'VE PROGRESSED FROM THE LOWER RANKS TO THE TOP 8...
DOES THIS GIRL EVER STOP ...!!?

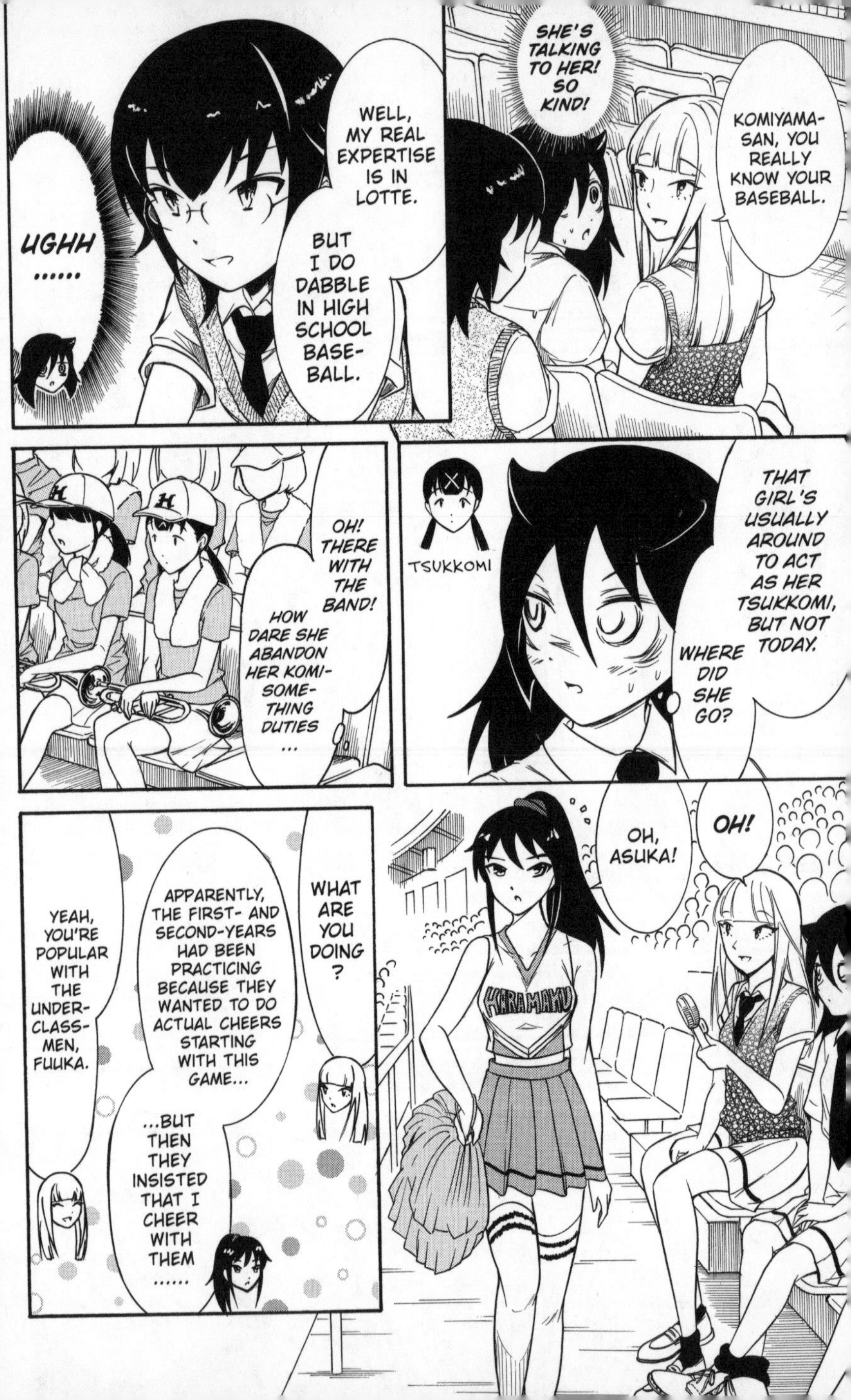
KOMIYAMA-SAN, YOU REALLY KNOW YOUR BASEBALL.
SHE'S TALKING TO HER! SO KIND!
WELL, MY REAL EXPERTISE IS IN LOTTE.
BUT I DO DABBLE IN HIGH SCHOOL BASE-BALL.
UGHH ......
THAT GIRL'S USUALLY AROUND TO ACT AS HER TSUKKOMI, BUT NOT TODAY.
WHERE DID SHE GO?
TSUKKOMI
OH! THERE WITH THE BAND!
HOW DARE SHE ABANDON HER KOMI-SOMETHING DUTIES ...
OH!
OH, ASUKA!
KIRAMAKU
WHAT ARE YOU DOING?
APPARENTLY, THE FIRST- AND SECOND-YEARS HAD BEEN PRACTICING BECAUSE THEY WANTED TO DO ACTUAL CHEERS STARTING WITH THIS GAME...
...BUT THEN THEY INSISTED THAT I CHEER WITH THEM ......
YEAH, YOU'RE POPULAR WITH THE UNDER-CLASS-MEN, FUUKA.

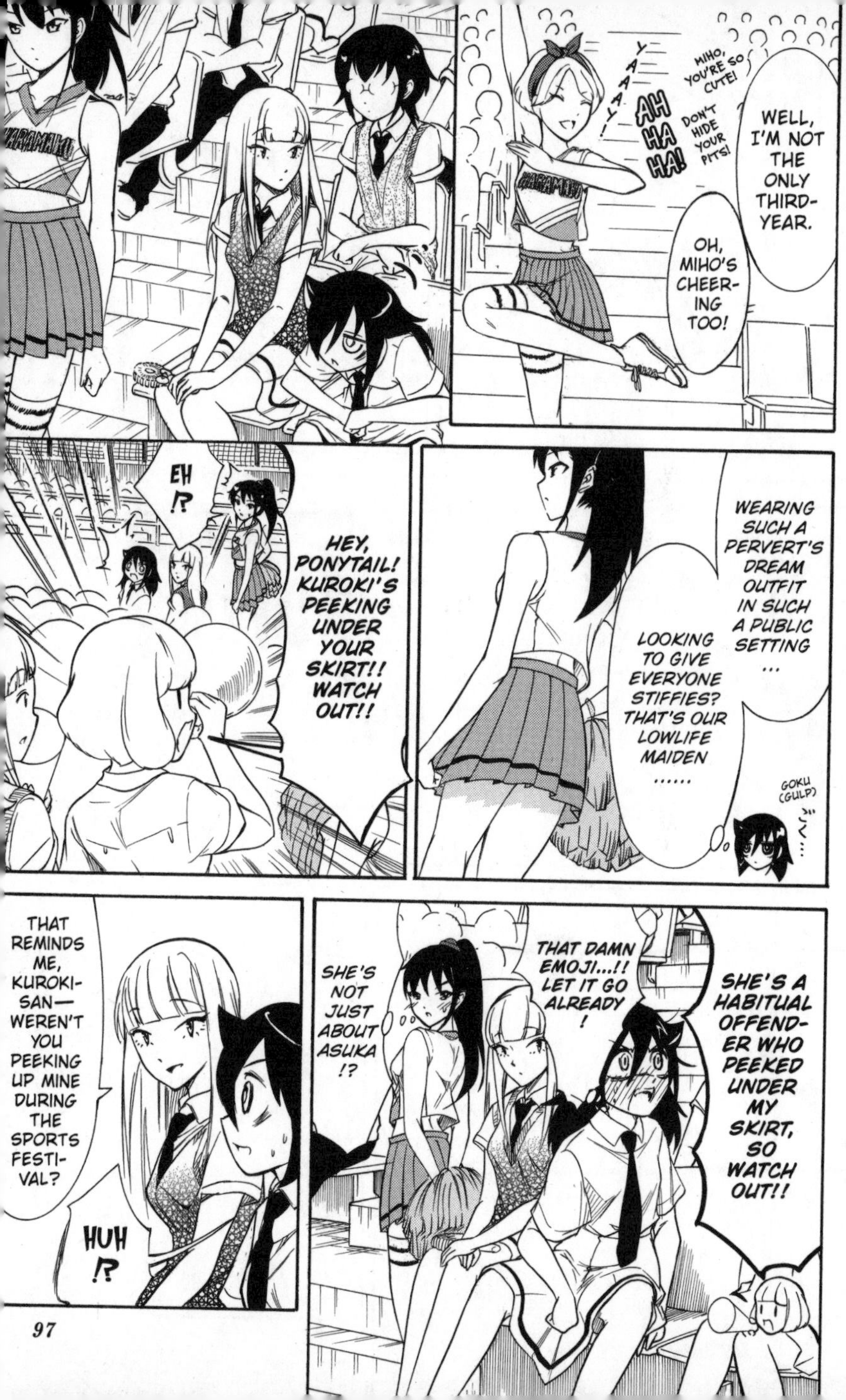
WELL, I'M NOT THE ONLY THIRD-YEAR.
MIHO, YOU'RE SO CUTE!
DON'T HIDE YOUR PITS!
AH HA HA!
YAAAAY!
OH, MIHO'S CHEERING TOO!
WEARING SUCH A PERVERT'S DREAM OUTFIT IN SUCH A PUBLIC SETTING...
LOOKING TO GIVE EVERYONE STIFFIES? THAT'S OUR LOWLIFE MAIDEN......
GOKU (GULP)
ごく…
EH !?
HEY, PONYTAIL! KUROKI'S PEEKING UNDER YOUR SKIRT!! WATCH OUT!!
SHE'S A HABITUAL OFFENDER WHO PEEKED UNDER MY SKIRT, SO WATCH OUT!!
THAT DAMN EMOJI...!! LET IT GO ALREADY!
SHE'S NOT JUST ABOUT ASUKA !?
THAT REMINDS ME, KUROKI-SAN—WEREN'T YOU PEEKING UP MINE DURING THE SPORTS FESTIVAL?
HUH !?

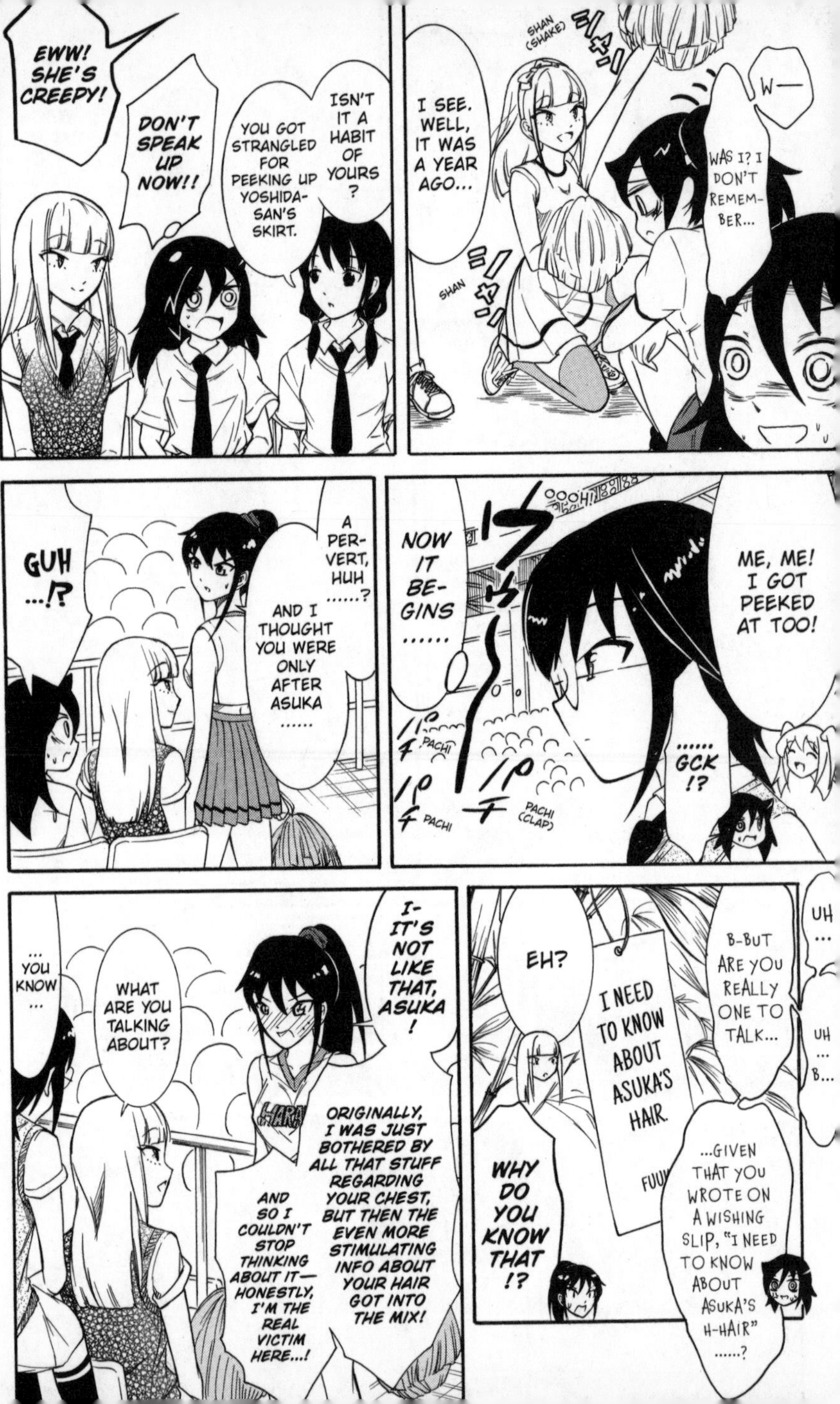
W—
WAS I? I DON'T REMEMBER...
SHAN (SHAKE)
I SEE. WELL, IT WAS A YEAR AGO...
SHAN
ISN'T IT A HABIT OF YOURS?
YOU GOT STRANGLED FOR PEEKING UP YOSHIDA-SAN'S SKIRT.
DON'T SPEAK UP NOW!!
EWW! SHE'S CREEPY!
ME, ME! I GOT PEEKED AT TOO!
NOW IT BEGINS......
......GCK!?
PACHI
PACHI (CLAP)
PACHI
A PERVERT, HUH......?
AND I THOUGHT YOU WERE ONLY AFTER ASUKA......
GUH...!?
UH... UH... B...
B-BUT ARE YOU REALLY ONE TO TALK...
EH?
I NEED TO KNOW ABOUT ASUKA'S HAIR.
...GIVEN THAT YOU WROTE ON A WISHING SLIP, "I NEED TO KNOW ABOUT ASUKA'S H-HAIR"......?
WHY DO YOU KNOW THAT!?
I-IT'S NOT LIKE THAT, ASUKA!
ORIGINALLY, I WAS JUST BOTHERED BY ALL THAT STUFF REGARDING YOUR CHEST, BUT THEN THE EVEN MORE STIMULATING INFO ABOUT YOUR HAIR GOT INTO THE MIX!
AND SO I COULDN'T STOP THINKING ABOUT IT—HONESTLY, I'M THE REAL VICTIM HERE...!
WHAT ARE YOU TALKING ABOUT?
...YOU KNOW...

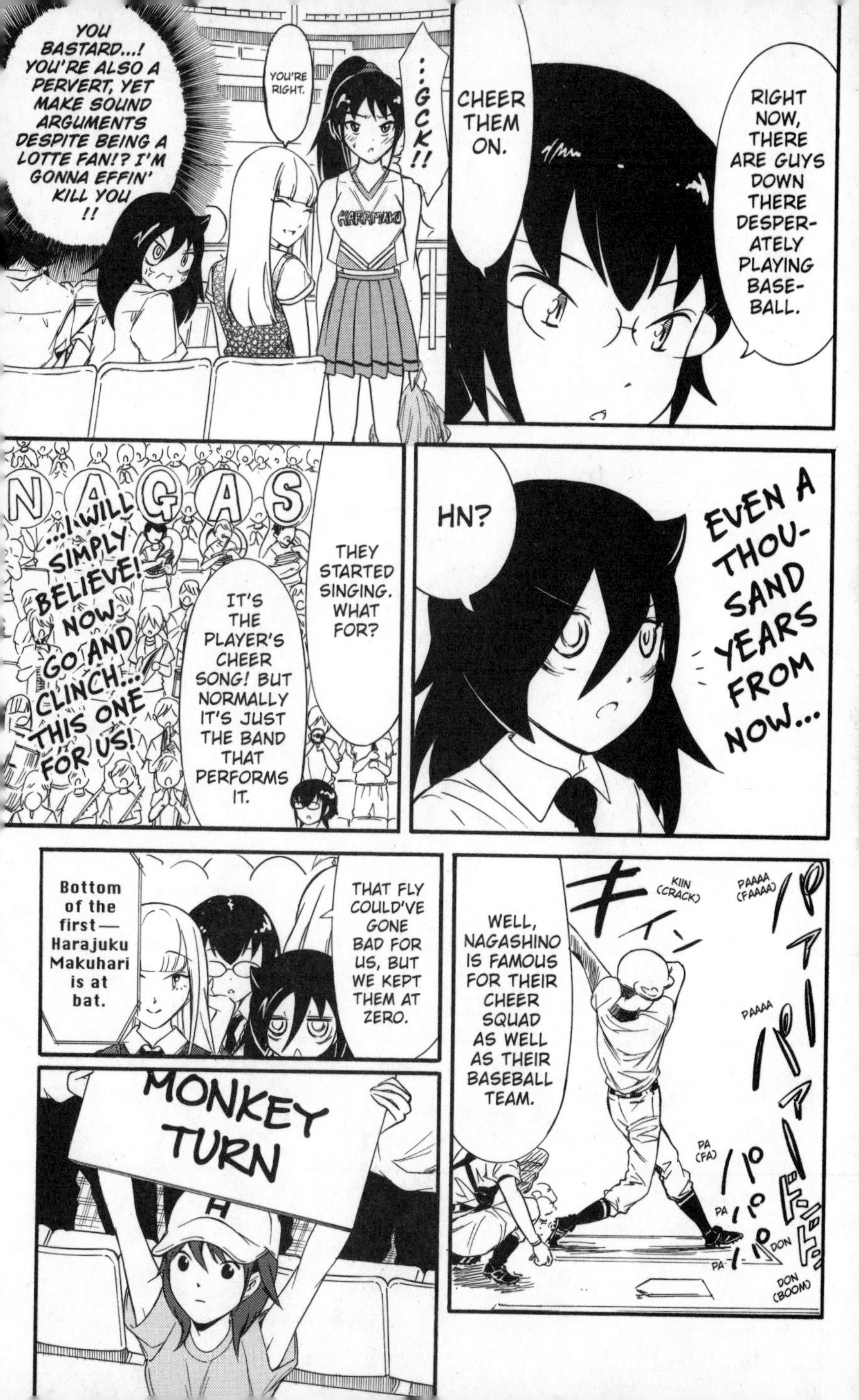
RIGHT NOW, THERE ARE GUYS DOWN THERE DESPERATELY PLAYING BASEBALL.
CHEER THEM ON.
...GCK!!
YOU'RE RIGHT.
YOU BASTARD...! YOU'RE ALSO A PERVERT, YET MAKE SOUND ARGUMENTS DESPITE BEING A LOTTE FAN!? I'M GONNA EFFIN' KILL YOU!!
HARAMAKU
EVEN A THOUSAND YEARS FROM NOW...
HN?
THEY STARTED SINGING. WHAT FOR?
IT'S THE PLAYER'S CHEER SONG! BUT NORMALLY IT'S JUST THE BAND THAT PERFORMS IT.
N A G A S
...I WILL SIMPLY BELIEVE! NOW GO AND CLINCH... THIS ONE FOR US!
KIIN (CRACK)
PAAAA (FAAAA)
WELL, NAGASHINO IS FAMOUS FOR THEIR CHEER SQUAD AS WELL AS THEIR BASEBALL TEAM.
PAAAA
PA (FA)
PA
PA
DON
DON (BOOM)
THAT FLY COULD'VE GONE BAD FOR US, BUT WE KEPT THEM AT ZERO.
Bottom of the first—Harajuku Makuhari is at bat.
MONKEY TURN

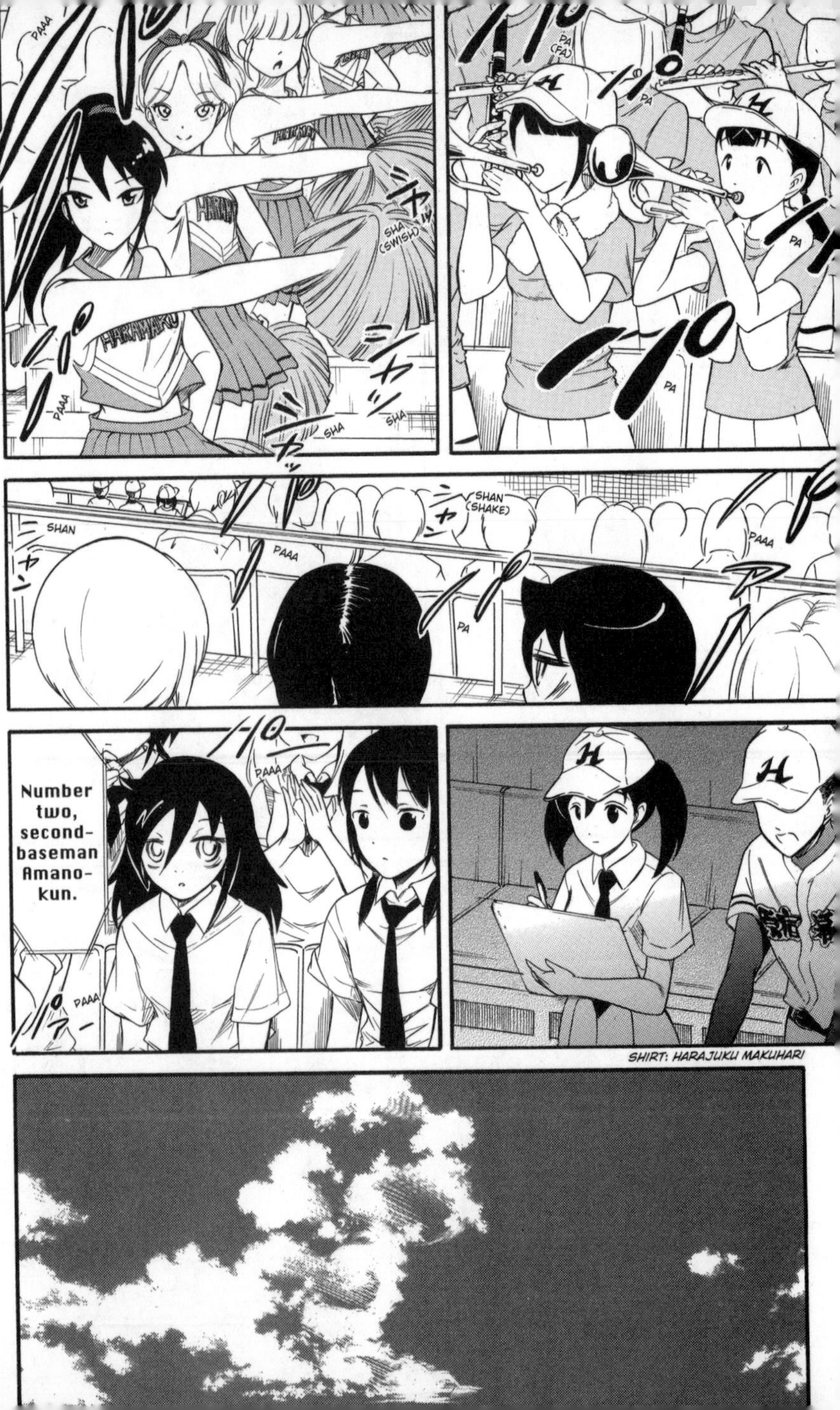
PA (FA)
PA
PA
PA
PAAA
SHA (SWISH)
SHA
SHA
PAAA
PAAA
SHAN (SHAKE)
PA
PAAA
SHAN
PAAA
Number two, second-baseman Amano-kun.
PAAA
SHIRT: HARAJUKU MAKUHARI

Grounder to short-shop! Runners can't move!

THEY'RE EVEN SHOWING THIS ON TV!

IF JUST CHIBA TV.

IT'S EASY FOR EVEN ME TO FOL-LOW.

The batter is number seven...

Nagashino High runners on second and third.

KIIN (CRACK)

YEAH!

TEAM	1	2	3	4	5	6	7	8	9	10	R	H	E
NAGASHINO	0	0	0	1	0	1	1	0	0		3	9	0
HARAJUKU MAKUHARI	0	0	0	0	0	0	0				0	3	2

QUIT TALKING LIKE YOU'RE READING A SCRIPT! IT'S IRRITAT-ING!

HONESTLY, THEIR GAME IS FAR BEYOND OURS QUALITY-WISE. ESPECIALLY IN BASE-RUNNING AND DEFENSE.

WE'VE DONE QUITE WELL TO LIMIT THEIR RUNS TO THREE.

FINAL INNING ALREADY... UNLIKE LAST YEAR, THIS WENT QUICK.

SHIRT: HARAJUKU MAKUHARI

...Number 3, right fielder, Fukuzawa-kun!

Bottom of the ninth, at bat for Harajuku Makuri High School is...

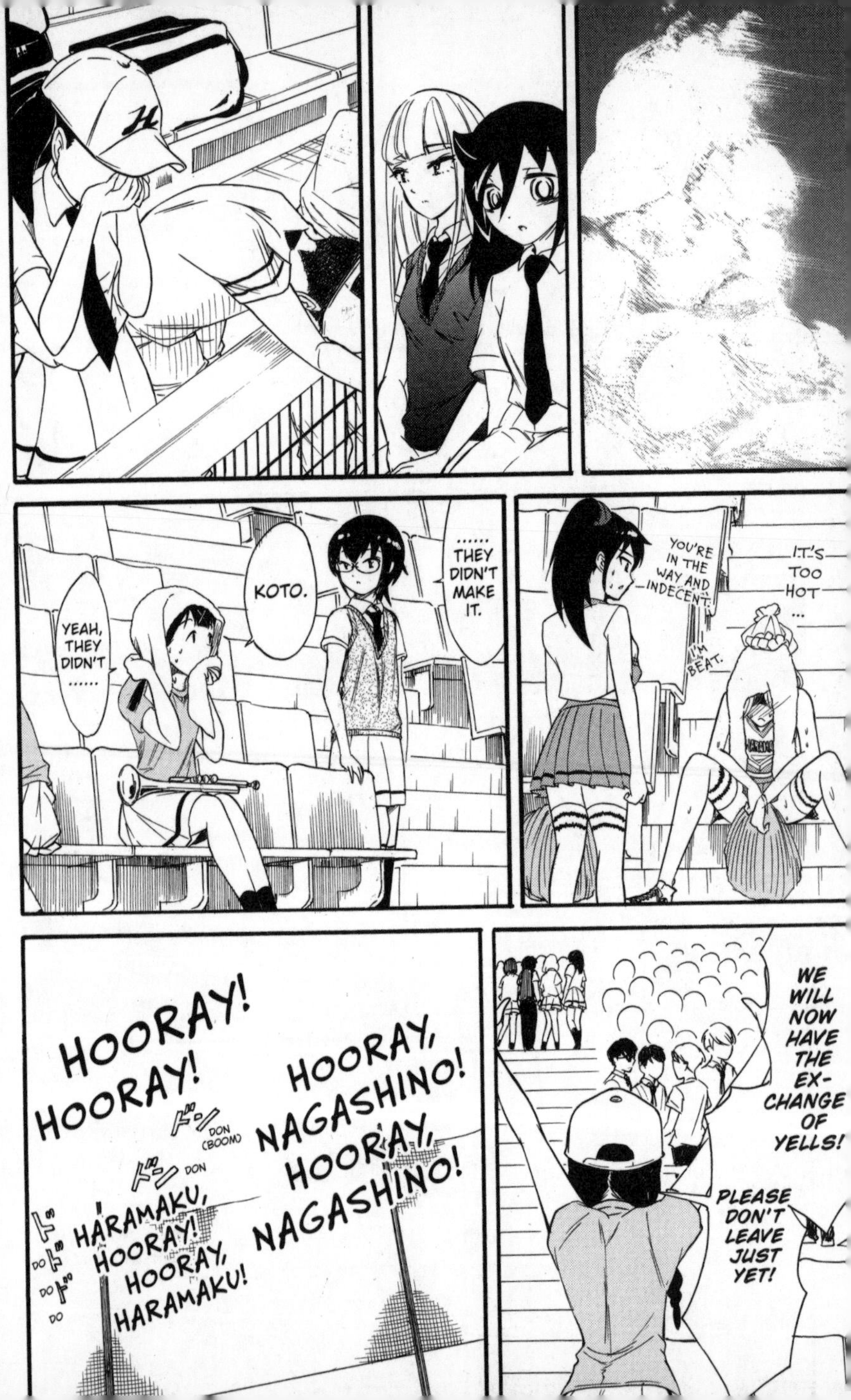
IT'S TOO HOT ...
YOU'RE IN THE WAY AND INDECENT.
I'M BEAT.
...... THEY DIDN'T MAKE IT.
KOTO.
YEAH, THEY DIDN'T ......
WE WILL NOW HAVE THE EX-CHANGE OF YELLS!
PLEASE DON'T LEAVE JUST YET!
HOORAY, NAGASHINO! HOORAY, NAGASHINO!
HOORAY! HOORAY!
ドン DON (BOOM)
ドン DON
HARAMAKU, HOORAY! HOORAY, HARAMAKU!
ド DO ド DO ド DO

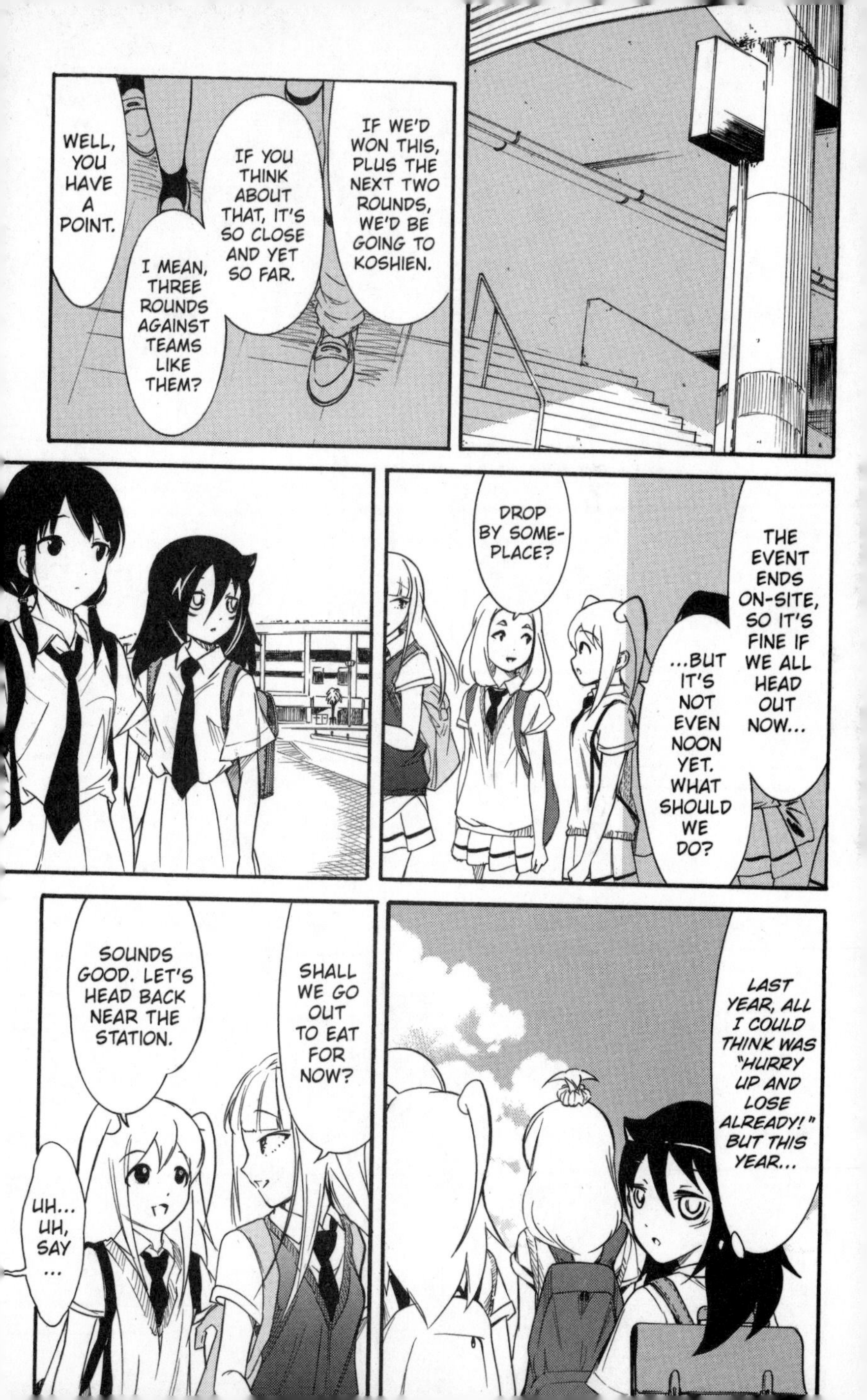
IF WE'D WON THIS, PLUS THE NEXT TWO ROUNDS, WE'D BE GOING TO KOSHIEN.
IF YOU THINK ABOUT THAT, IT'S SO CLOSE AND YET SO FAR.
I MEAN, THREE ROUNDS AGAINST TEAMS LIKE THEM?
WELL, YOU HAVE A POINT.
THE EVENT ENDS ON-SITE, SO IT'S FINE IF WE ALL HEAD OUT NOW...
...BUT IT'S NOT EVEN NOON YET. WHAT SHOULD WE DO?
DROP BY SOME-PLACE?
LAST YEAR, ALL I COULD THINK WAS "HURRY UP AND LOSE ALREADY!" BUT THIS YEAR...
SHALL WE GO OUT TO EAT FOR NOW?
SOUNDS GOOD. LET'S HEAD BACK NEAR THE STATION.
UH... UH, SAY...

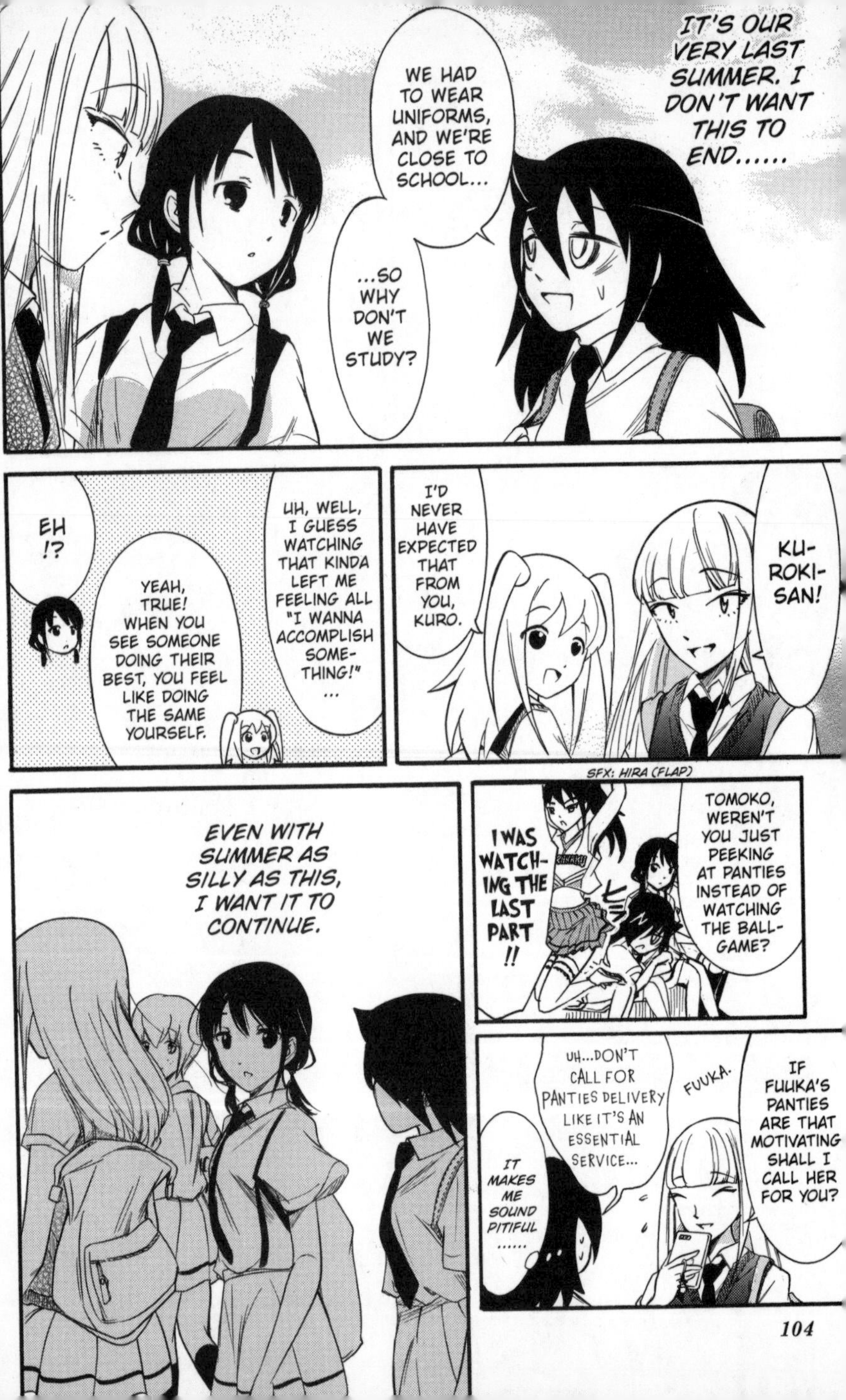
IT'S OUR VERY LAST SUMMER. I DON'T WANT THIS TO END......
WE HAD TO WEAR UNIFORMS, AND WE'RE CLOSE TO SCHOOL...
...SO WHY DON'T WE STUDY?
KU-ROKI-SAN!
I'D NEVER HAVE EXPECTED THAT FROM YOU, KURO.
UH, WELL, I GUESS WATCHING THAT KINDA LEFT ME FEELING ALL "I WANNA ACCOMPLISH SOME-THING!" ...
YEAH, TRUE! WHEN YOU SEE SOMEONE DOING THEIR BEST, YOU FEEL LIKE DOING THE SAME YOURSELF.
EH !?
SFX: HIRA (FLAP)
TOMOKO, WEREN'T YOU JUST PEEKING AT PANTIES INSTEAD OF WATCHING THE BALL-GAME?
I WAS WATCH-ING THE LAST PART !!
IF FUUKA'S PANTIES ARE THAT MOTIVATING SHALL I CALL HER FOR YOU?
FUUKA.
UH...DON'T CALL FOR PANTIES DELIVERY LIKE IT'S AN ESSENTIAL SERVICE...
IT MAKES ME SOUND PITIFUL ......
EVEN WITH SUMMER AS SILLY AS THIS, I WANT IT TO CONTINUE.

TRANSLATION NOTES

PAGE 6
DoRe, the brand name on the juice boxes here, is a parody of *Dole*.

PAGE 22
In Japanese, Ucchi compared the word *kimoi* ("creepy") to the word *yabai*, an adjective that primarily means "dangerous" but has been adopted by young people for positive connotations in a "so good it's dangerous" sense. For example, in Special Chapter 8 (Volume 15), Hina's two nerd-girl friends in middle school constantly used the word in reference to the anime *Tiger and Bunny*.

PAGES 23-25
Hina is suggesting the **AEON Mall** (Makuhari branch) or Makuhari **Techno Garden** as places to drop by for a quick bite to eat. It appears they went with AEON Mall, which would be a closer walk and has a food court with many snack options.

PAGE 32
Tanabata is a star festival celebrated on July 7 in Japan as the one day a year when the celestial weaver Orihime (the star Vega) and the cowherd Hikoboshi (the star Altair) can cross the Milky Way, which separates them, before returning to their hard and skillful work for the rest of the year. As we see in the chapter, there's a tradition of writing wishes on colorful slips of paper and tying them to stalks of bamboo. Befitting the origin story, the wishes are often related to development of skills and success, as well as romance.

PAGE 33
Chiba Prefectural Qualifiers refers to the Chiba Prefecture stage of the National High School Baseball Championship, a massive event each summer in Japan.

PAGE 35
In the original Japanese, Tomoko's using the net-slang term NTR here, which reads as *netore*, meaning to seduce someone, usually someone in a relationship with someone else. As manga aficionados may be aware, NTR is also used as a genre in manga called *netorare*, which is the passive form of *netore*, meaning the main character is the one getting their lover stolen.

PAGE 40
The **kendo girl** stereotype is a girl who's serious and athletic, with long, black hair in a ponytail. Not all actual "kendo girls" in manga and anime fit this stereotype, but it's easy to find characters who do.

Koshien is the Osaka stadium where the finals for the National High School Baseball Tournament are held.

PAGE 47
Shanto! is a parody of the *Chanto!* TV weather report that runs on weekdays on CBC TV.

PAGE 56
Dala is another parody variant of *Dole*.

PAGE 66
The prefectural sub-tournaments of the National High School Baseball Tournament usually take place in late July. Also in late July are the prefectural legs of the All-Japan Band Competition, which have high school divisions as well as grade school, middle school, and workplaces. Itou certainly would be exhausted...

PAGE 68
Intensive sleepaway training camps have long been a summer activity for Japanese students who participate in sports, but in more recent years, college-test prep schools have begun to offer their own version of the experience, based around studying instead of sports. This also explains Ucchi's misunderstanding on Page 71.

PAGE 69
Kuroki House is a parody of *Terrace House (Boys x Girls Next Door)*, a Japanese reality series on Netflix that began in late 2012, running for two years and spawning four follow-up seasons in various locales.

PAGE 73
Ultimate Lowlife Maiden, or *Gesu no Kiwami Otome*, is the name of a well-known four-person Japanese rock band. The bassist of the group actually appeared on *Terrace House* in December 2018.

Fuuka's **"I want to join you...after all. When do we leave?"** lines are a reference to the manga *Jojo's Bizarre Adventure*. The lines she's referring to are from *Stardust Crusaders*, Chapter 8, and they've become a running gag and basis of fan-art jokes.

PAGE 77
Akagi and **Third-Year Class-B Inpachi-sensei** are both mah-jongg manga. *Inpachi-sensei* ran in the *Modern Mah-jongg* magazine and on its website until late 2019.

PAGE 84
The drinks they buy are common vending-machine drinks in Japan, with the names either partially covered or altered: **CALPIS SODA**, **ITO-EN Barley Tea**, **POCARI**, and **KOCHAKADEN**.

PAGE 85
A **deer scarer** (*shishi odoshi*) is a fixture of many traditional Japanese gardens: a bamboo tube arranged to fill with water until it tilts down to strike a rock with a distinct sound as it empties out, before tilting back up to fill again.

PAGE 88
Shonan is the coastal region of Kanagawa Prefecture, which faces Sagami Bay instead of Tokyo Bay, and thus has relatively clean beaches while still being about an hour away from Tokyo. **Odaiba** is a large artificial island in Tokyo Bay, right by central Tokyo, and though it has lots of available leisure activities, the water quality would not be as good as less-urbanized Shonan.

PAGE 94
ZOZO Marine Stadium is a portmanteau of the current name-sponsor, ZOZO, and the previous one, QVC.

As for the ads, "Ishukke" is a parody of "Agekke," an HR consulting firm; "bayfin5" is an alteration of "bayfm78," a radio station based in Chiba City; the rest are more slight shortenings or making the actual name less legible: Chiba Bank, Keiyo Bank, Shinnihon Corporation.

PAGE 95
Nagashino High School is referring to Narashino High School, in Narashino, northwest of Makuhari, which is famous for both their baseball team and their band. **Kisaragi High School** is referring to Kisarazu (Sogo) High School, another top-ranked baseball school farther down the Chiba peninsula. The name might also be a call back to Kisaragi Girls' High from the 1998 girls' baseball anime *Princess Nine*.

PAGE 96
Tsukkomi is a Japanese term for the "straight man" in a comedy duo, who comments on the silly things the *boke* ("dunce") member of the duo says. It's also being used here to highlight Komi, whose name comprises the latter half of the word.

PAGE 99
In Japanese, Tomoko uses the verb *buchikorogasu* (I'm gonna roll you over), when what she actually means is *buchikorosu* (I'm gonna kill you). By adding the extra *ga*, Tomoko's violent declaration is now PG, so it's a bit like using the word "heck" to avoid cursing, or in this case, "effin'."

The song the other school fans sing starts out as a couple lines from the Arashi song "One Love" (with "thousand years" instead of the actual song's "hundred years"), but the last part is an addition specifically telling the player to hit the ball, etc. Such lines seem to be a practice used for cheer songs for the Nagoya Chunichi Dragons, but it's a bit controversial since it uses *omae*, a ruder word for "you," which indirectly encourages kids to say it.

Monkey Turn refers to a tune "SG RUSH *Yuushousen*" that plays on the pachislo-game spin-off of the late '90s/early 2000s hydroplane-racing manga and anime *Monkey Turn*. This tune was adopted as a fight tune for the Chiba Lotte Marines starting in 2011, and also by high school bands the following year. This is what Haramaku's band is playing on the next page.

TRANSLATION NOTES ....

PAGE 109
Play Gal is a parody of the Shueisha men's magazine *Weekly Playboy*. The one shown is specifically based on the Nov. 4, 2019 issue.

PAGE 110
Center is the common name for the National Center Test for University Admissions, Japan's dominant standardized exam used by public universities and some private ones. The more prestigious universities use the Center test in addition to a harder one of their own. There are separate tests for each subject, and Tomoko is studying books of past Center exam questions for both English and Japanese History.

For the day Tomoko imagines, she spends the morning playing a **Fallout** game on her PS4, and late at night she's flailing on the floor, a reference to **Kaiji** from the gambling manga by the same name, who also flails on the floor with the SFX *jita jita* whenever he's frustrated.

PAGE 116
Yes, Tomoko uses "standby" as a verb here. The verb is most well-known from its usage in the series *Mobile Suit Gundam*.

PAGE 118
The original Japanese line for "I want this to be done with already..." is a reference to main character Misuzu's final lines in *Air*, the visual novel and anime by Key.

PAGE 119
Li'l Collector is a reference to *Matomaru-kun*, a brand of eraser for which the eraser dust collects into a single lump.

PAGE 121
"All-Seasons Quin-" is probably a combination of *Spring, Summer, Fall, Winter Octet*, another web manga, and *Kamisama to Quintet*, a manga published in *Manga Time Kirara*.

The anime itself is possibly referring to *Wasteful Days of High School Girls*, which aired summer 2019 and is also based on a four-panel web manga. The character designs are somewhat different, but the character descriptions are similar, with an emotionless girl and a half-Japanese, half-Australian girl.

In Japanese, Tomoko calls the **"stinky pits"** character *Wakiga*, which means "bad armpit odor," an issue commonly associated with foreigners, since it's less common for Japanese people and others of East Asian descent (lucky them). The **"show a little while back"** that she's mixing up with this one is probably *Asobi Asobase*, which aired in summer 2018 and had a character named Olivia. Olivia speaks broken Japanese to pretend to be an American transfer student even though she actually grew up in Japan.

PAGE 134
Komi's expression while demanding a ride from Yoshida appears to be a parody of the unhinged facial expressions made by the character Amamiya in the 18+ indie visual novel *Sakusei Byoutau*.

PAGE 135
In the super-long-running Shonen Jump police-station gag manga with a superlong name (*Kochikame* for short), it was a running gag for Chief Ohara, boss of the main character, Ryoutsu, to come bursting into the building, angrily brandishing some sort of weapon, and yelling, "Where's that idiot Ryoutsu!? Where'd he go!?" or some variation thereof.

PAGE 136
In the **"definitely a cleats-up tackle at me!"** line, the verb Tomoki uses, *kezuru*, has a bit of a specific meaning in soccer: a defensive player deliberately aiming for the offensive player's foot with a tackle. It's legal if they only hit the ball to get it away but a serious foul and potential card if they deliberately aim for the player.

PAGE 140
Loft/Plus One is a pub in Shinjuku also used as a venue for live music, improv, and talk events.

Freestyle Dungeon is a Japanese variety show featuring freestyle rap battles. Challengers on the show are called "Monsters," so the "Monster Room" is basically the room where the challengers wait for their turn.

PAGE 141
Icco Tanigawa is a pun on "Nico Tanigawa," treating the *nica/niko* as the word meaning "two items," so the equivalent with only one of the pair there is *icca/ikko* (one item).

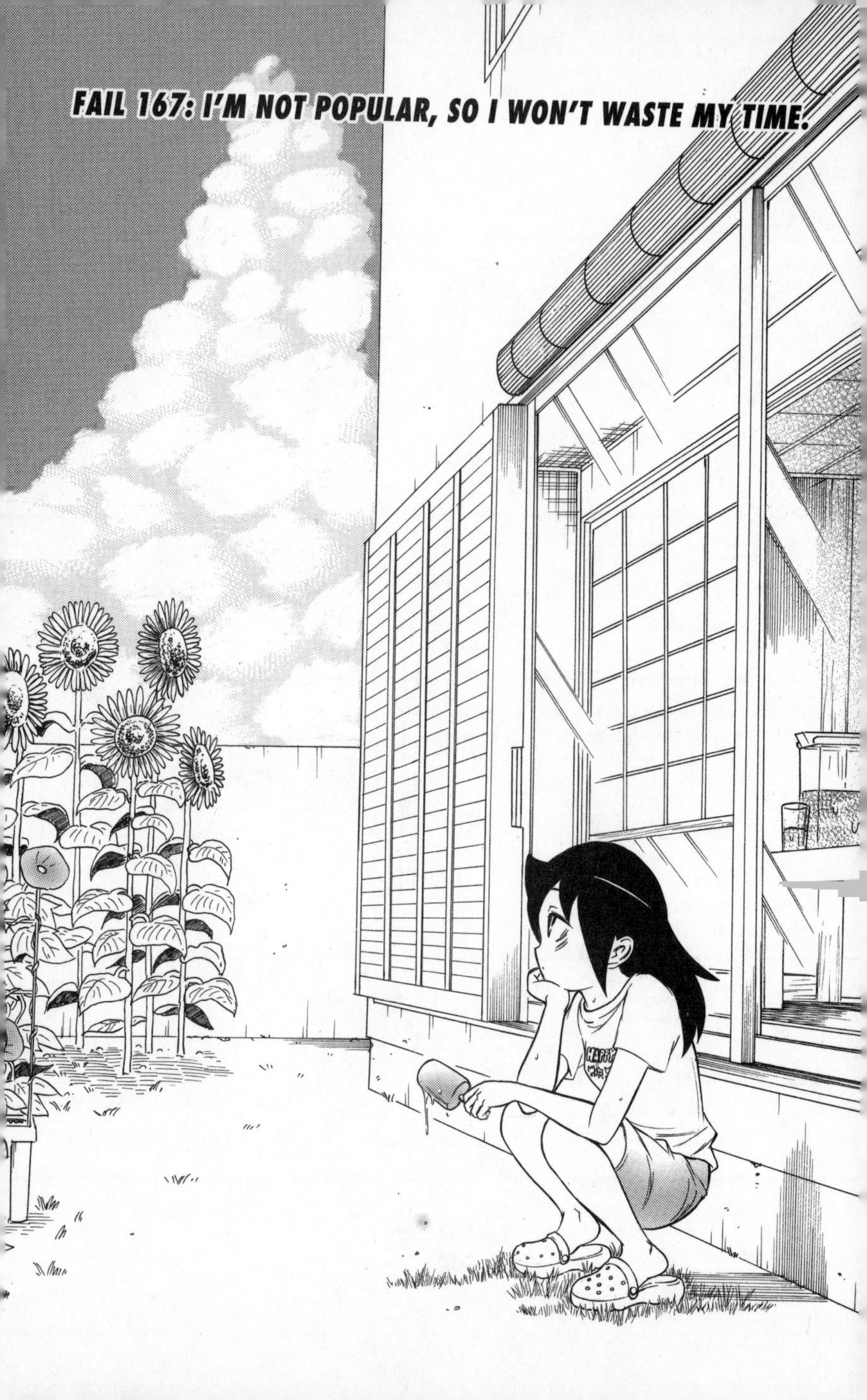
FAIL 167: I'M NOT POPULAR, SO I WON'T WASTE MY TIME.

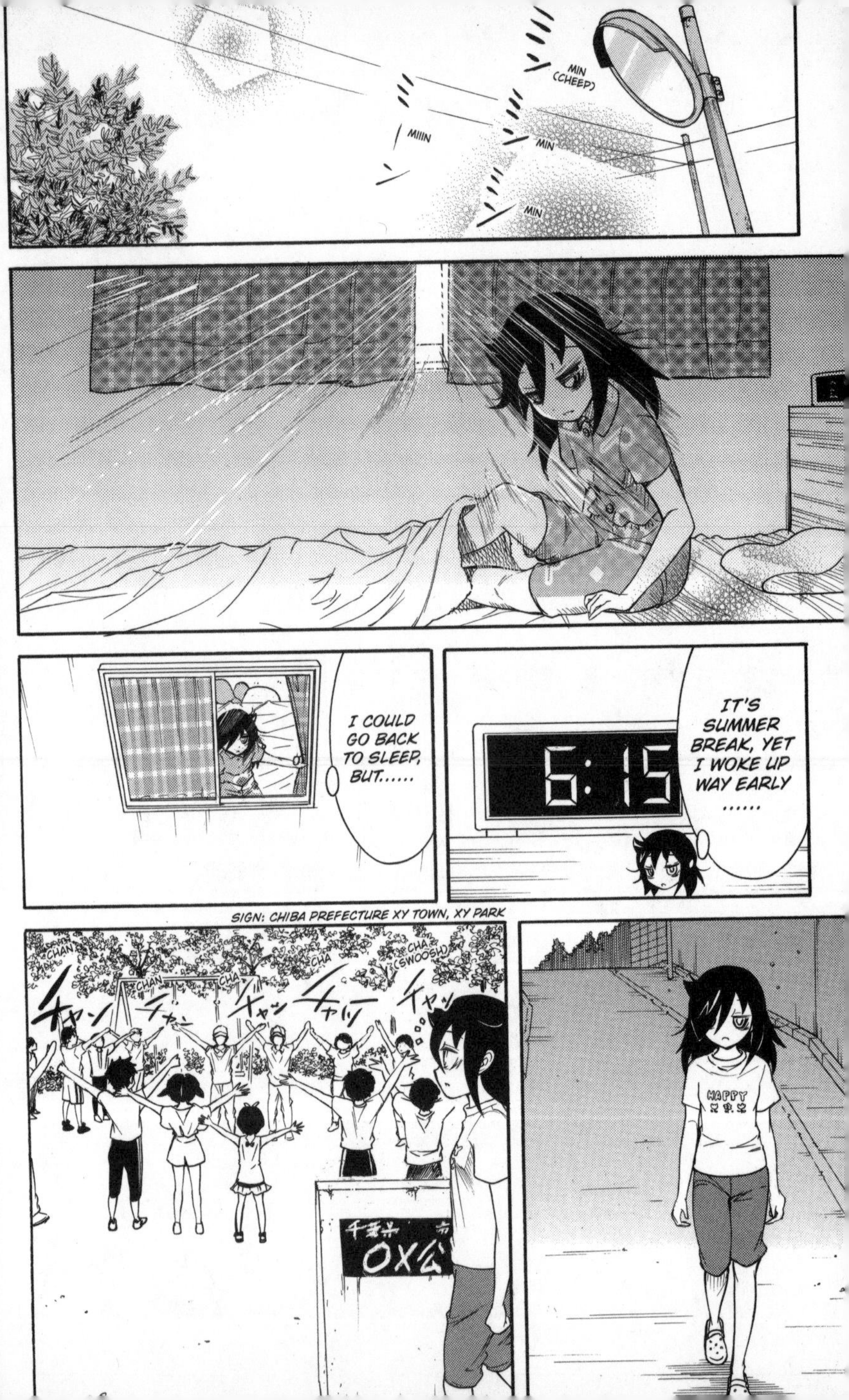
MIN (CHEEP)
MIN
MIIN
MIN
IT'S SUMMER BREAK, YET I WOKE UP WAY EARLY ......
I COULD GO BACK TO SLEEP, BUT......
SIGN: CHIBA PREFECTURE XY TOWN, XY PARK
CHA (SWOOSH)
CHA
CHA
CHAN
CHAN

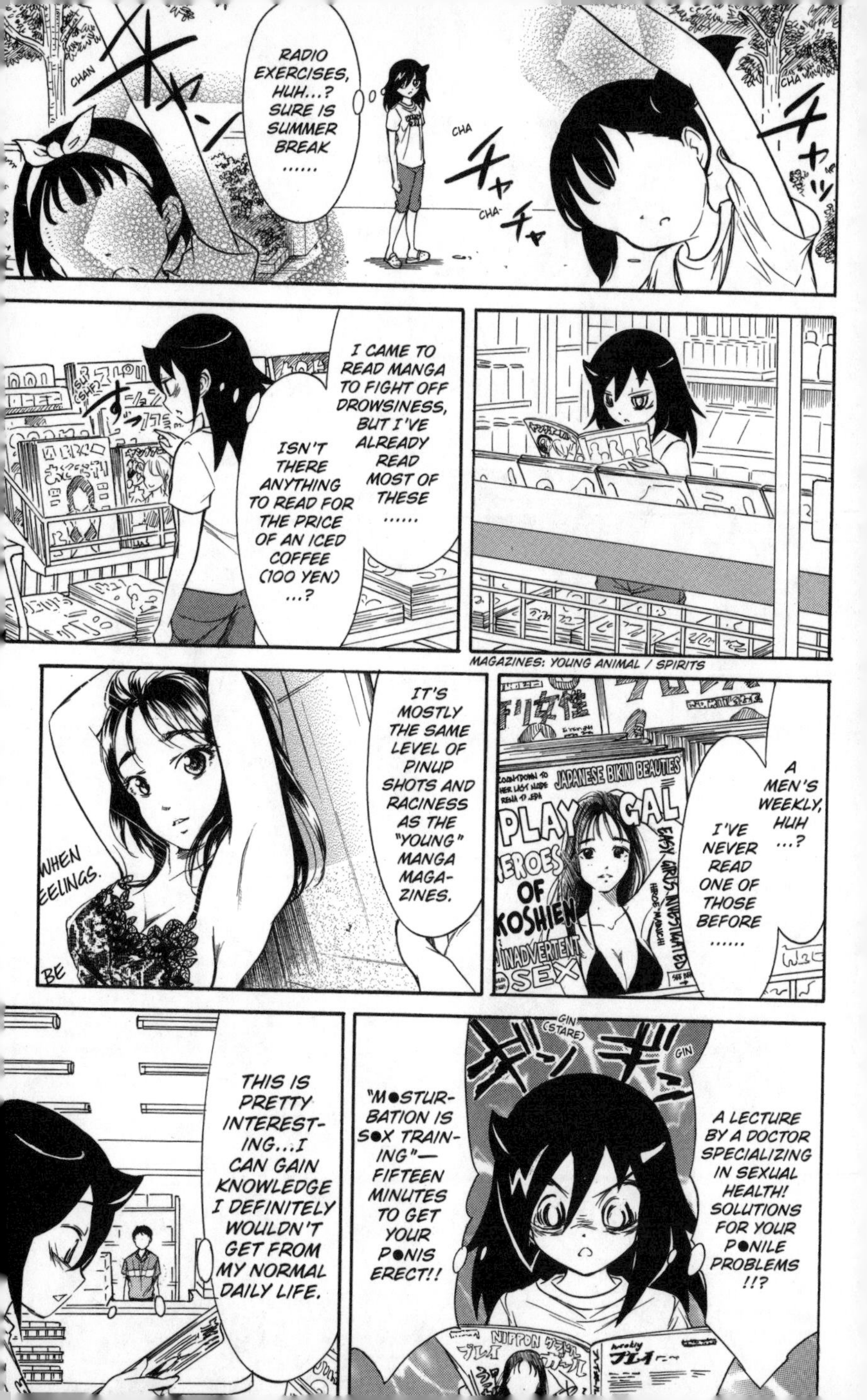
CHA
CHA
CHA-
RADIO EXERCISES, HUH...? SURE IS SUMMER BREAK ......
CHAN
I CAME TO READ MANGA TO FIGHT OFF DROWSINESS, BUT I'VE ALREADY READ MOST OF THESE ......
ISN'T THERE ANYTHING TO READ FOR THE PRICE OF AN ICED COFFEE (100 YEN) ...?
MAGAZINES: YOUNG ANIMAL / SPIRITS
JAPANESE BIKINI BEAUTIES
PLAY GAL
EASY GIRLS INVESTIGATED
EROES OF KOSHIEN
INADVERTENT SEX
A MEN'S WEEKLY, HUH ...?
I'VE NEVER READ ONE OF THOSE BEFORE ......
IT'S MOSTLY THE SAME LEVEL OF PINUP SHOTS AND RACINESS AS THE "YOUNG" MANGA MAGA-ZINES.
GIN (STARE)
GIN
A LECTURE BY A DOCTOR SPECIALIZING IN SEXUAL HEALTH! SOLUTIONS FOR YOUR P●NILE PROBLEMS !!?
"M●STUR-BATION IS S●X TRAIN-ING"— FIFTEEN MINUTES TO GET YOUR P●NIS ERECT!!
NIPPON
THIS IS PRETTY INTEREST-ING...I CAN GAIN KNOWLEDGE I DEFINITELY WOULDN'T GET FROM MY NORMAL DAILY LIFE.

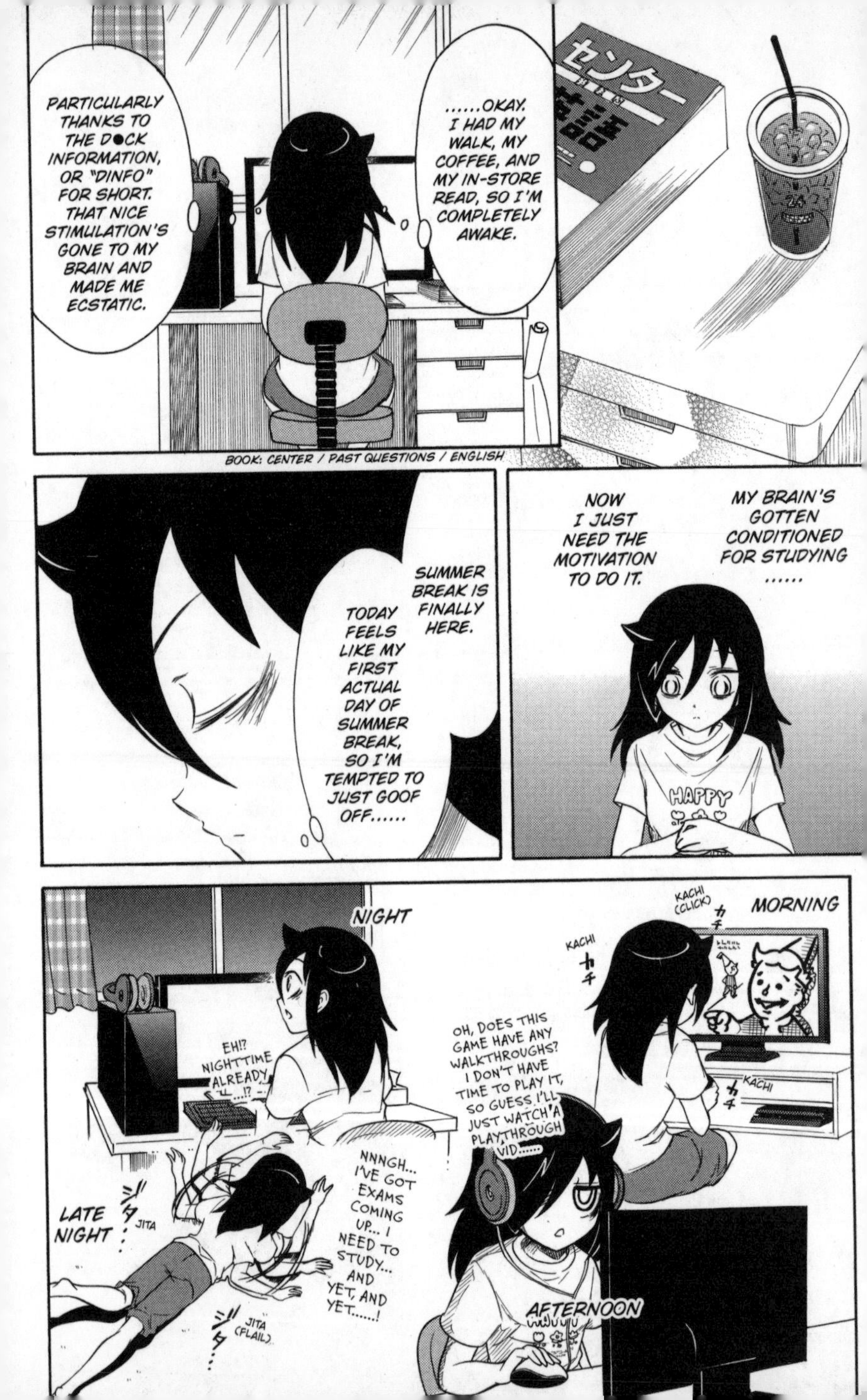
......OKAY. I HAD MY WALK, MY COFFEE, AND MY IN-STORE READ, SO I'M COMPLETELY AWAKE.
PARTICULARLY THANKS TO THE D●CK INFORMATION, OR "DINFO" FOR SHORT. THAT NICE STIMULATION'S GONE TO MY BRAIN AND MADE ME ECSTATIC.
BOOK: CENTER / PAST QUESTIONS / ENGLISH
MY BRAIN'S GOTTEN CONDITIONED FOR STUDYING ......
NOW I JUST NEED THE MOTIVATION TO DO IT.
SUMMER BREAK IS FINALLY HERE.
TODAY FEELS LIKE MY FIRST ACTUAL DAY OF SUMMER BREAK, SO I'M TEMPTED TO JUST GOOF OFF......
MORNING
KACHI (CLICK)
KACHI
KACHI
AFTERNOON
OH, DOES THIS GAME HAVE ANY WALKTHROUGHS? I DON'T HAVE TIME TO PLAY IT, SO GUESS I'LL JUST WATCH A PLAYTHROUGH VID......
NIGHT
EH!? NIGHTTIME ALREADY...!?
LATE NIGHT
JITA
NNNGH... I'VE GOT EXAMS COMING UP... I NEED TO STUDY... AND YET, AND YET......!
JITA (FLAIL)

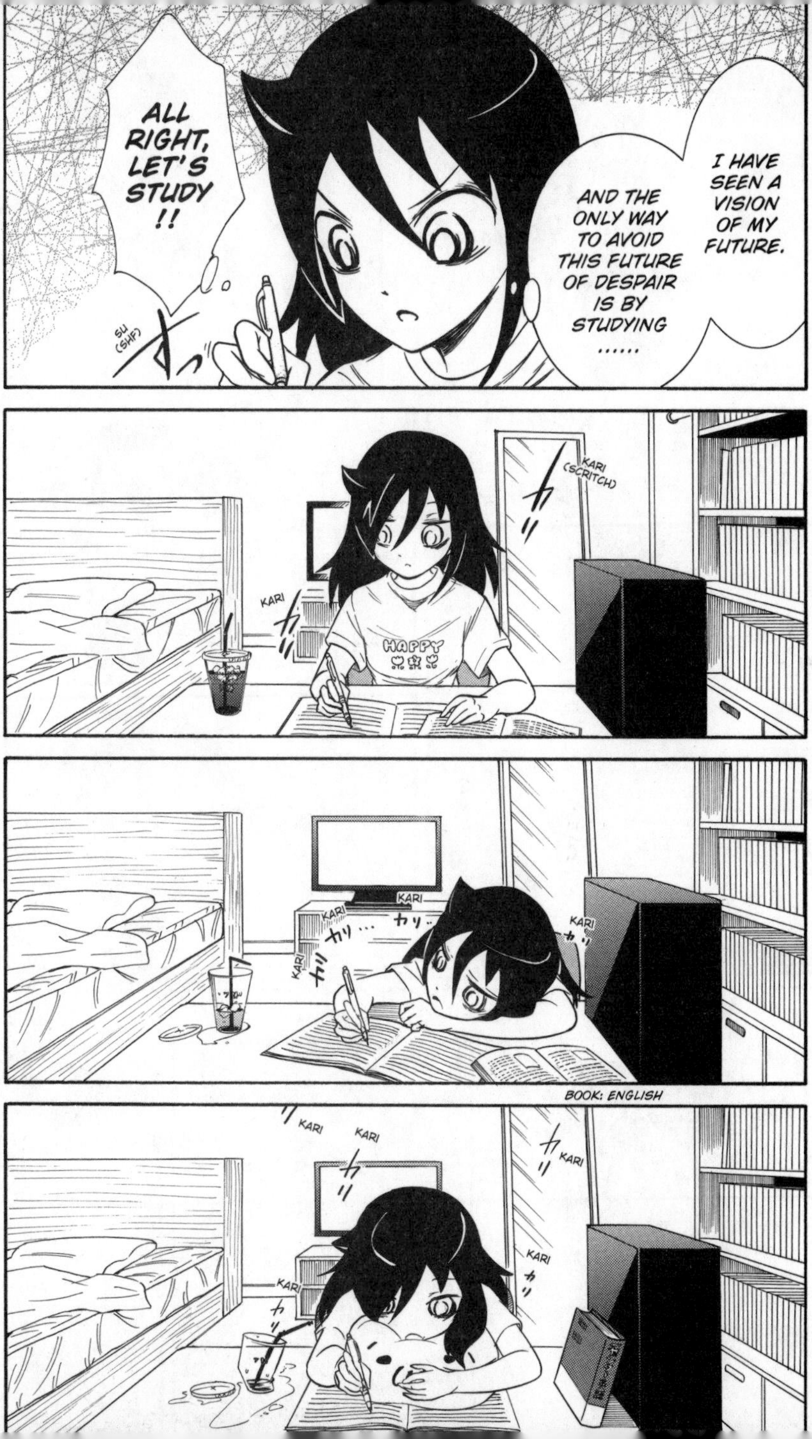
I HAVE SEEN A VISION OF MY FUTURE.
AND THE ONLY WAY TO AVOID THIS FUTURE OF DESPAIR IS BY STUDYING ......
ALL RIGHT, LET'S STUDY !!
SU (SHF)
KARI (SCRITCH)
KARI
HAPPY
KARI
KARI
KARI
KARI
KARI
KARI
KARI
KARI
BOOK: ENGLISH

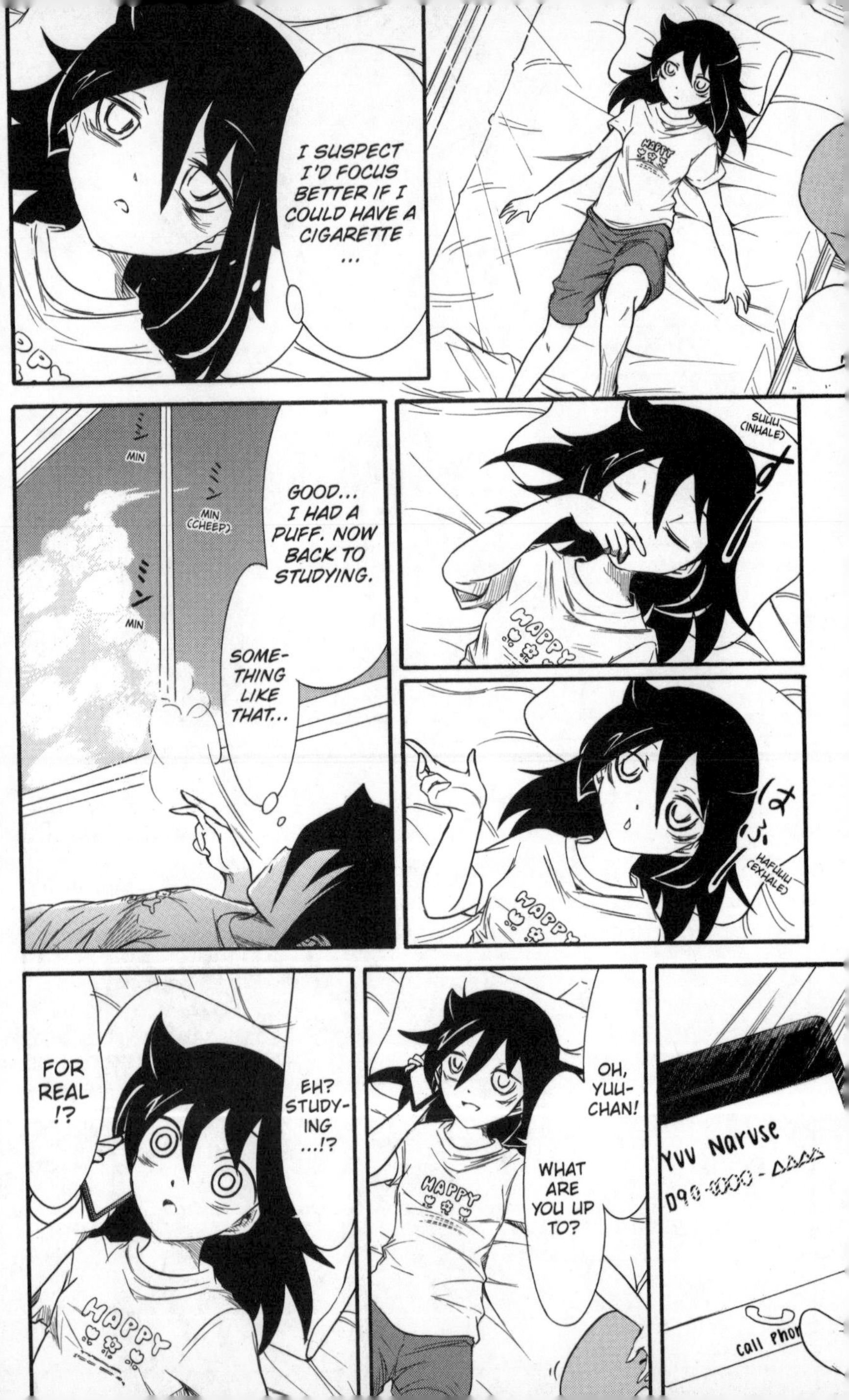
I SUSPECT I'D FOCUS BETTER IF I COULD HAVE A CIGARETTE ...
す
SUUU (INHALE)
はふ
HAFUUU (EXHALE)
ミン
MIN
ミン
MIN (CHEEP)
ミン
MIN
GOOD... I HAD A PUFF. NOW BACK TO STUDYING.
SOMETHING LIKE THAT...
Yuu Naruse
Call Phon
OH, YUU-CHAN!
WHAT ARE YOU UP TO?
EH? STUDYING ...!?
FOR REAL !?

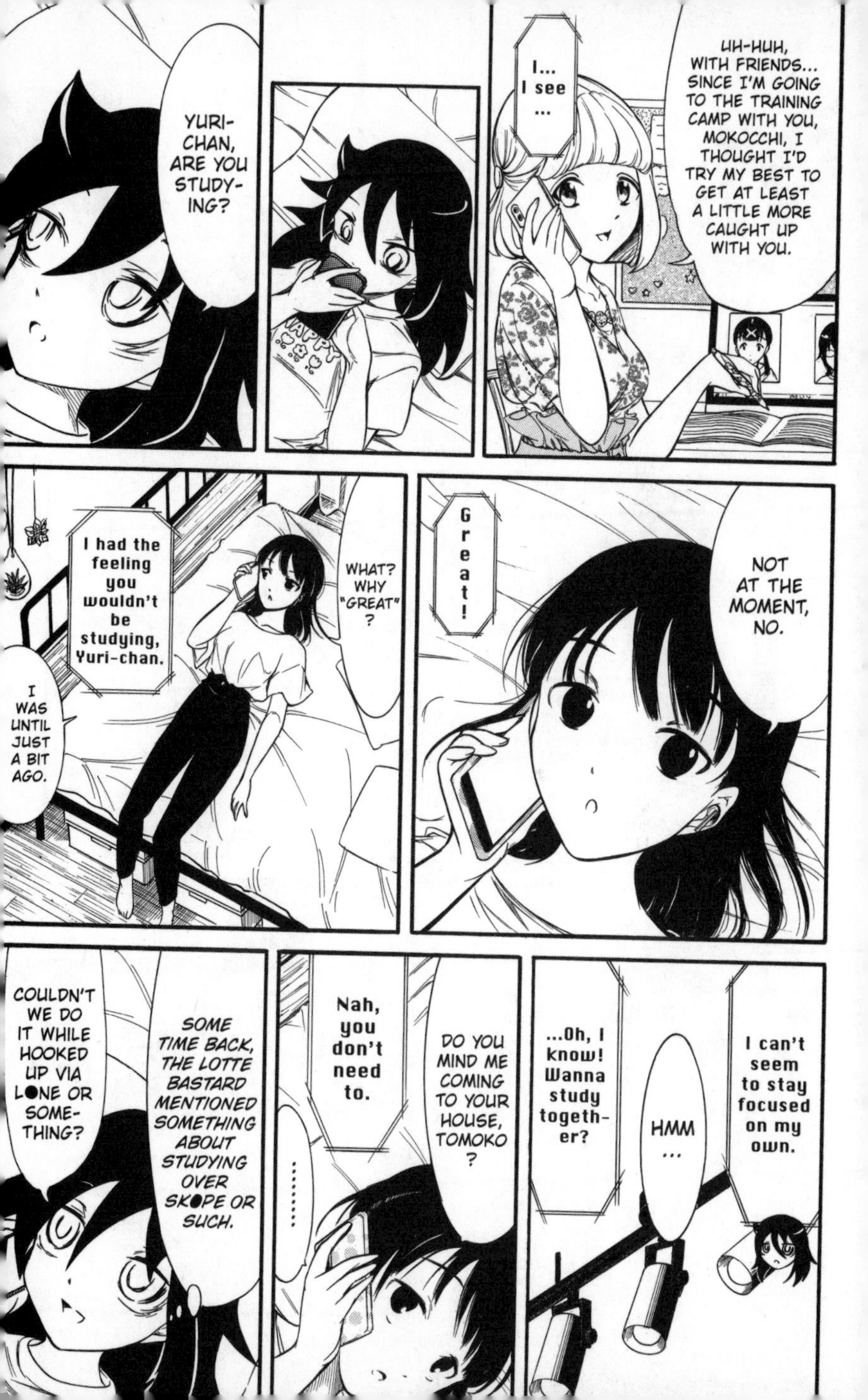
UH-HUH, WITH FRIENDS... SINCE I'M GOING TO THE TRAINING CAMP WITH YOU, MOKOCCHI, I THOUGHT I'D TRY MY BEST TO GET AT LEAST A LITTLE MORE CAUGHT UP WITH YOU.
I... I see ...
YURI-CHAN, ARE YOU STUDYING?
NOT AT THE MOMENT, NO.
Great!
WHAT? WHY "GREAT"?
I had the feeling you wouldn't be studying, Yuri-chan.
I WAS UNTIL JUST A BIT AGO.
I can't seem to stay focused on my own.
HMM...
...Oh, I know! Wanna study together?
DO YOU MIND ME COMING TO YOUR HOUSE, TOMOKO?
Nah, you don't need to.
....
SOME TIME BACK, THE LOTTE BASTARD MENTIONED SOMETHING ABOUT STUDYING OVER SKOPE OR SUCH.
COULDN'T WE DO IT WHILE HOOKED UP VIA L●NE OR SOMETHING?

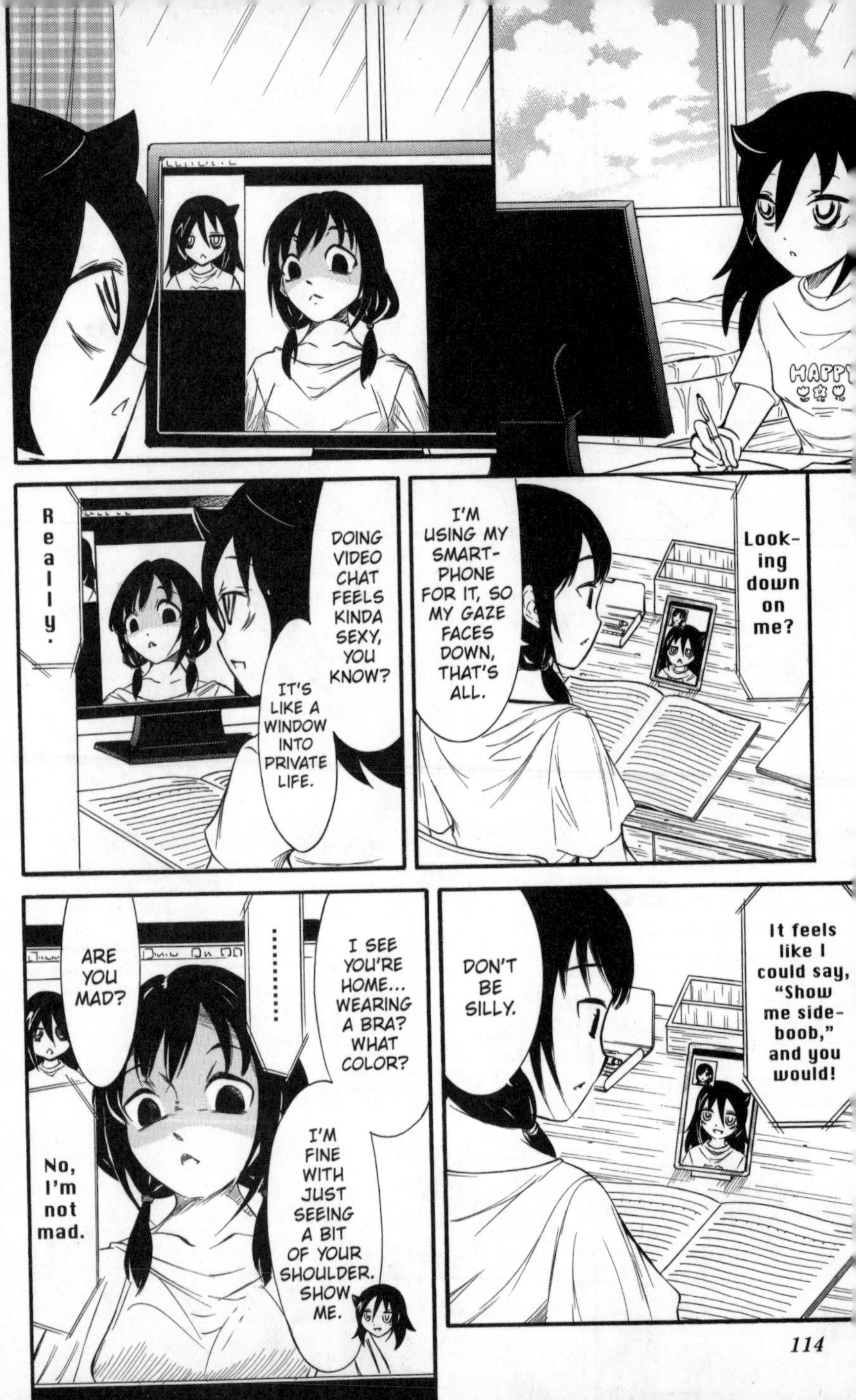
Looking down on me?
I'M USING MY SMARTPHONE FOR IT, SO MY GAZE FACES DOWN, THAT'S ALL.
DOING VIDEO CHAT FEELS KINDA SEXY, YOU KNOW?
IT'S LIKE A WINDOW INTO PRIVATE LIFE.
Really.
It feels like I could say, "Show me side-boob," and you would!
DON'T BE SILLY.
I SEE YOU'RE HOME... WEARING A BRA? WHAT COLOR?
I'M FINE WITH JUST SEEING A BIT OF YOUR SHOULDER. SHOW ME.
....
ARE YOU MAD?
No, I'm not mad.

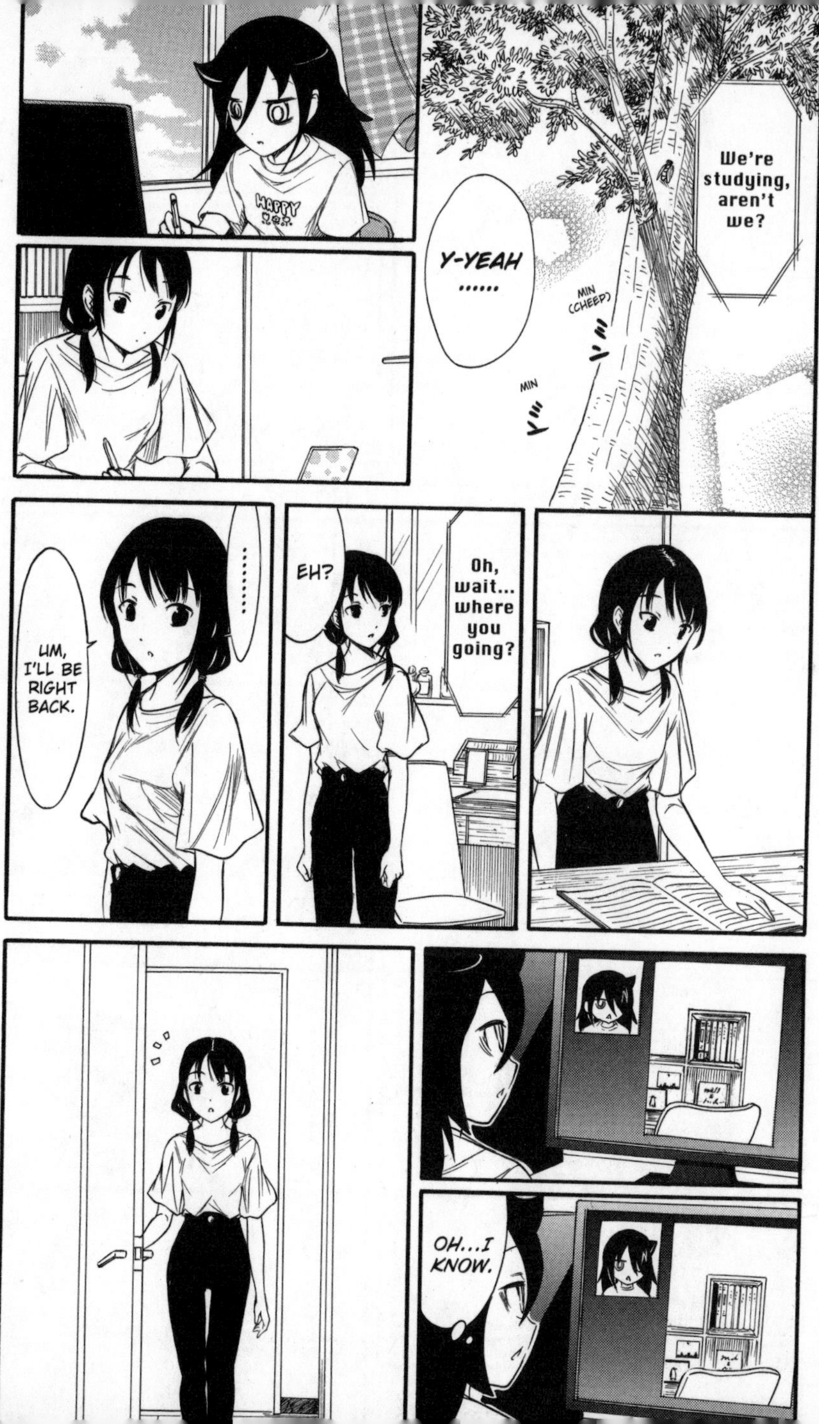
We're studying, aren't we?
Y-YEAH ......
MIN (CHEEP)
MIN
Oh, wait... where you going?
EH?
......
UM, I'LL BE RIGHT BACK.
OH...I KNOW.

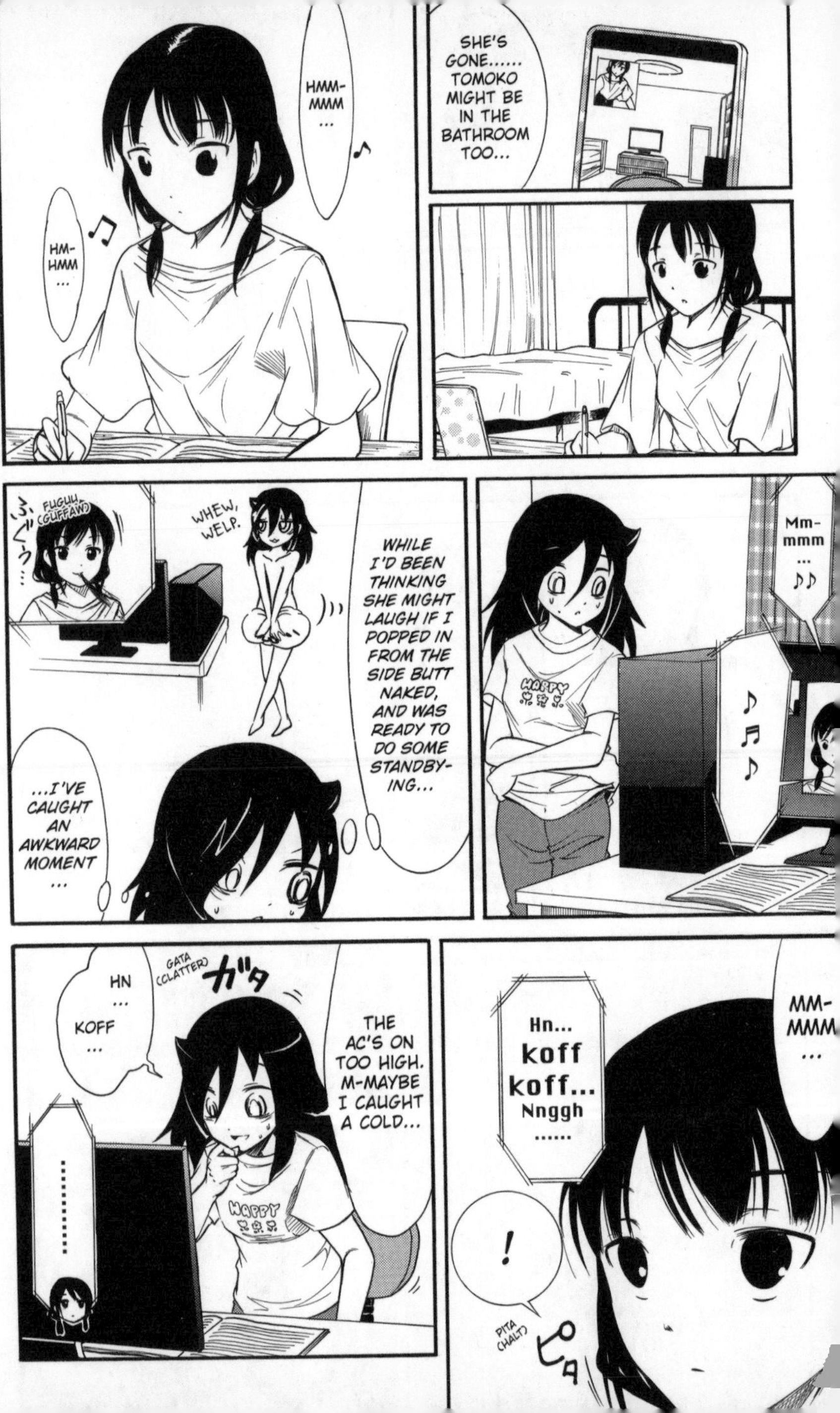
SHE'S GONE...... TOMOKO MIGHT BE IN THE BATHROOM TOO...
HMM-MMM ...
♪
HM-HMM ...
♪
Mm-mmm ... ♪♪
♪ ♬ ♪
WHILE I'D BEEN THINKING SHE MIGHT LAUGH IF I POPPED IN FROM THE SIDE BUTT NAKED, AND WAS READY TO DO SOME STANDBY-ING...
WHEW, WELP.
ふぐぅ… FUGUU (GUFFAWD)
...I'VE CAUGHT AN AWKWARD MOMENT ...
MM-MMM ...
Hn... koff koff... Nnggh ......
!
ピタ PITA (HALT)
ガタ GATA (CLATTER)
HN ... KOFF ...
THE AC'S ON TOO HIGH. M-MAYBE I CAUGHT A COLD...
......

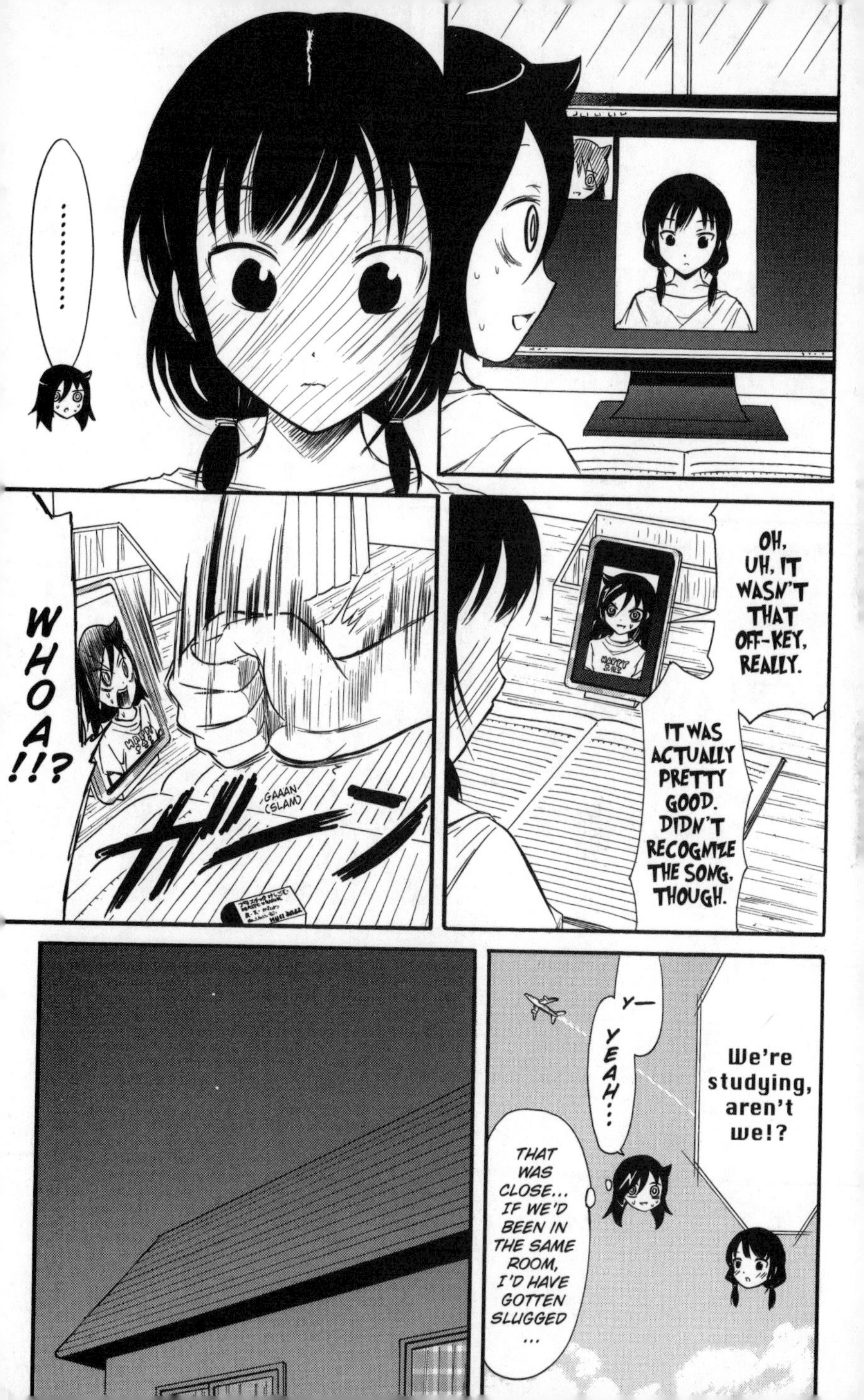

....
OH, UH, IT WASN'T THAT OFF-KEY, REALLY.
IT WAS ACTUALLY PRETTY GOOD. DIDN'T RECOGNIZE THE SONG, THOUGH.
WHOA!!?
GAAAN (SLAM)
We're studying, aren't we!?
Y— YEAH...
THAT WAS CLOSE... IF WE'D BEEN IN THE SAME ROOM, I'D HAVE GOTTEN SLUGGED...

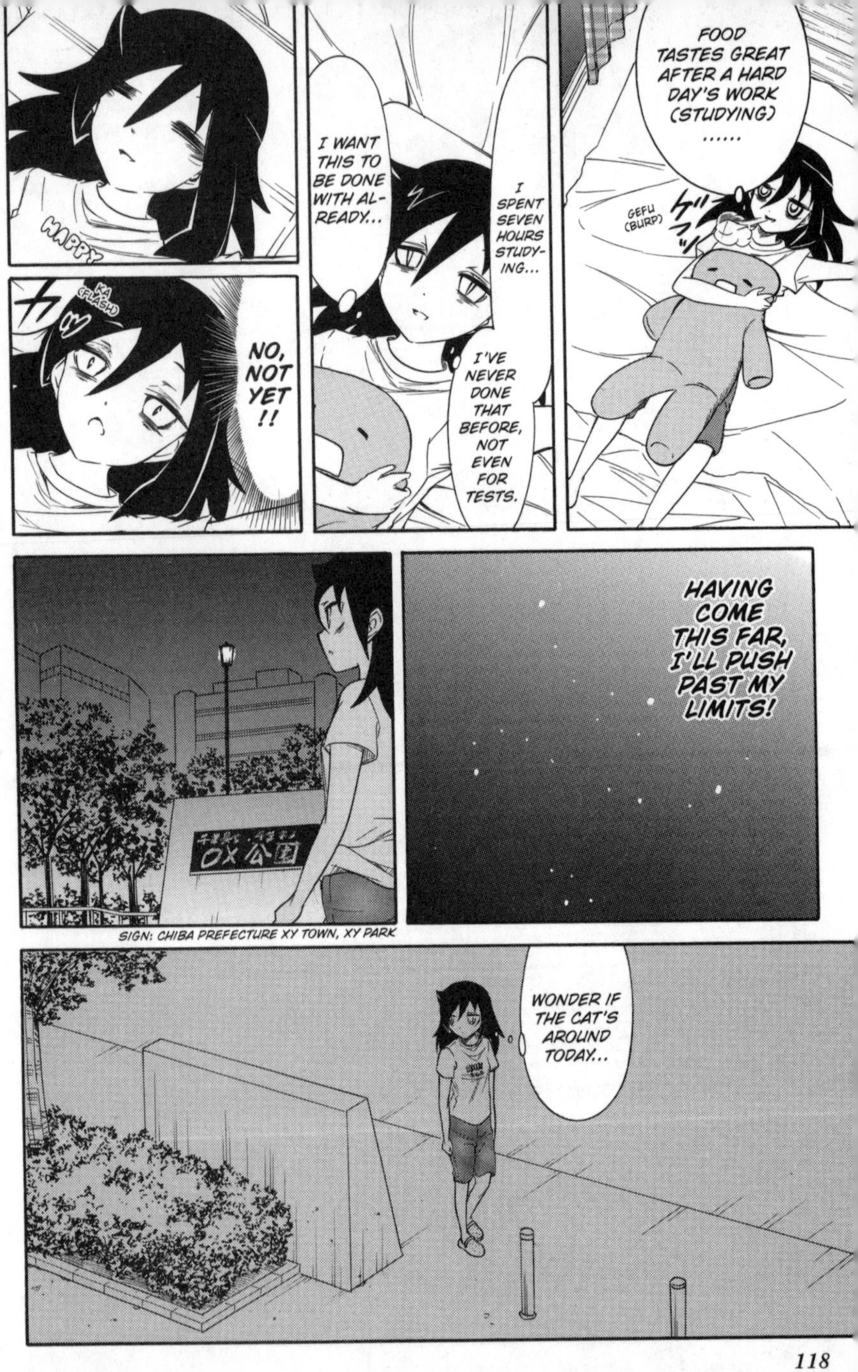
FOOD TASTES GREAT AFTER A HARD DAY'S WORK (STUDYING) ......
GEFU (BURP)
I SPENT SEVEN HOURS STUDYING...
I WANT THIS TO BE DONE WITH ALREADY...
I'VE NEVER DONE THAT BEFORE, NOT EVEN FOR TESTS.
HAPPY
KA (FLASH)
NO, NOT YET !!
HAVING COME THIS FAR, I'LL PUSH PAST MY LIMITS!
SIGN: CHIBA PREFECTURE XY TOWN, XY PARK
WONDER IF THE CAT'S AROUND TODAY...

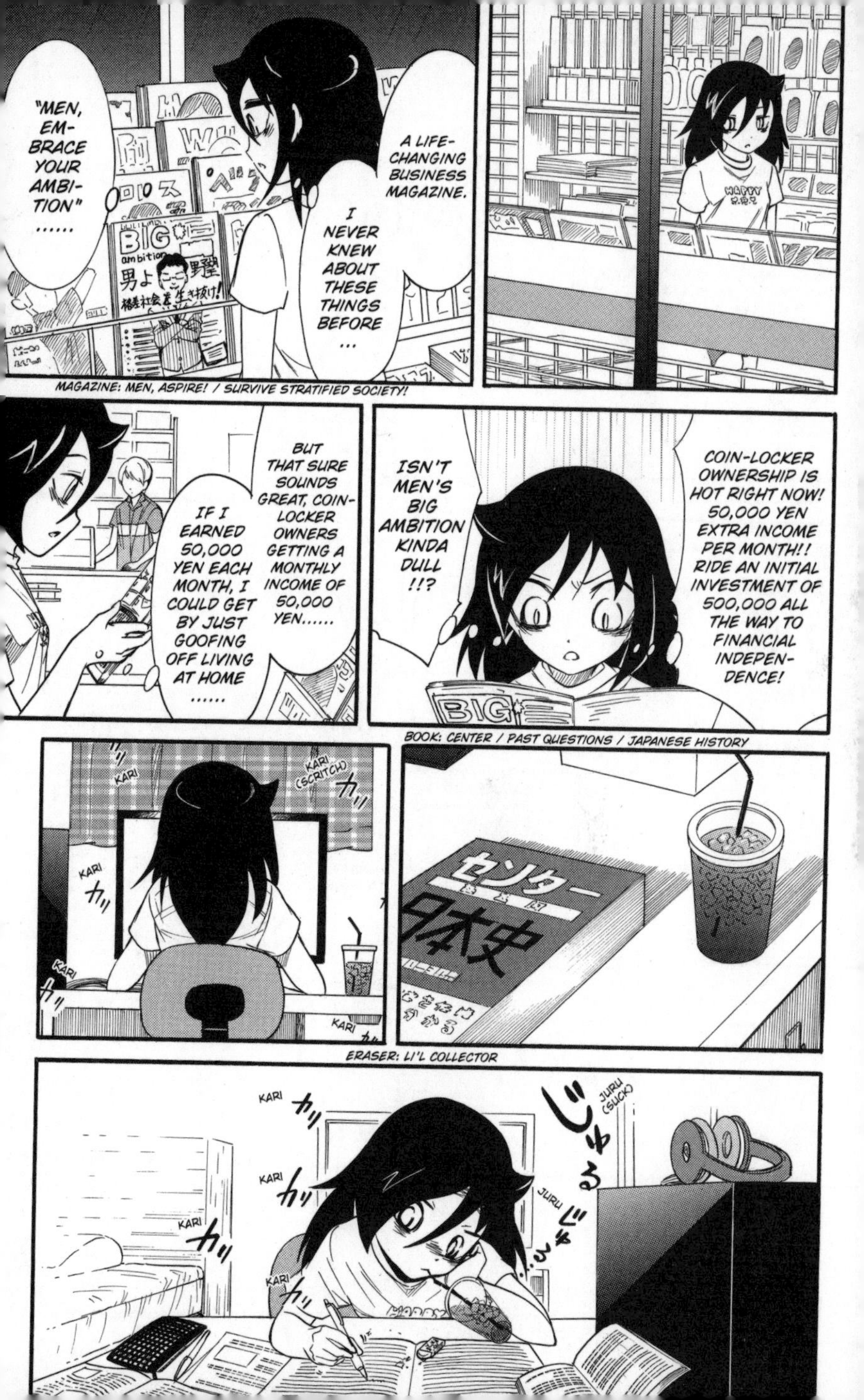
A LIFE-CHANGING BUSINESS MAGAZINE.
I NEVER KNEW ABOUT THESE THINGS BEFORE ...
"MEN, EMBRACE YOUR AMBITION" ......
BIG ambition
MAGAZINE: MEN, ASPIRE! / SURVIVE STRATIFIED SOCIETY!
COIN-LOCKER OWNERSHIP IS HOT RIGHT NOW! 50,000 YEN EXTRA INCOME PER MONTH!! RIDE AN INITIAL INVESTMENT OF 500,000 ALL THE WAY TO FINANCIAL INDEPENDENCE!
ISN'T MEN'S BIG AMBITION KINDA DULL !!?
BUT THAT SURE SOUNDS GREAT, COIN-LOCKER OWNERS GETTING A MONTHLY INCOME OF 50,000 YEN......
IF I EARNED 50,000 YEN EACH MONTH, I COULD GET BY JUST GOOFING OFF LIVING AT HOME ......
BIG
BOOK: CENTER / PAST QUESTIONS / JAPANESE HISTORY
KARI
KARI (SCRITCH)
KARI
KARI
KARI
ERASER: LI'L COLLECTOR
JURU (SUCK)
KARI
KARI
JURU
KARI
KARI

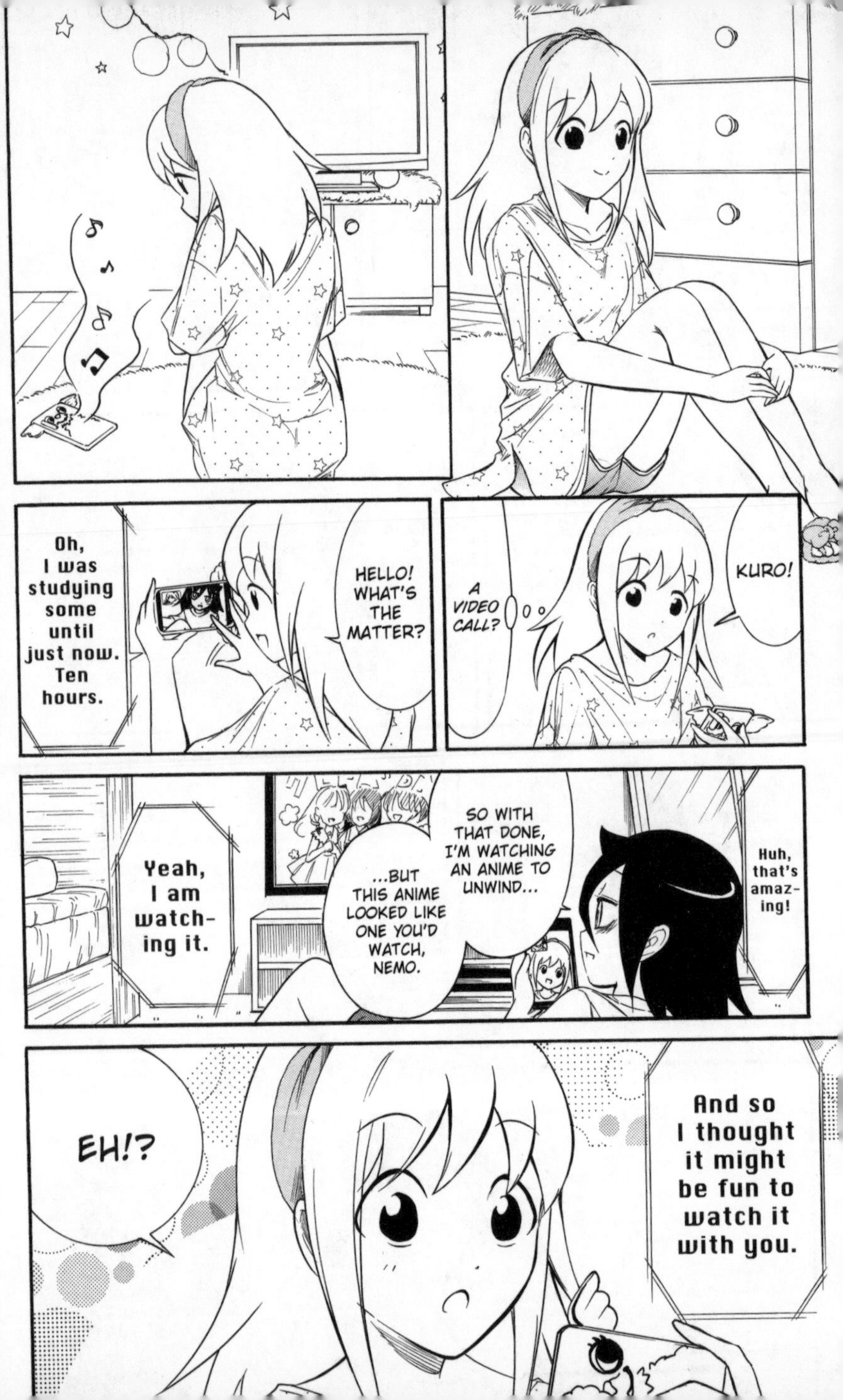
KURO!
A VIDEO CALL?
HELLO! WHAT'S THE MATTER?
Oh, I was studying some until just now. Ten hours.
Huh, that's amaz-ing!
SO WITH THAT DONE, I'M WATCHING AN ANIME TO UNWIND...
...BUT THIS ANIME LOOKED LIKE ONE YOU'D WATCH, NEMO.
Yeah, I am watch-ing it.
And so I thought it might be fun to watch it with you.
EH!?

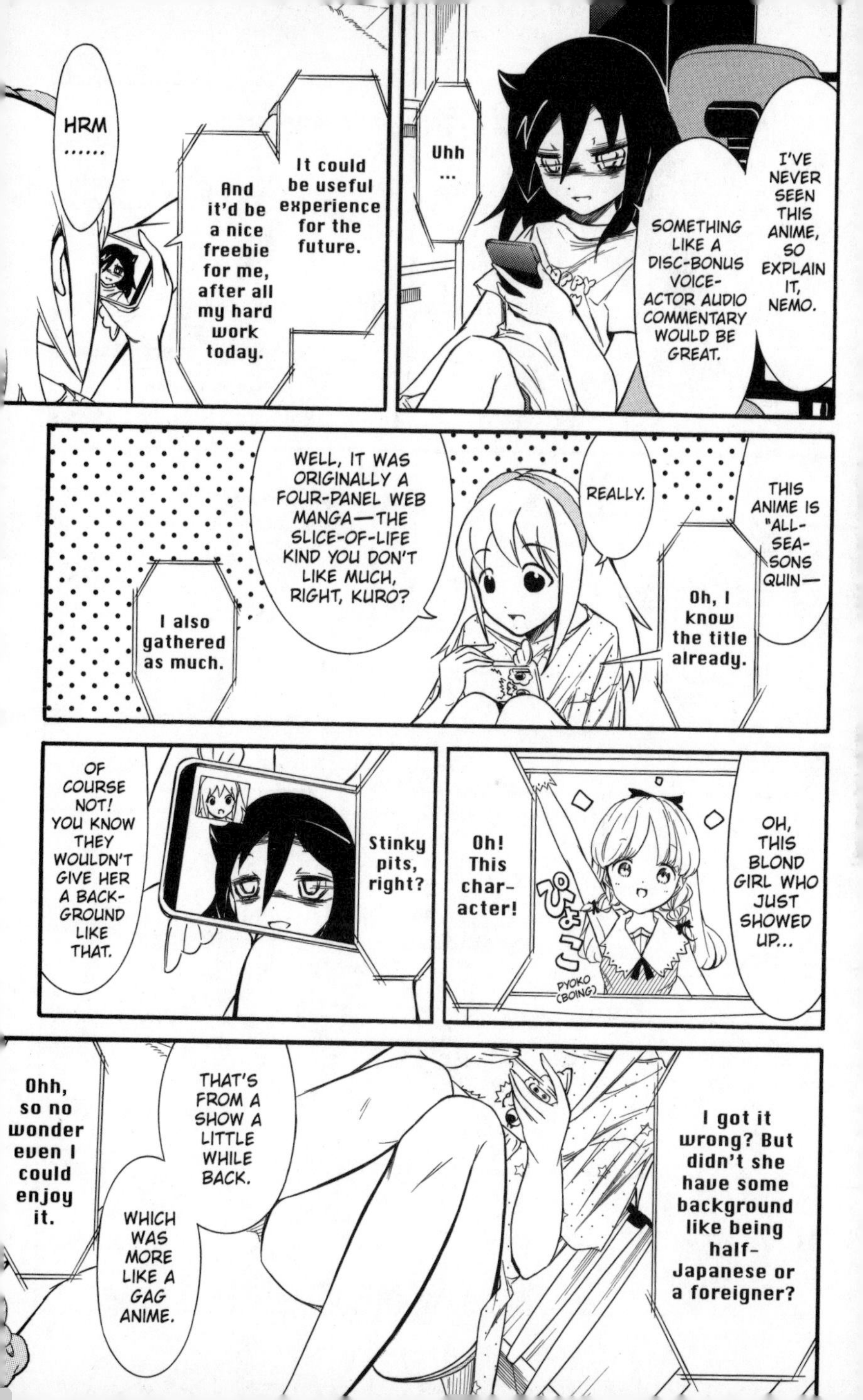
I'VE NEVER SEEN THIS ANIME, SO EXPLAIN IT, NEMO.
SOMETHING LIKE A DISC-BONUS VOICE-ACTOR AUDIO COMMENTARY WOULD BE GREAT.
Uhh ...
It could be useful experience for the future.
And it'd be a nice freebie for me, after all my hard work today.
HRM ......
THIS ANIME IS "ALL-SEASONS QUIN—
Oh, I know the title already.
REALLY.
WELL, IT WAS ORIGINALLY A FOUR-PANEL WEB MANGA—THE SLICE-OF-LIFE KIND YOU DON'T LIKE MUCH, RIGHT, KURO?
I also gathered as much.
OH, THIS BLOND GIRL WHO JUST SHOWED UP...
Oh! This character!
ぴょこ
PYOKO (BOING)
Stinky pits, right?
OF COURSE NOT! YOU KNOW THEY WOULDN'T GIVE HER A BACKGROUND LIKE THAT.
I got it wrong? But didn't she have some background like being half-Japanese or a foreigner?
THAT'S FROM A SHOW A LITTLE WHILE BACK.
WHICH WAS MORE LIKE A GAG ANIME.
Ohh, so no wonder even I could enjoy it.

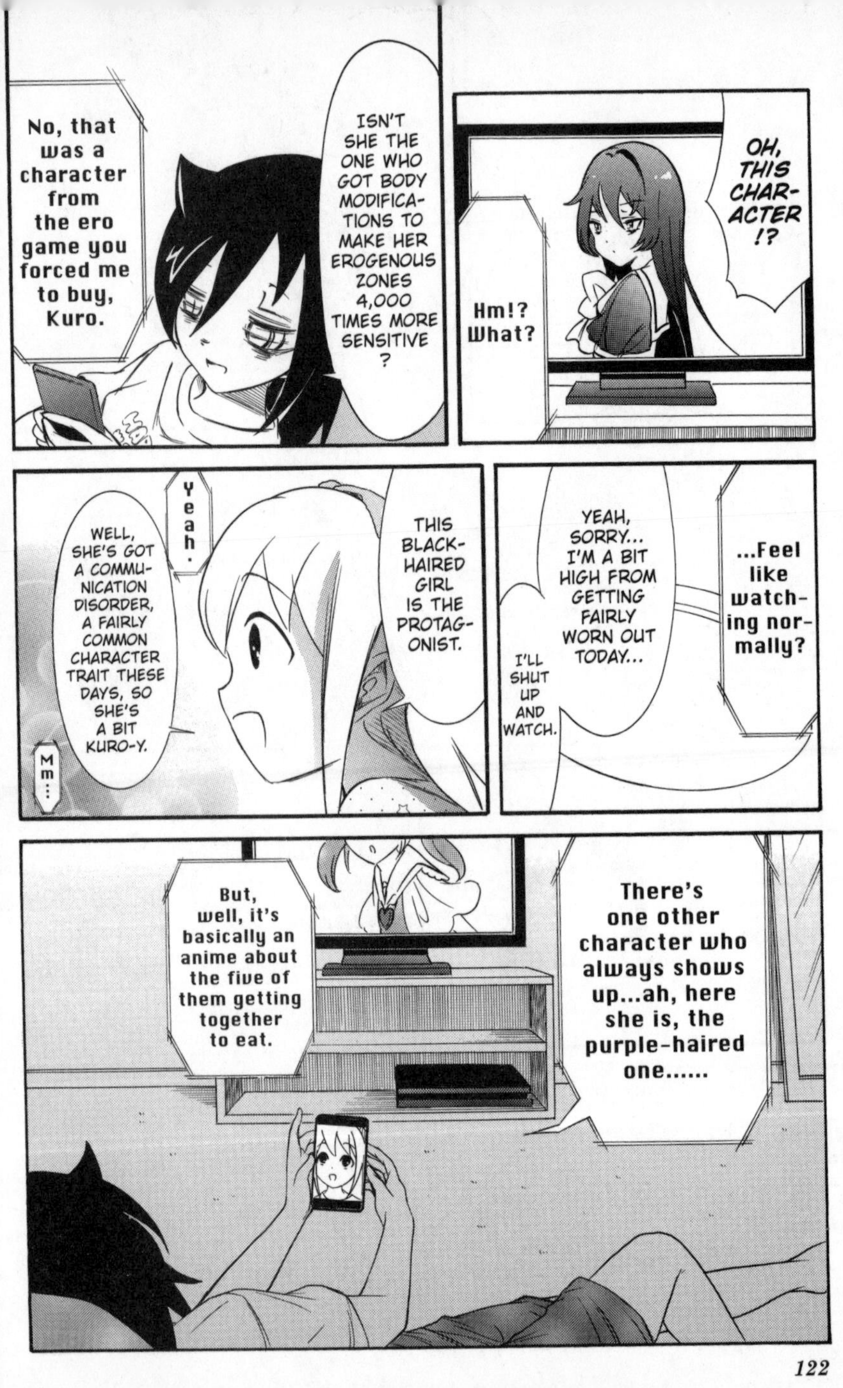
OH, THIS CHARACTER!?
Hm!? What?
ISN'T SHE THE ONE WHO GOT BODY MODIFICATIONS TO MAKE HER EROGENOUS ZONES 4,000 TIMES MORE SENSITIVE?
No, that was a character from the ero game you forced me to buy, Kuro.
...Feel like watching normally?
YEAH, SORRY... I'M A BIT HIGH FROM GETTING FAIRLY WORN OUT TODAY...
I'LL SHUT UP AND WATCH.
THIS BLACK-HAIRED GIRL IS THE PROTAGONIST.
Yeah.
WELL, SHE'S GOT A COMMUNICATION DISORDER, A FAIRLY COMMON CHARACTER TRAIT THESE DAYS, SO SHE'S A BIT KURO-Y.
Mm...
There's one other character who always shows up...ah, here she is, the purple-haired one......
But, well, it's basically an anime about the five of them getting together to eat.

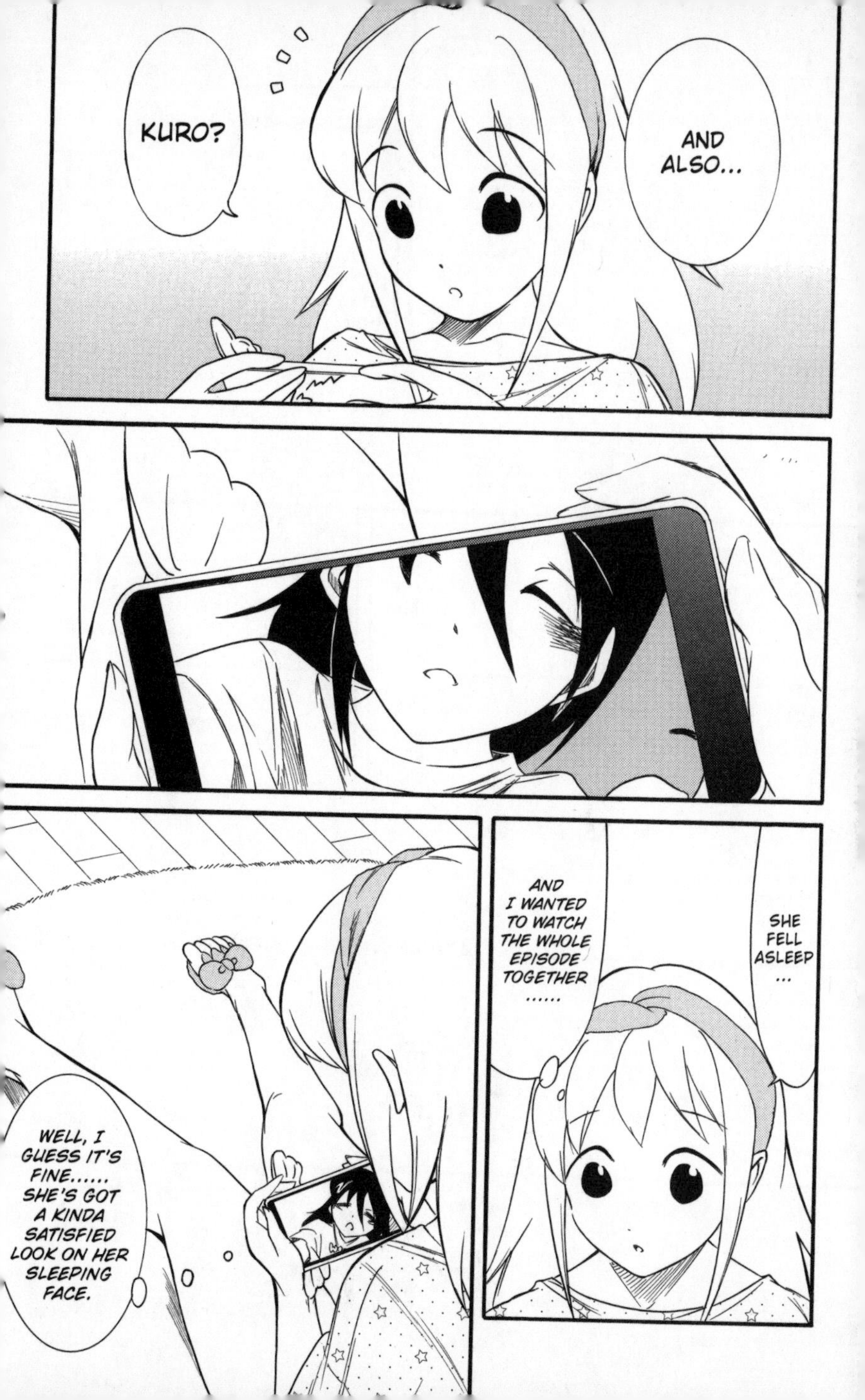
AND ALSO...
KURO?
SHE FELL ASLEEP ...
AND I WANTED TO WATCH THE WHOLE EPISODE TOGETHER ......
WELL, I GUESS IT'S FINE...... SHE'S GOT A KINDA SATISFIED LOOK ON HER SLEEPING FACE.

No Matter How I Look at It, It's You Guys' Fault I'm Not Popular!

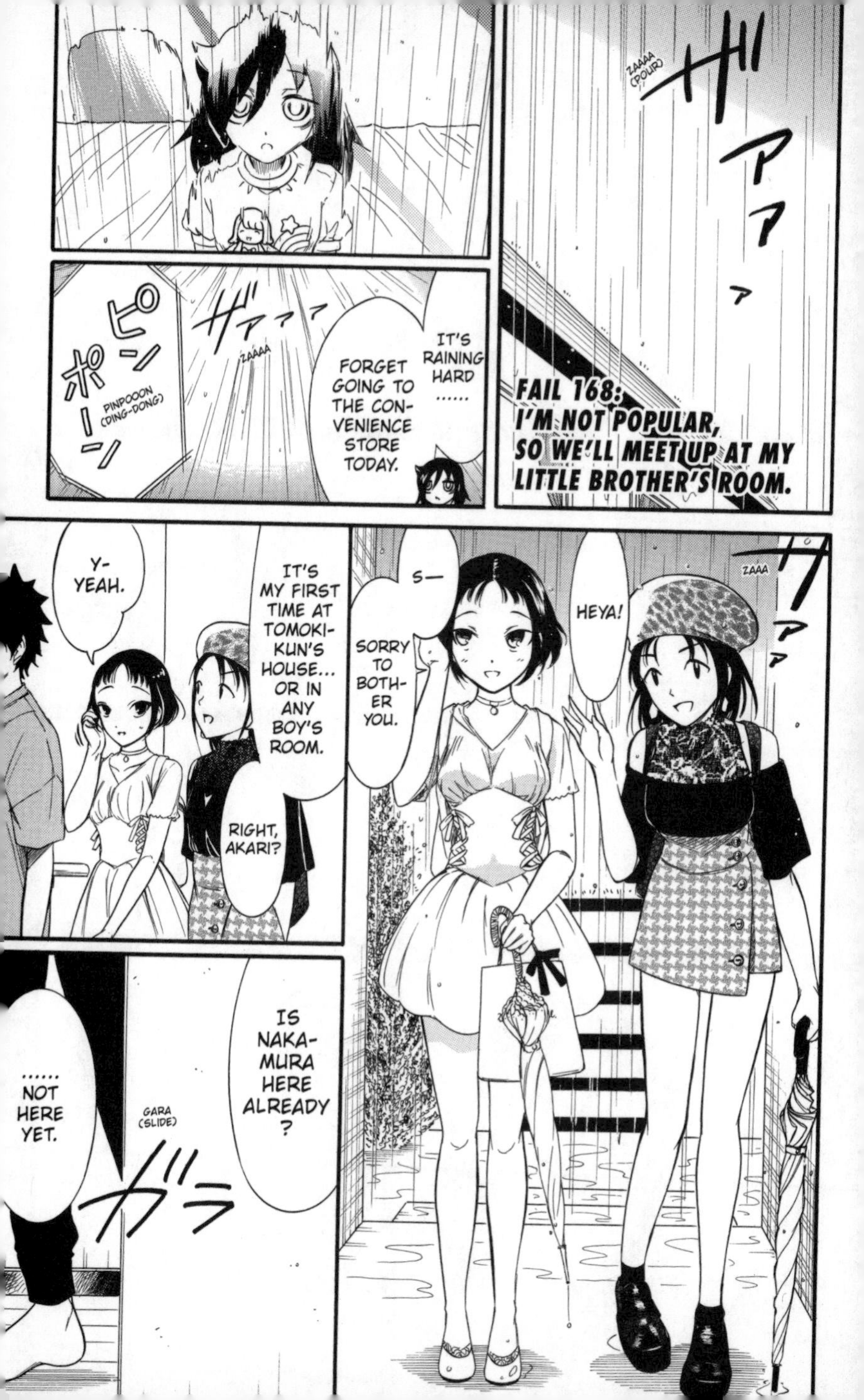
ZAAAA (POUR)
FAIL 168: I'M NOT POPULAR, SO WE'LL MEET UP AT MY LITTLE BROTHER'S ROOM.
IT'S RAINING HARD ......
FORGET GOING TO THE CON-VENIENCE STORE TODAY.
ZAAAA
PINPOOON (DING-DONG)
ZAAA
HEYA!
S—
SORRY TO BOTH-ER YOU.
IT'S MY FIRST TIME AT TOMOKI-KUN'S HOUSE... OR IN ANY BOY'S ROOM.
RIGHT, AKARI?
Y-YEAH.
IS NAKA-MURA HERE ALREADY?
GARA (SLIDE)
...... NOT HERE YET.

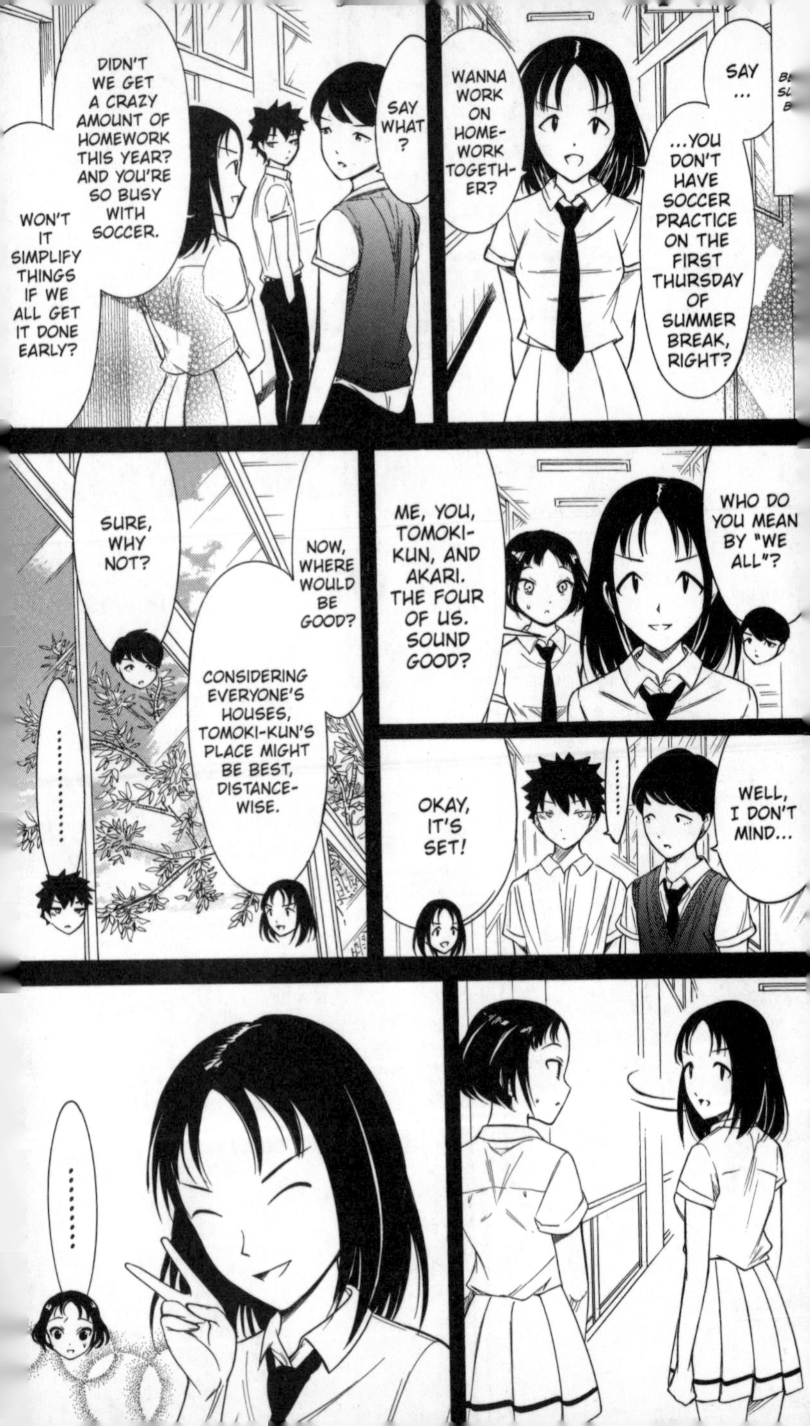
SAY ...
...YOU DON'T HAVE SOCCER PRACTICE ON THE FIRST THURSDAY OF SUMMER BREAK, RIGHT?
WANNA WORK ON HOME-WORK TOGETH-ER?
SAY WHAT?
DIDN'T WE GET A CRAZY AMOUNT OF HOMEWORK THIS YEAR? AND YOU'RE SO BUSY WITH SOCCER.
WON'T IT SIMPLIFY THINGS IF WE ALL GET IT DONE EARLY?
WHO DO YOU MEAN BY "WE ALL"?
ME, YOU, TOMOKI-KUN, AND AKARI. THE FOUR OF US. SOUND GOOD?
WELL, I DON'T MIND...
......
OKAY, IT'S SET!
NOW, WHERE WOULD BE GOOD?
SURE, WHY NOT?
CONSIDERING EVERYONE'S HOUSES, TOMOKI-KUN'S PLACE MIGHT BE BEST, DISTANCE-WISE.
....
....

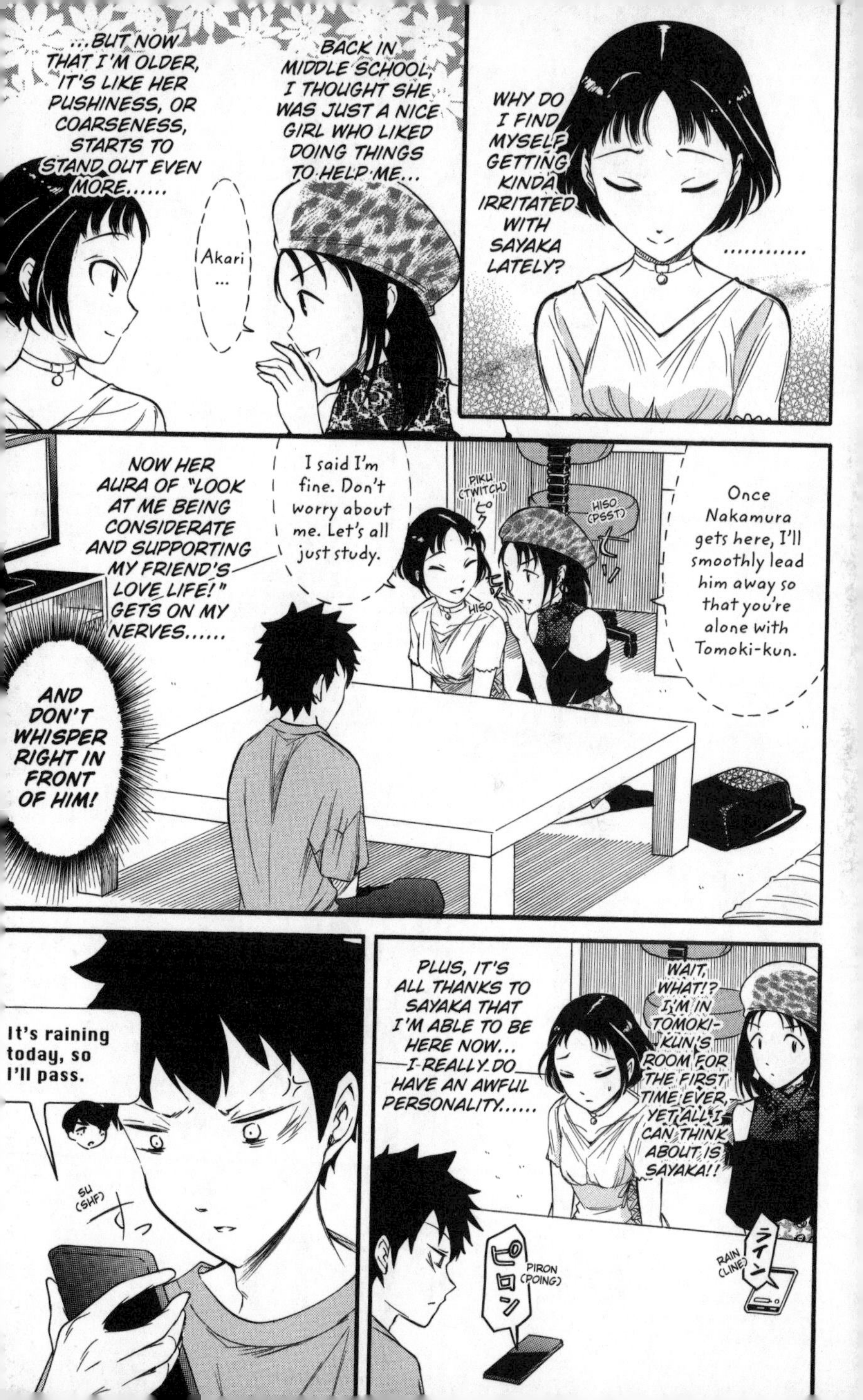
WHY DO I FIND MYSELF GETTING KINDA IRRITATED WITH SAYAKA LATELY?
....
BACK IN MIDDLE SCHOOL, I THOUGHT SHE WAS JUST A NICE GIRL WHO LIKED DOING THINGS TO HELP ME...
...BUT NOW THAT I'M OLDER, IT'S LIKE HER PUSHINESS, OR COARSENESS, STARTS TO STAND OUT EVEN MORE......
Akari ...
Once Nakamura gets here, I'll smoothly lead him away so that you're alone with Tomoki-kun.
HISO (PSST)
HISO
PIKU (TWITCH)
I said I'm fine. Don't worry about me. Let's all just study.
NOW HER AURA OF "LOOK AT ME BEING CONSIDERATE AND SUPPORTING MY FRIEND'S LOVE LIFE!" GETS ON MY NERVES......
AND DON'T WHISPER RIGHT IN FRONT OF HIM!
WAIT, WHAT!? I'M IN TOMOKI-KUN'S ROOM FOR THE FIRST TIME EVER, YET ALL I CAN THINK ABOUT IS SAYAKA!!
PLUS, IT'S ALL THANKS TO SAYAKA THAT I'M ABLE TO BE HERE NOW... I REALLY DO HAVE AN AWFUL PERSONALITY......
RAIN (LINE)
ライン
PIRON (POING)
ピロン
It's raining today, so I'll pass.
SU (SHF)

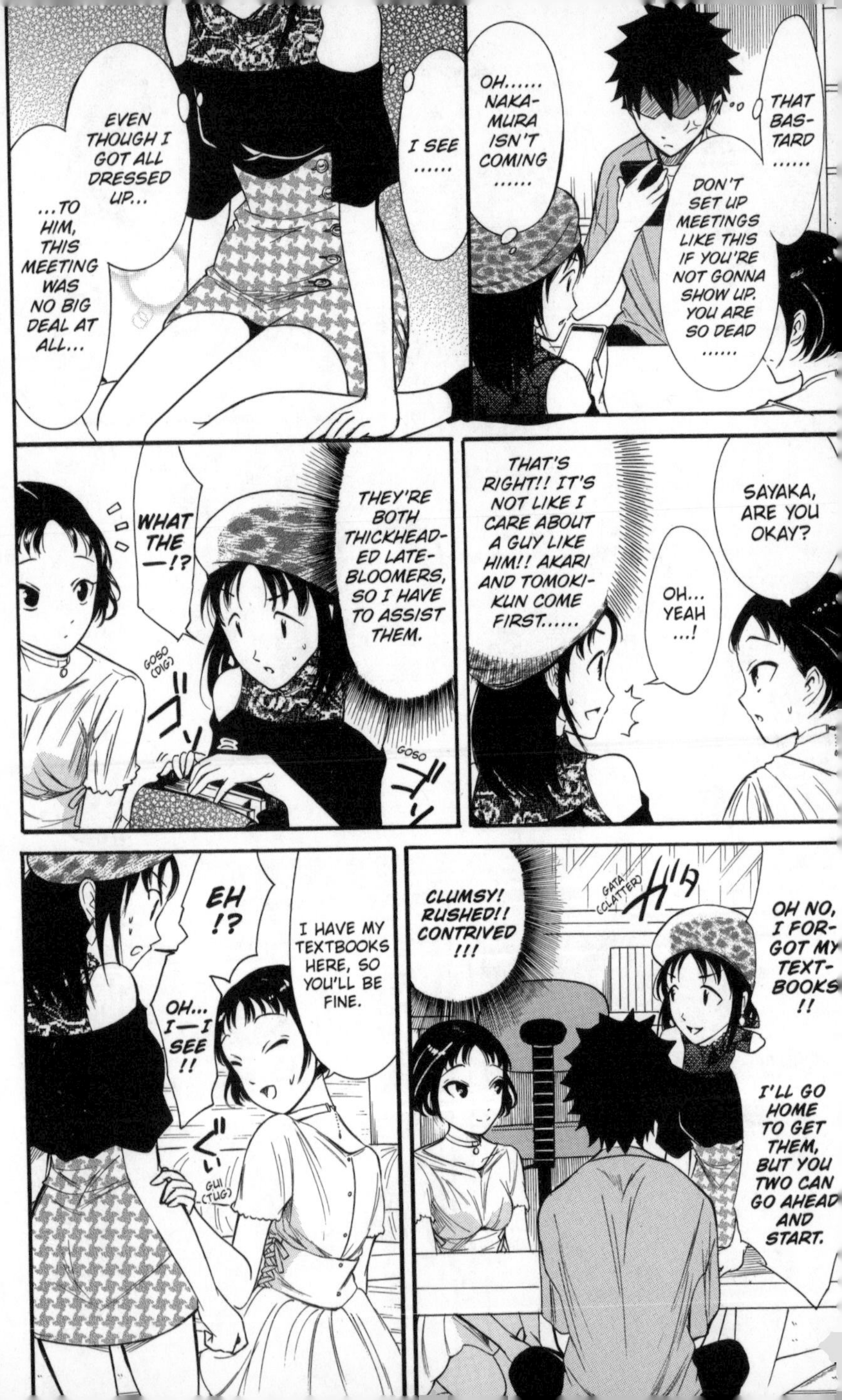
THAT BASTARD......
DON'T SET UP MEETINGS LIKE THIS IF YOU'RE NOT GONNA SHOW UP. YOU ARE SO DEAD......
OH...... NAKAMURA ISN'T COMING......
I SEE......
EVEN THOUGH I GOT ALL DRESSED UP...
...TO HIM, THIS MEETING WAS NO BIG DEAL AT ALL...
SAYAKA, ARE YOU OKAY?
OH... YEAH ...!
THAT'S RIGHT!! IT'S NOT LIKE I CARE ABOUT A GUY LIKE HIM!! AKARI AND TOMOKI-KUN COME FIRST......
THEY'RE BOTH THICKHEADED LATE-BLOOMERS, SO I HAVE TO ASSIST THEM.
WHAT THE—!?
GOSO (DIG)
GOSO
OH NO, I FORGOT MY TEXTBOOKS!!
GATA (CLATTER)
CLUMSY! RUSHED!! CONTRIVED!!!
I'LL GO HOME TO GET THEM, BUT YOU TWO CAN GO AHEAD AND START.
I HAVE MY TEXTBOOKS HERE, SO YOU'LL BE FINE.
EH!?
OH... I—I SEE!!
GUI (TUG)

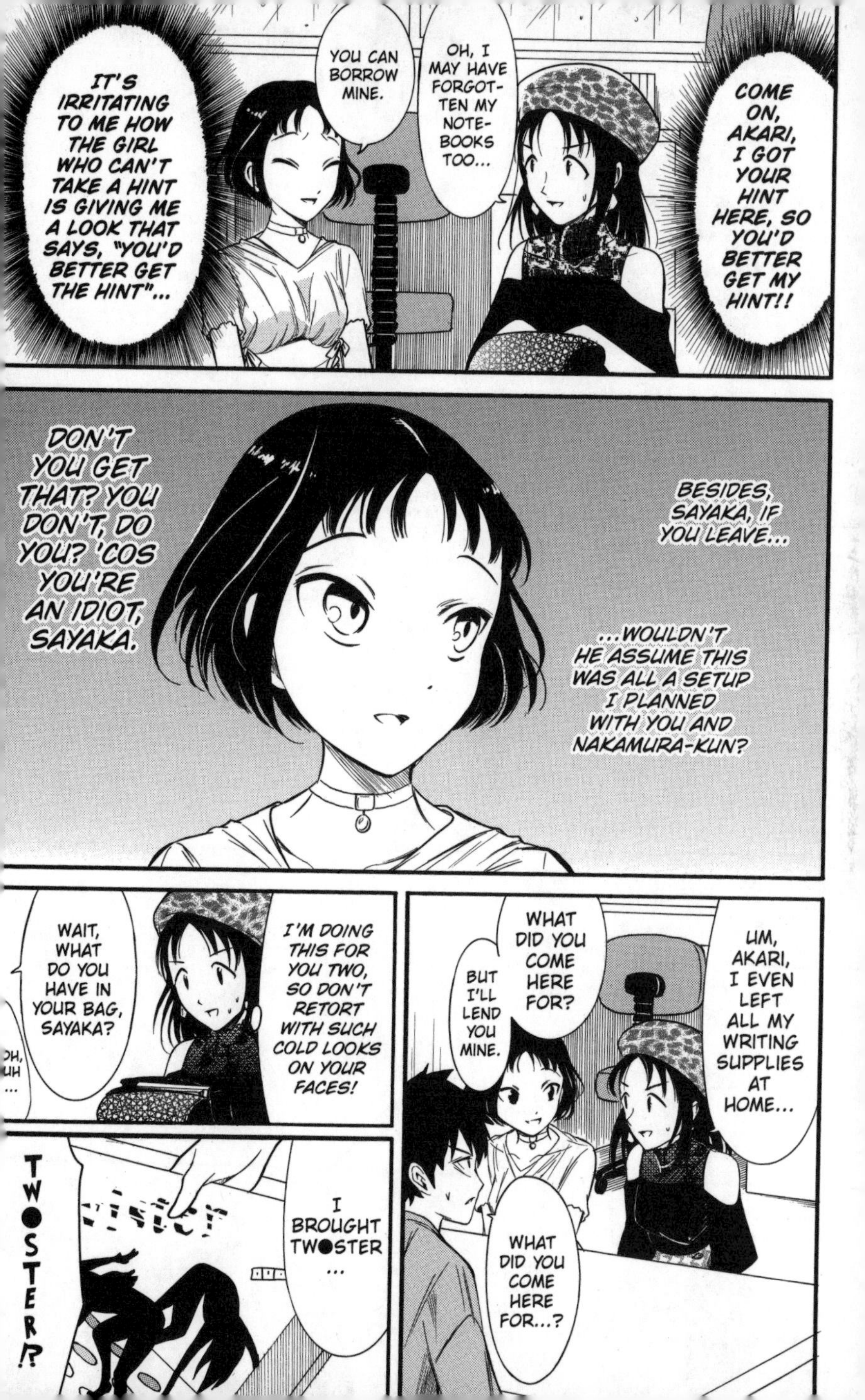
COME ON, AKARI, I GOT YOUR HINT HERE, SO YOU'D BETTER GET MY HINT!!
OH, I MAY HAVE FORGOT-TEN MY NOTE-BOOKS TOO...
YOU CAN BORROW MINE.
IT'S IRRITATING TO ME HOW THE GIRL WHO CAN'T TAKE A HINT IS GIVING ME A LOOK THAT SAYS, "YOU'D BETTER GET THE HINT"...
BESIDES, SAYAKA, IF YOU LEAVE...
...WOULDN'T HE ASSUME THIS WAS ALL A SETUP I PLANNED WITH YOU AND NAKAMURA-KUN?
DON'T YOU GET THAT? YOU DON'T, DO YOU? 'COS YOU'RE AN IDIOT, SAYAKA.
UM, AKARI, I EVEN LEFT ALL MY WRITING SUPPLIES AT HOME...
WHAT DID YOU COME HERE FOR?
BUT I'LL LEND YOU MINE.
WHAT DID YOU COME HERE FOR...?
I'M DOING THIS FOR YOU TWO, SO DON'T RETORT WITH SUCH COLD LOOKS ON YOUR FACES!
WAIT, WHAT DO YOU HAVE IN YOUR BAG, SAYAKA?
OH, UH...
I BROUGHT TW●STER...
TW●STER!?

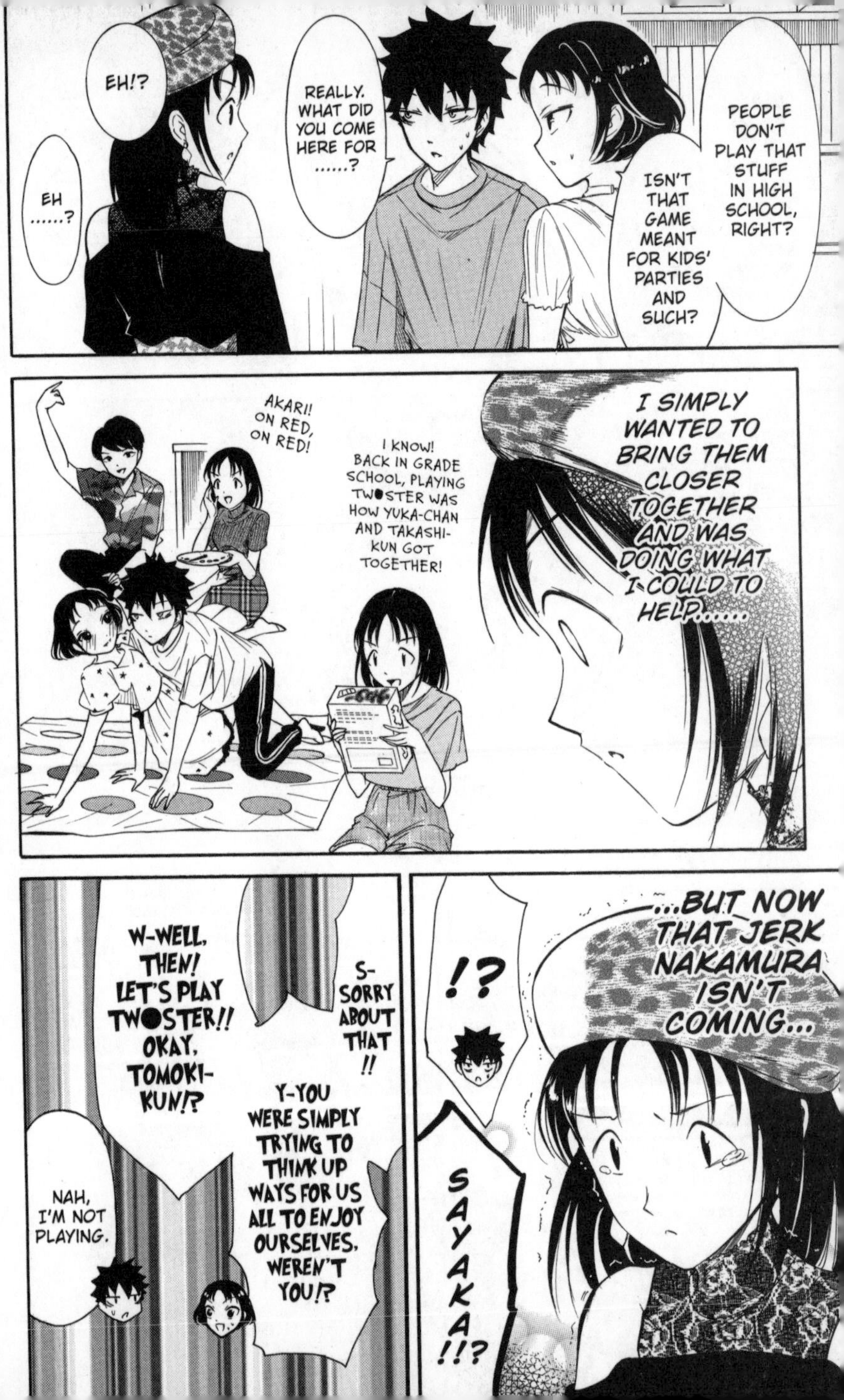
PEOPLE DON'T PLAY THAT STUFF IN HIGH SCHOOL, RIGHT?
ISN'T THAT GAME MEANT FOR KIDS' PARTIES AND SUCH?
REALLY. WHAT DID YOU COME HERE FOR ......?
EH!?
EH ......?
I SIMPLY WANTED TO BRING THEM CLOSER TOGETHER AND WAS DOING WHAT I COULD TO HELP......
I KNOW! BACK IN GRADE SCHOOL, PLAYING TWOSTER WAS HOW YUKA-CHAN AND TAKASHI-KUN GOT TOGETHER!
AKARI!! ON RED, ON RED!
...BUT NOW THAT JERK NAKAMURA ISN'T COMING...
!?
SAYAKA!!?
S-SORRY ABOUT THAT!!
W-WELL, THEN! LET'S PLAY TWOSTER!! OKAY, TOMOKI-KUN!?
Y-YOU WERE SIMPLY TRYING TO THINK UP WAYS FOR US ALL TO ENJOY OURSELVES, WEREN'T YOU!?
NAH, I'M NOT PLAYING.

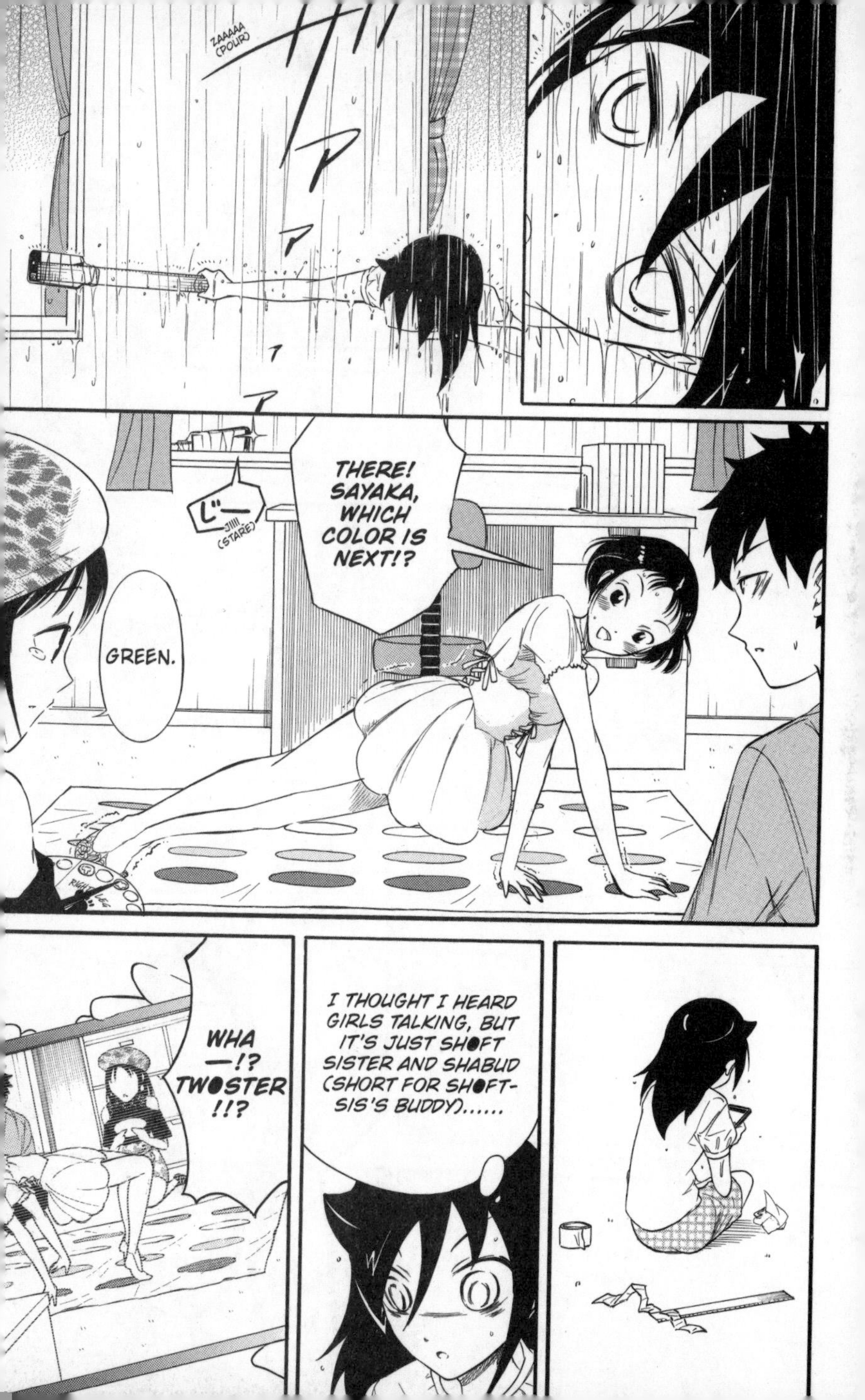
ZAAAAA (POUR)
THERE! SAYAKA, WHICH COLOR IS NEXT!?
じー
JIIII (STARE)
GREEN.
I THOUGHT I HEARD GIRLS TALKING, BUT IT'S JUST SHOFT SISTER AND SHABUD (SHORT FOR SHOFT-SIS'S BUDDY)......
WHA—!? TWOSTER!!?

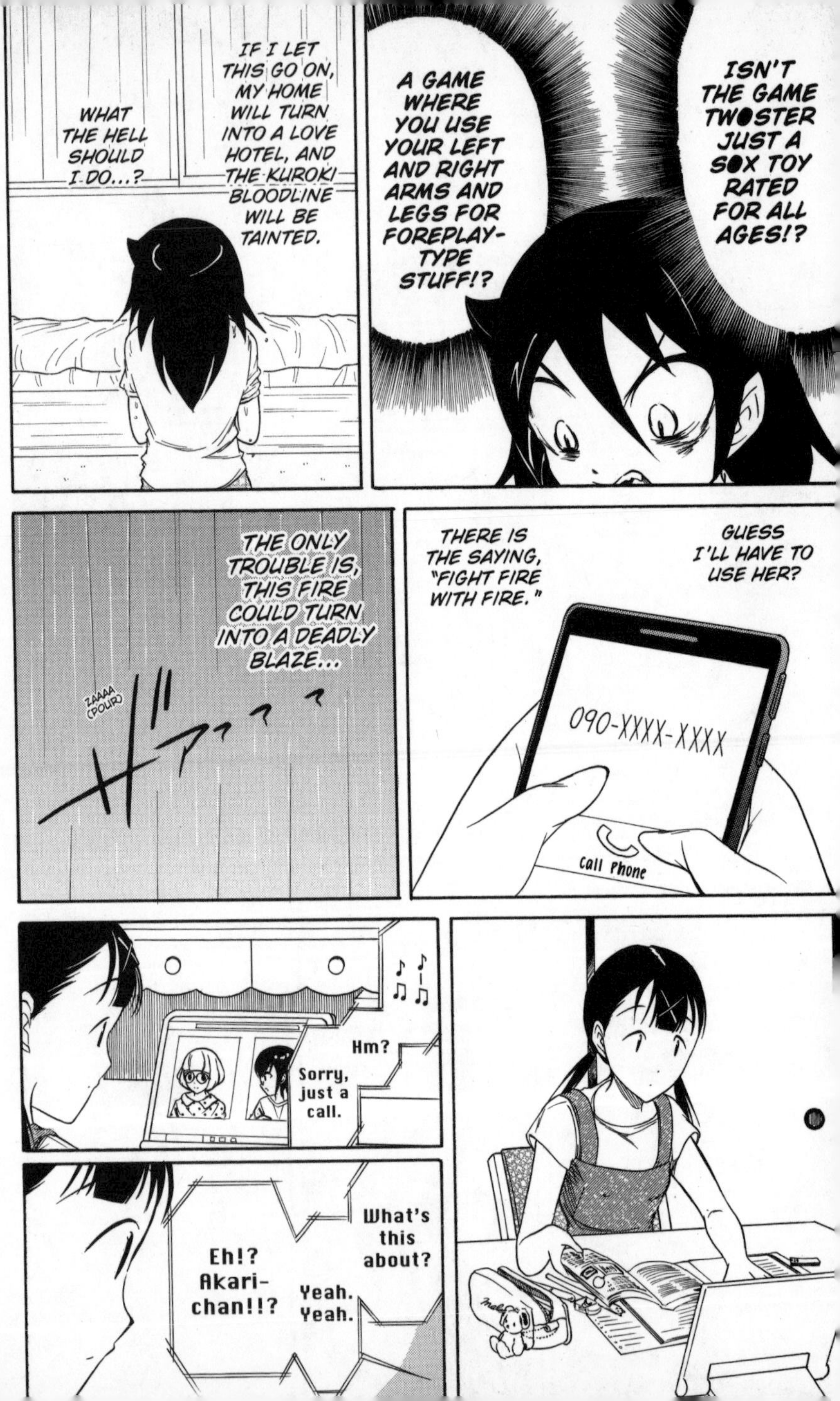
ISN'T THE GAME TWOSTER JUST A S●X TOY RATED FOR ALL AGES!?
A GAME WHERE YOU USE YOUR LEFT AND RIGHT ARMS AND LEGS FOR FOREPLAY-TYPE STUFF!?
IF I LET THIS GO ON, MY HOME WILL TURN INTO A LOVE HOTEL, AND THE KUROKI BLOODLINE WILL BE TAINTED.
WHAT THE HELL SHOULD I DO...?
GUESS I'LL HAVE TO USE HER?
THERE IS THE SAYING, "FIGHT FIRE WITH FIRE."
090-XXXX-XXXX
Call Phone
THE ONLY TROUBLE IS, THIS FIRE COULD TURN INTO A DEADLY BLAZE...
ZAAAA (POUR)
Hm?
Sorry, just a call.
What's this about?
Eh!? Akari-chan!!?
Yeah. Yeah.

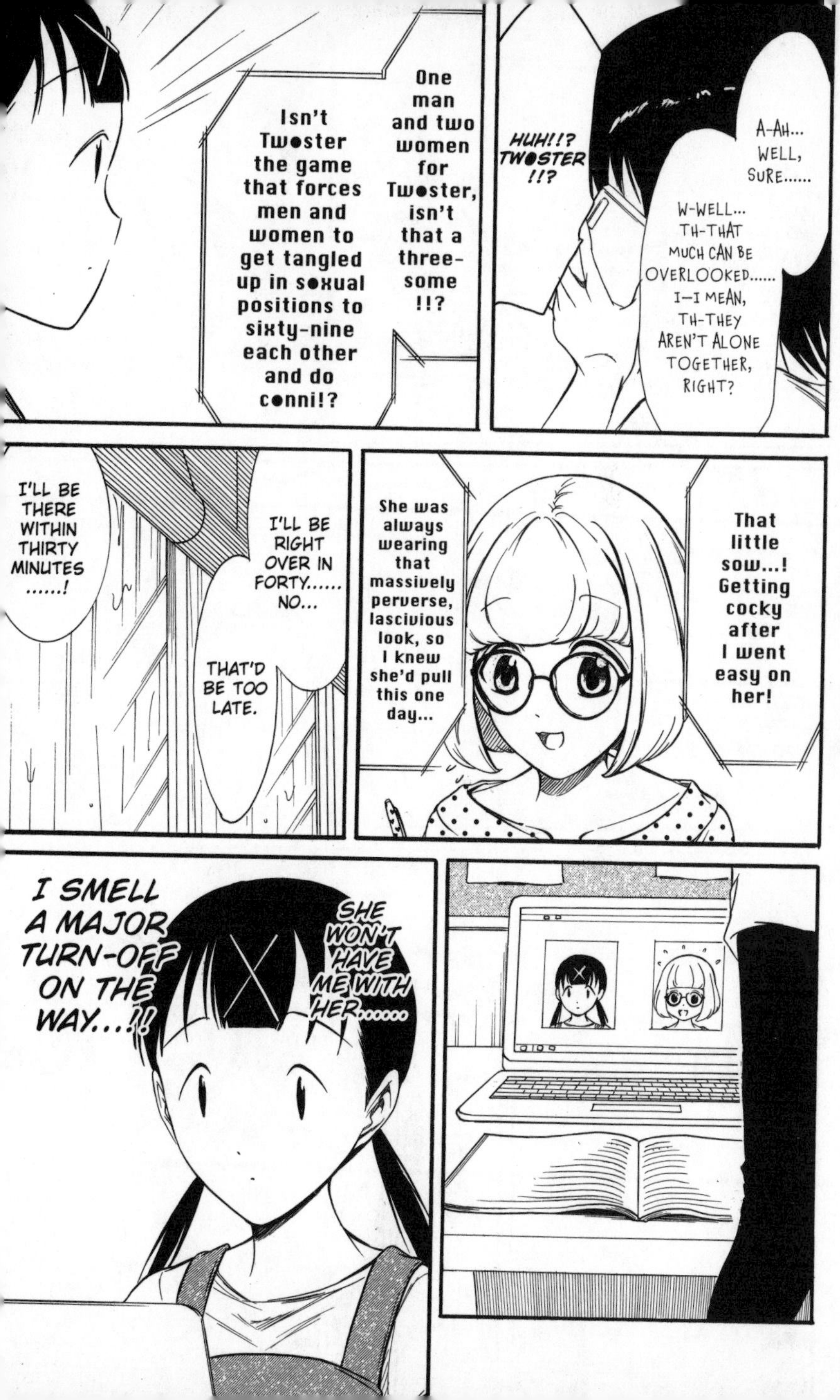
A-AH... WELL, SURE......
W-WELL... TH-THAT MUCH CAN BE OVERLOOKED...... I—I MEAN, TH-THEY AREN'T ALONE TOGETHER, RIGHT?
HUH!!? TW●STER !!?
One man and two women for Tw●ster, isn't that a three-some !!?
Isn't Tw●ster the game that forces men and women to get tangled up in s●xual positions to sixty-nine each other and do c●nni!?
That little sow...! Getting cocky after I went easy on her!
She was always wearing that massively perverse, lascivious look, so I knew she'd pull this one day...
I'LL BE RIGHT OVER IN FORTY...... NO...
THAT'D BE TOO LATE.
I'LL BE THERE WITHIN THIRTY MINUTES ......!
SHE WON'T HAVE ME WITH HER.......
I SMELL A MAJOR TURN-OFF ON THE WAY...!!

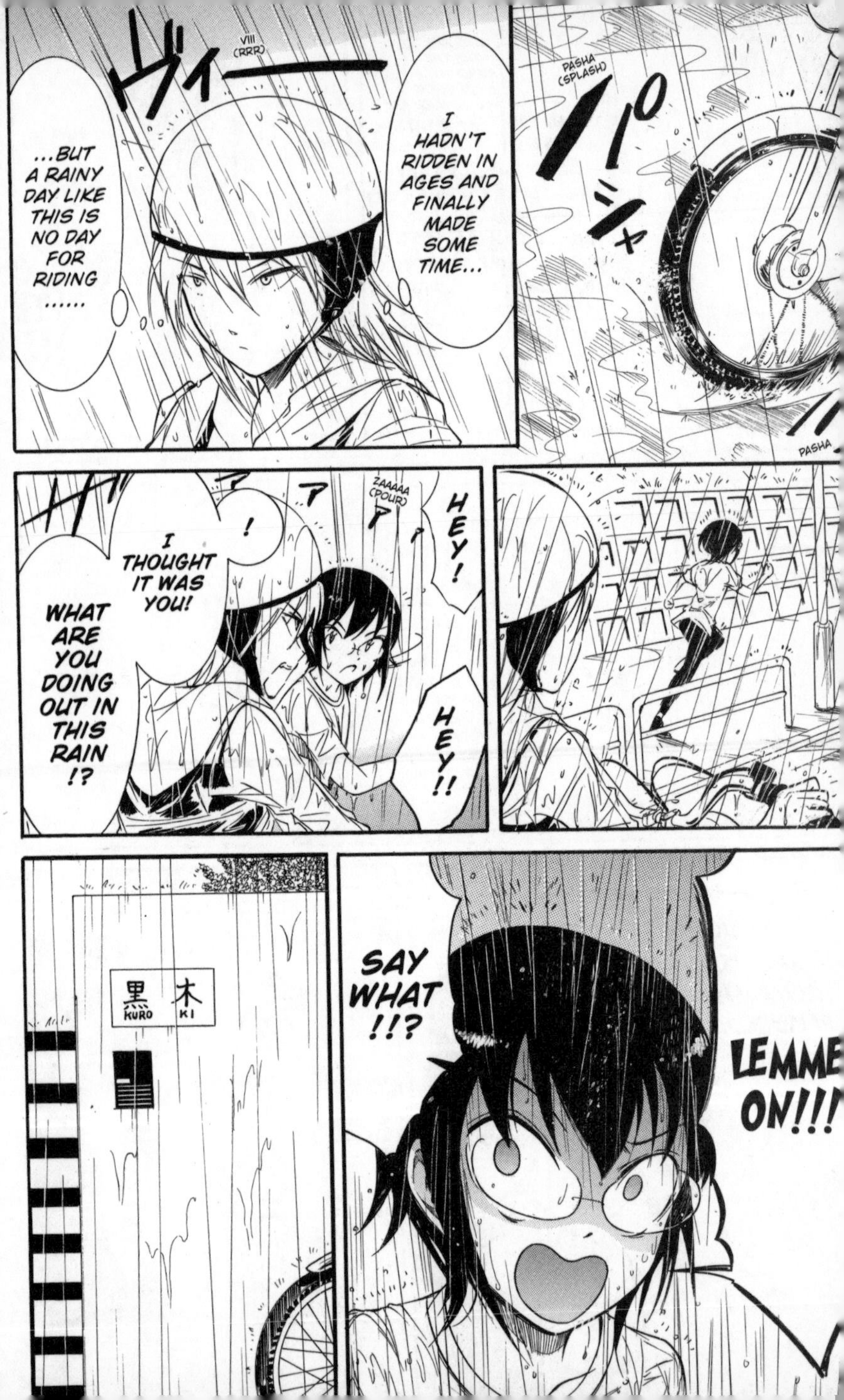
PASHA (SPLASH)
PASHA
VIII (RRR)
I HADN'T RIDDEN IN AGES AND FINALLY MADE SOME TIME...
...BUT A RAINY DAY LIKE THIS IS NO DAY FOR RIDING ......
ZAAAAA (POUR)
HEY!
HEY!!
!
I THOUGHT IT WAS YOU!
WHAT ARE YOU DOING OUT IN THIS RAIN !?
LEMME ON!!!
SAY WHAT !!?
黒木
KURO KI

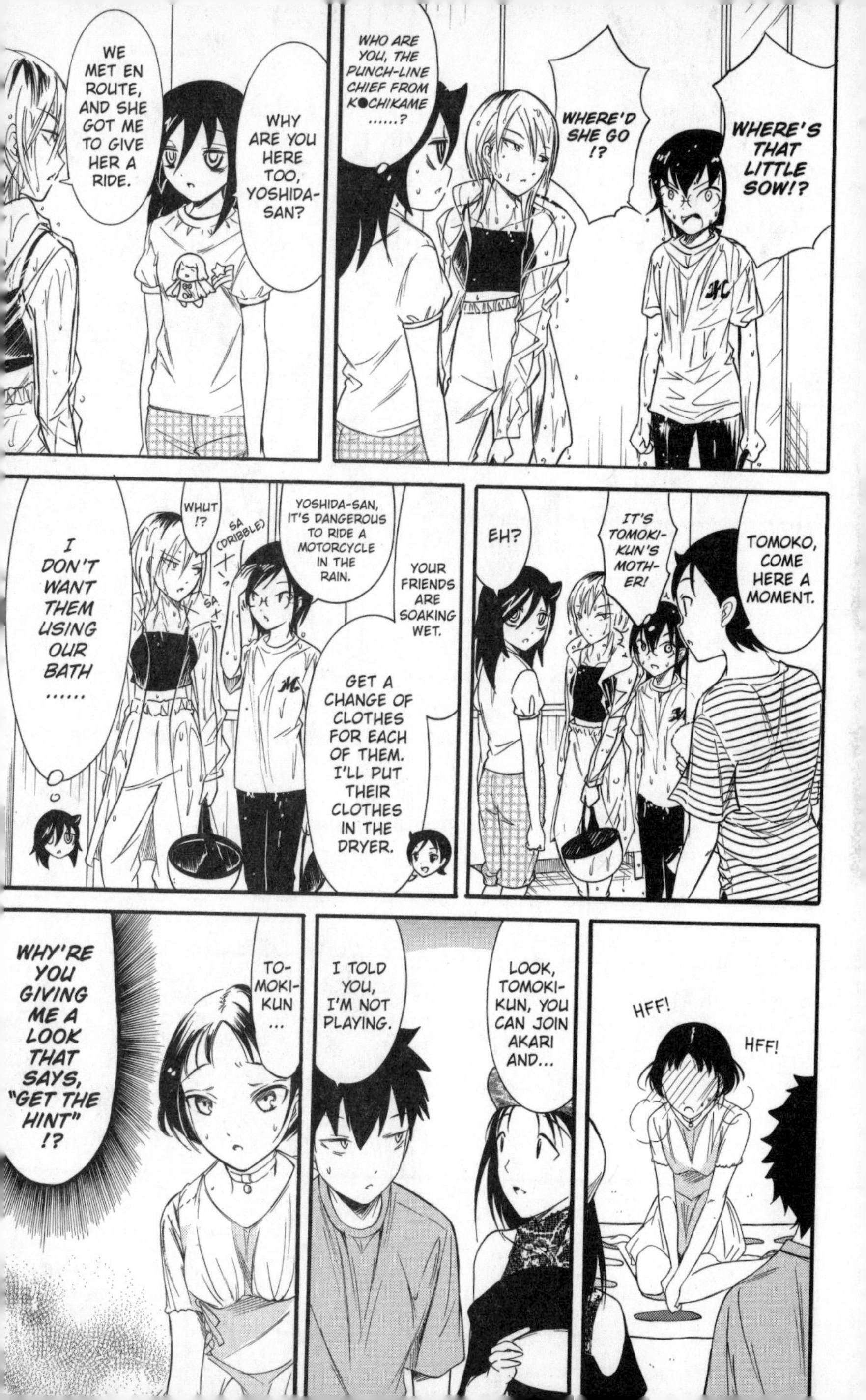
WHERE'S THAT LITTLE SOW!?
WHERE'D SHE GO !?
WHO ARE YOU, THE PUNCH-LINE CHIEF FROM K●CHIKAME ......?
WHY ARE YOU HERE TOO, YOSHIDA-SAN?
WE MET EN ROUTE, AND SHE GOT ME TO GIVE HER A RIDE.
TOMOKO, COME HERE A MOMENT.
IT'S TOMOKI-KUN'S MOTH-ER!
EH?
YOSHIDA-SAN, IT'S DANGEROUS TO RIDE A MOTORCYCLE IN THE RAIN.
YOUR FRIENDS ARE SOAKING WET.
GET A CHANGE OF CLOTHES FOR EACH OF THEM. I'LL PUT THEIR CLOTHES IN THE DRYER.
WHUT !?
SA (DRIBBLE)
SA
I DON'T WANT THEM USING OUR BATH ......
HFF!
HFF!
LOOK, TOMOKI-KUN, YOU CAN JOIN AKARI AND...
I TOLD YOU, I'M NOT PLAYING.
TO-MOKI-KUN ...
WHY'RE YOU GIVING ME A LOOK THAT SAYS, "GET THE HINT" !?

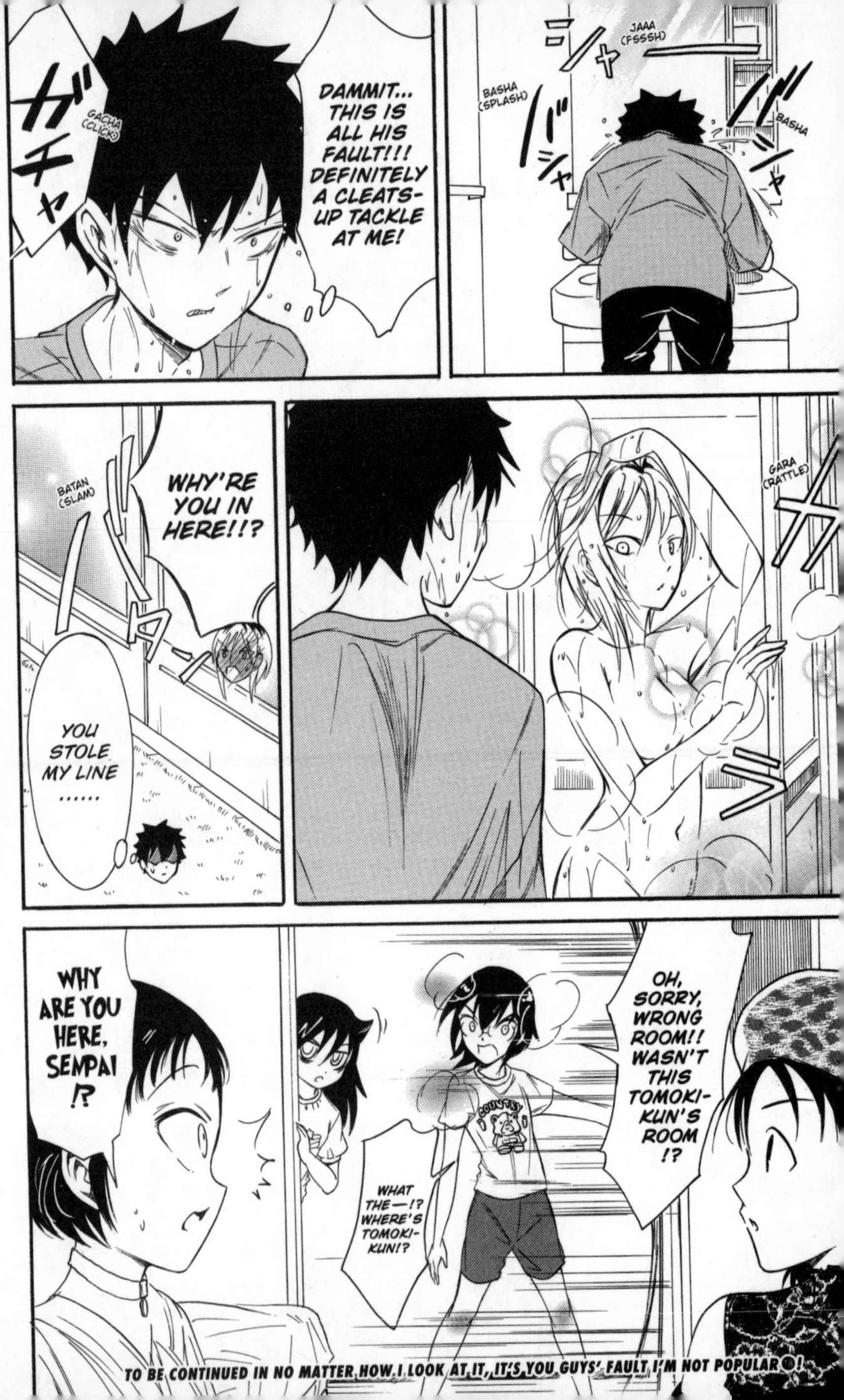
JAAA (FSSSH)
BASHA (SPLASH)
BASHA
GACHA (CLICK)
DAMMIT... THIS IS ALL HIS FAULT!!! DEFINITELY A CLEATS-UP TACKLE AT ME!
GARA (RATTLE)
WHY'RE YOU IN HERE!!?
BATAN (SLAM)
YOU STOLE MY LINE ......
OH, SORRY, WRONG ROOM!! WASN'T THIS TOMOKI-KUN'S ROOM !?
WHAT THE—!? WHERE'S TOMOKI-KUN!?
WHY ARE YOU HERE, SENPAI !?
TO BE CONTINUED IN NO MATTER HOW I LOOK AT IT, IT'S YOU GUYS' FAULT I'M NOT POPULAR ⑥!

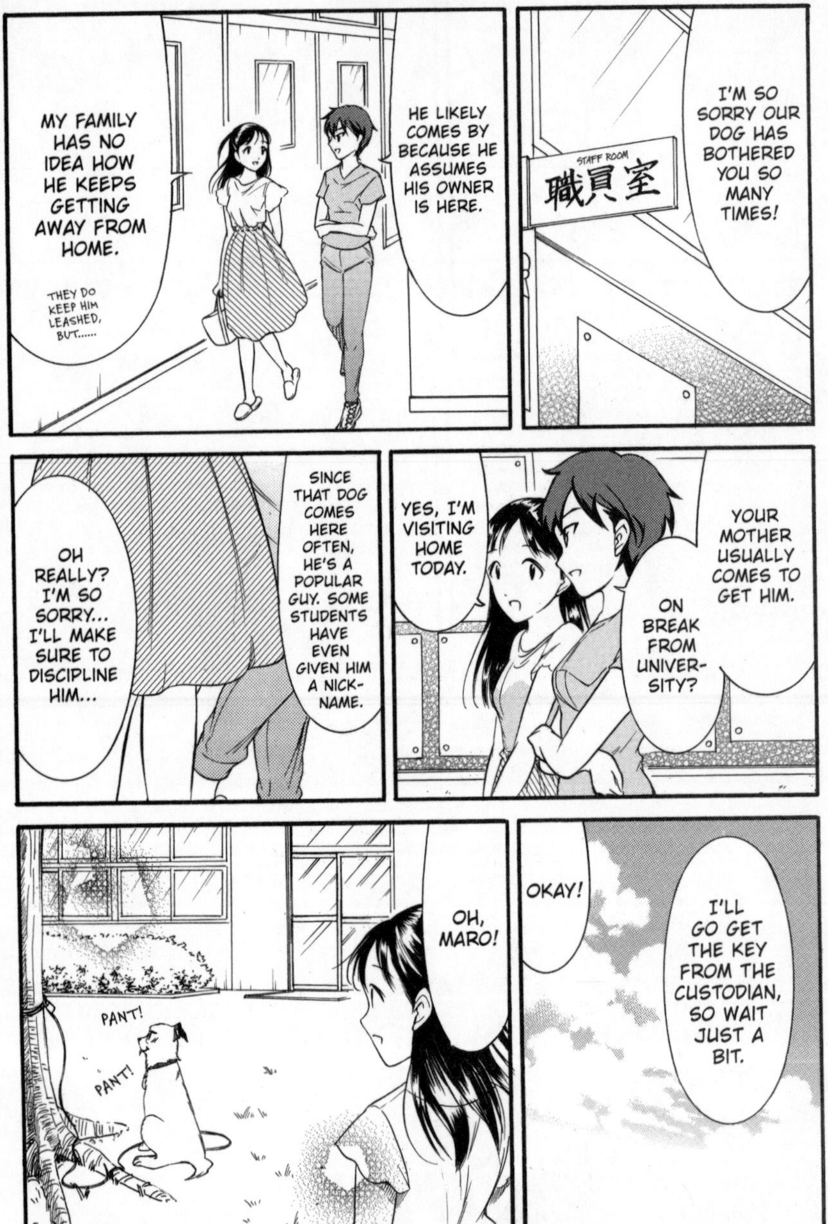
I'M SO SORRY OUR DOG HAS BOTHERED YOU SO MANY TIMES!
STAFF ROOM
職員室
HE LIKELY COMES BY BECAUSE HE ASSUMES HIS OWNER IS HERE.
MY FAMILY HAS NO IDEA HOW HE KEEPS GETTING AWAY FROM HOME.
THEY DO KEEP HIM LEASHED, BUT......
YOUR MOTHER USUALLY COMES TO GET HIM.
ON BREAK FROM UNIVERSITY?
YES, I'M VISITING HOME TODAY.
SINCE THAT DOG COMES HERE OFTEN, HE'S A POPULAR GUY. SOME STUDENTS HAVE EVEN GIVEN HIM A NICK-NAME.
OH REALLY? I'M SO SORRY... I'LL MAKE SURE TO DISCIPLINE HIM...
I'LL GO GET THE KEY FROM THE CUSTODIAN, SO WAIT JUST A BIT.
OKAY!
OH, MARO!
PANT!
PANT!

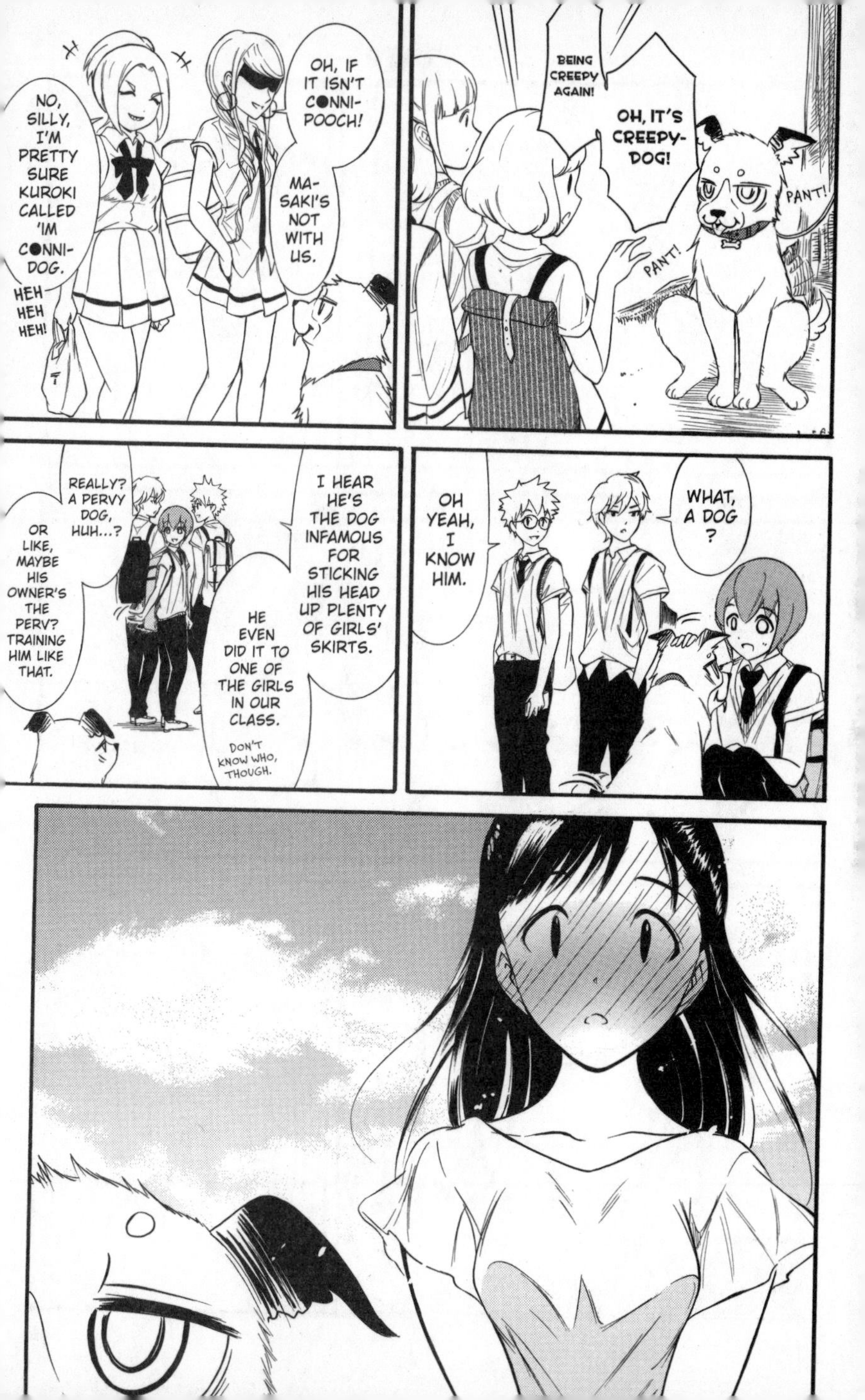
OH, IT'S CREEPY-DOG!
BEING CREEPY AGAIN!
PANT!
PANT!
OH, IF IT ISN'T CONNI-POOCH!
MA-SAKI'S NOT WITH US.
NO, SILLY, I'M PRETTY SURE KUROKI CALLED 'IM CONNI-DOG.
HEH HEH HEH!
WHAT, A DOG?
OH YEAH, I KNOW HIM.
I HEAR HE'S THE DOG INFAMOUS FOR STICKING HIS HEAD UP PLENTY OF GIRLS' SKIRTS.
HE EVEN DID IT TO ONE OF THE GIRLS IN OUR CLASS.
DON'T KNOW WHO, THOUGH.
REALLY? A PERVY DOG, HUH...?
OR LIKE, MAYBE HIS OWNER'S THE PERV? TRAINING HIM LIKE THAT.

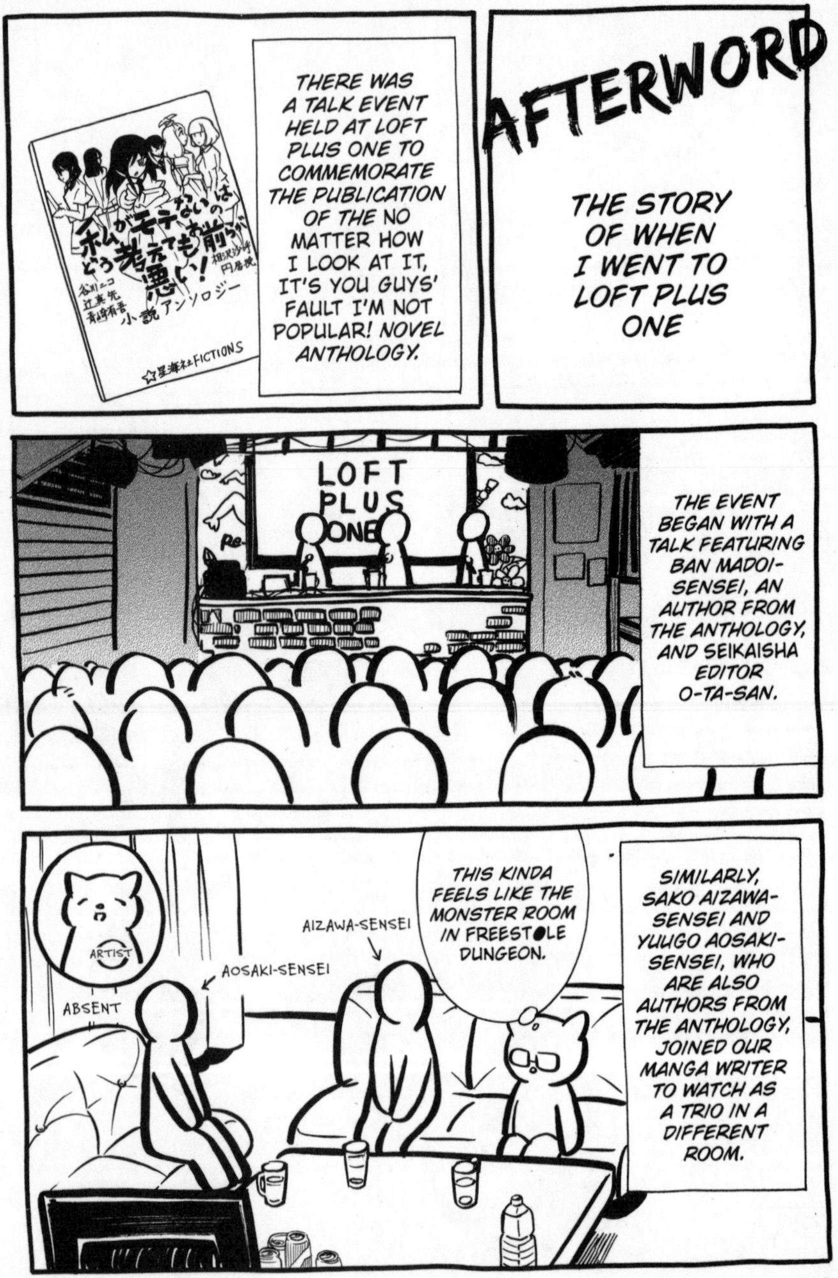
AFTERWORD
THE STORY OF WHEN I WENT TO LOFT PLUS ONE
THERE WAS A TALK EVENT HELD AT LOFT PLUS ONE TO COMMEMORATE THE PUBLICATION OF THE NO MATTER HOW I LOOK AT IT, IT'S YOU GUYS' FAULT I'M NOT POPULAR! NOVEL ANTHOLOGY.
私がモテないのはどう考えてもお前らが悪い！
相沢沙呼
円居挽
谷川ニコ
辻真先
青崎有吾
小説アンソロジー
☆星海社FICTIONS
THE EVENT BEGAN WITH A TALK FEATURING BAN MADOI-SENSEI, AN AUTHOR FROM THE ANTHOLOGY, AND SEIKAISHA EDITOR O-TA-SAN.
LOFT PLUS ONE
SIMILARLY, SAKO AIZAWA-SENSEI AND YUUGO AOSAKI-SENSEI, WHO ARE ALSO AUTHORS FROM THE ANTHOLOGY, JOINED OUR MANGA WRITER TO WATCH AS A TRIO IN A DIFFERENT ROOM.
THIS KINDA FEELS LIKE THE MONSTER ROOM IN FREESTOLE DUNGEON.
AIZAWA-SENSEI
AOSAKI-SENSEI
ARTIST
ABSENT

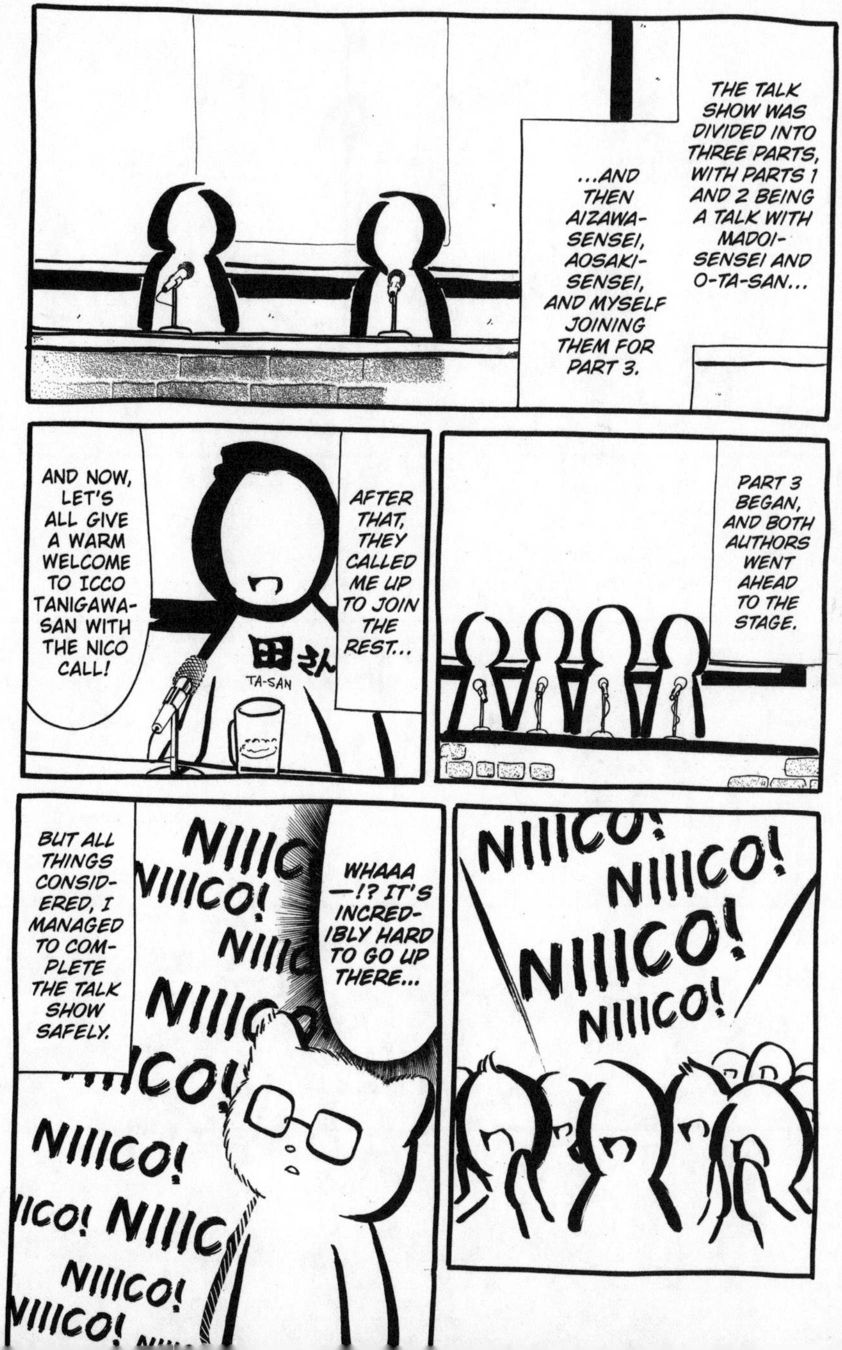
THE TALK SHOW WAS DIVIDED INTO THREE PARTS, WITH PARTS 1 AND 2 BEING A TALK WITH MADOI-SENSEI AND O-TA-SAN...
...AND THEN AIZAWA-SENSEI, AOSAKI-SENSEI, AND MYSELF JOINING THEM FOR PART 3.
PART 3 BEGAN, AND BOTH AUTHORS WENT AHEAD TO THE STAGE.
AFTER THAT, THEY CALLED ME UP TO JOIN THE REST...
AND NOW, LET'S ALL GIVE A WARM WELCOME TO ICCO TANIGAWA-SAN WITH THE NICO CALL!
田さん
TA-SAN
NIIICO!
NIIICO!
NIIICO!
NIIICO!
WHAAA—!? IT'S INCREDIBLY HARD TO GO UP THERE...
BUT ALL THINGS CONSIDERED, I MANAGED TO COMPLETE THE TALK SHOW SAFELY.
NIIICO!
NIIICO!
NIIICO!
NIIICO!

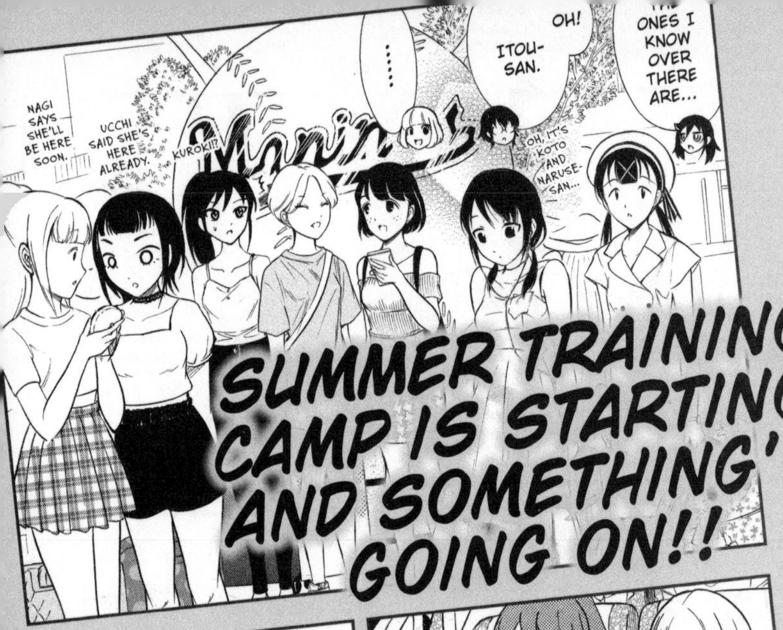
ONES I KNOW OVER THERE ARE...
OH!
ITOU-SAN.
......
OH, IT'S KOTO AND NARUSE-SAN...
KUROKI!?
UCCHI SAID SHE'S HERE ALREADY.
NAGI SAYS SHE'LL BE HERE SOON.

SUMMER TRAINING CAMP IS STARTING, AND SOMETHING'S GOING ON!!

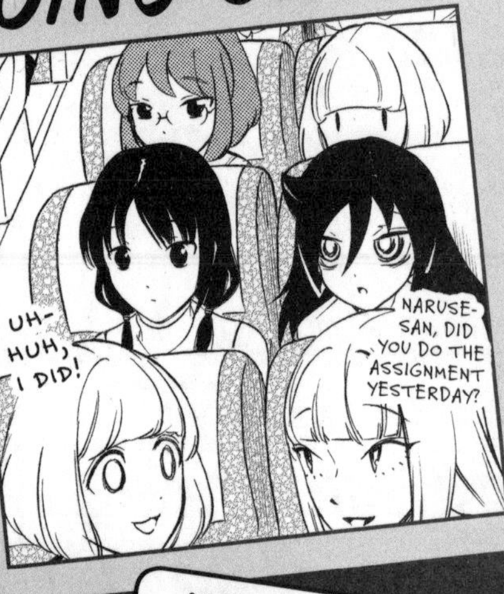
NARUSE-SAN, DID YOU DO THE ASSIGNMENT YESTERDAY?
UH-HUH, I DID!

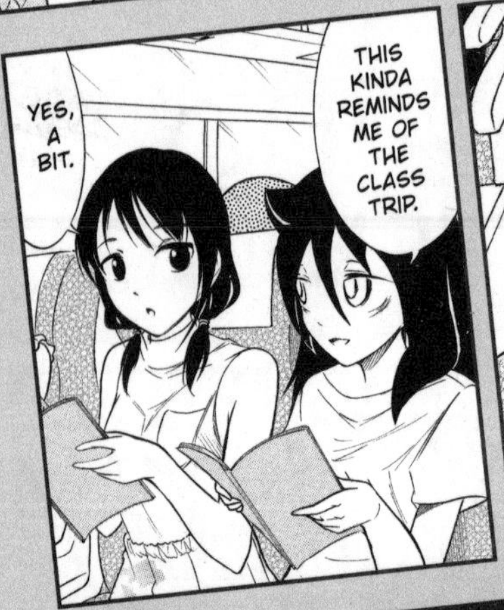
THIS KINDA REMINDS ME OF THE CLASS TRIP.
YES, A BIT.

NEXT: VOLUME 18

No Matter How I Look at It, It's You Guys' Fault I'm Not Popular!

COMING SOON!!

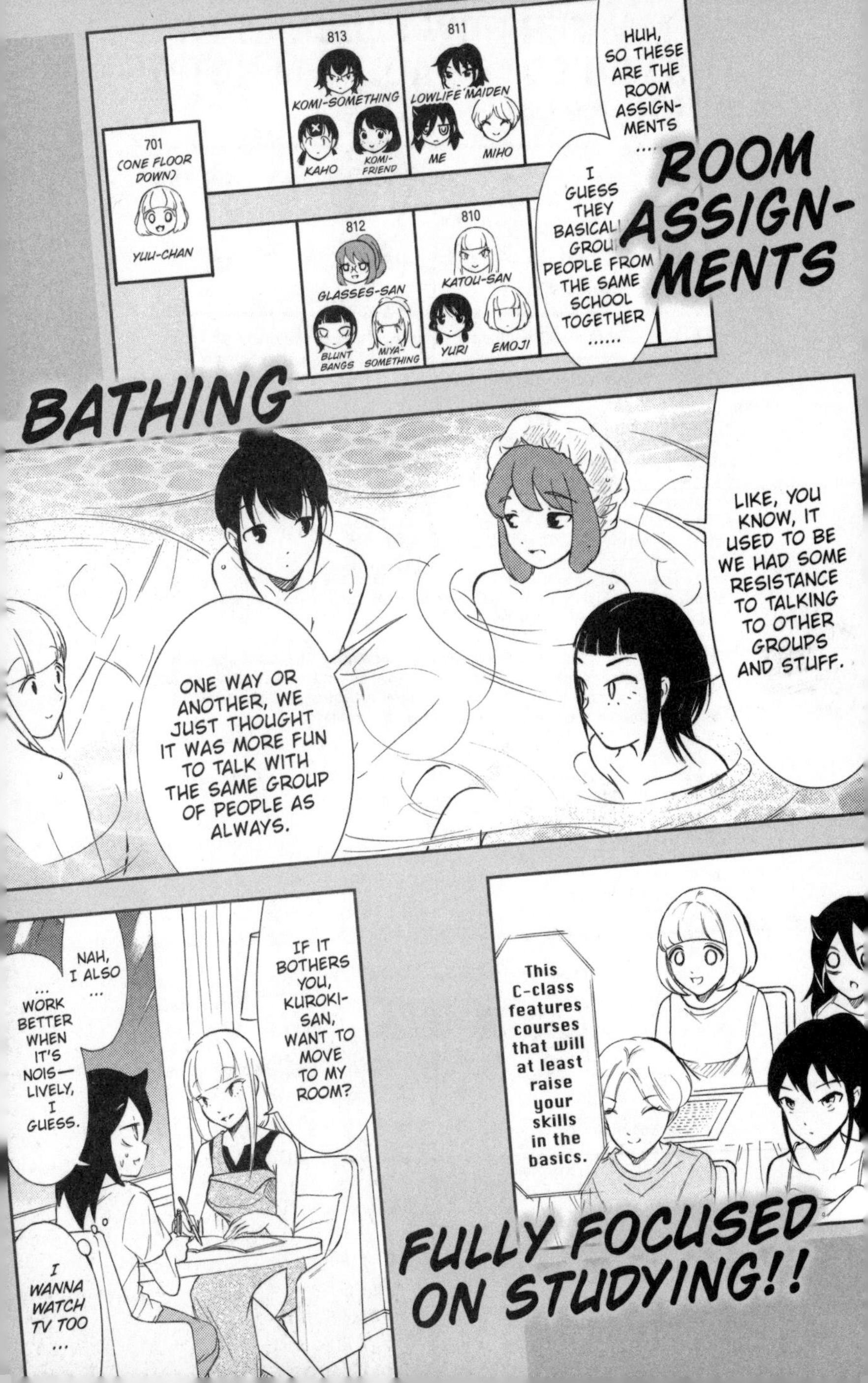
ROOM ASSIGN-MENTS
HUH, SO THESE ARE THE ROOM ASSIGN-MENTS ....
I GUESS THEY BASICAL GROU PEOPLE FROM THE SAME SCHOOL TOGETHER ......
811
LOWLIFE MAIDEN
ME
MIHO
813
KOMI-SOMETHING
KAHO
KOMI-FRIEND
810
KATOU-SAN
YURI
EMOJI
812
GLASSES-SAN
BLUNT BANGS
MIYA-SOMETHING
701
(ONE FLOOR DOWN)
YUU-CHAN
BATHING
LIKE, YOU KNOW, IT USED TO BE WE HAD SOME RESISTANCE TO TALKING TO OTHER GROUPS AND STUFF.
ONE WAY OR ANOTHER, WE JUST THOUGHT IT WAS MORE FUN TO TALK WITH THE SAME GROUP OF PEOPLE AS ALWAYS.
FULLY FOCUSED ON STUDYING!!
This C-class features courses that will at least raise your skills in the basics.
IF IT BOTHERS YOU, KUROKI-SAN, WANT TO MOVE TO MY ROOM?
NAH, I ALSO ...
... WORK BETTER WHEN IT'S NOIS— LIVELY, I GUESS.
I WANNA WATCH TV TOO ...

NO MATTER HOW I LOOK AT IT, IT'S YOU GUYS' FAULT I'M NOT POPULAR! ⑰

Nico Tanigawa

Translation/Adaptation: Krista Shipley, Karie Shipley
Lettering: Bianca Pistillo

This book is a work of fiction. Names, characters, places, and incidents are the product of the author's imagination or are used fictitiously. Any resemblance to actual events, locales, or persons, living or dead, is coincidental.

WATASHI GA MOTENAI NOWA DOU KANGAETEMO OMAERA GA WARUI! Volume 17 © 2020 Nico Tanigawa / SQUARE ENIX CO., LTD. First published in Japan in 2020 by SQUARE ENIX CO., LTD. English translation rights arranged with SQUARE ENIX CO., LTD. and Yen Press, LLC through Tuttle-Mori Agency, Inc., Tokyo.

English translation ©2020 by SQUARE ENIX CO., LTD.

Yen Press, LLC supports the right to free expression and the value of copyright. The purpose of copyright is to encourage writers and artists to produce the creative works that enrich our culture.

The scanning, uploading, and distribution of this book without permission is a theft of the author's intellectual property. If you would like permission to use material from the book (other than for review purposes), please contact the publisher. Thank you for your support of the author's rights.

Yen Press
150 West 30th Street, 19th Floor
New York, NY 10001

Visit us!
⁄ yenpress.com
⁄ facebook.com/yenpress
⁄ twitter.com/yenpress
⁄ yenpress.tumblr.com
⁄ instagram.com/yenpress

First Yen Press Edition: November 2020

Yen Press is an imprint of Yen Press, LLC.
The Yen Press name and logo are trademarks of Yen Press, LLC.

The publisher is not responsible for websites (or their content) that are not owned by the publisher.

Library of Congress Control Number: 2013498929

ISBNs: 978-1-9753-1789-8 (paperback)
       978-1-9753-1790-4 (ebook)

10 9 8 7 6 5 4 3 2 1

WOR

Printed in the United States of America